*The Creator's Healing Power—
Restoring the Broken to Beautiful*

The Creator's Healing Power— Restoring the Broken to Beautiful

Bible Studies to Nurture the Creative Spirit Within

Jody Thomae

THE CREATOR'S HEALING POWER—RESTORING THE BROKEN TO BEAUTIFUL

Bible Studies to Nurture the Creative Spirit Within

Copyright © 2018 Jody Thomae. Ashland, Ohio. All rights reserved. Except for brief quotations in publications or reviews, no part of this book may be reproduced in any manner without prior written permission from the author. Contact jodythomae@zoominternet.net.

Printed by CreateSpace, An Amazon.com Company.

ISBN: 978-1717016461

Unless otherwise noted, all scripture passages are from THE HOLY BIBLE, NEW INTERNATIONAL VERSION®, NIV® Copyright 1973, 1978, 1984, 2011 by Biblica, Inc.™ Used by permission. All rights reserved worldwide.

Other translations used and indicated:
The Amplified® Bible (AMP) Copyright 2015 by The Lockman Foundation. Used by permission. www.Lockman.org.

The ESV® Bible (The Holy Bible, English Standard Version®) Copyright 2001 by Crossway, a publishing ministry of Good News Publishers. ESV® Text Edition: 2011.

Scripture quotations marked (GNT) are from the Good News Translation in Today's English Version-Second Edition Copyright © 1992 by American Bible Society. Used by Permission.

Holy Bible, New Living Translation (NLT) Copyright 1996, 2004, 2015 by Tyndale House Foundation. Used by permission of Tyndale House Publishers Inc., Carol Stream, Illinois. All rights reserved.

The Message (MSG) Copyright 1993, 1994, 1995, 1996, 2000, 2001, 2002 by Eugene H. Peterson. Used by permission of NavPress Publishing Group.

Revised Standard Version of the Bible (RSV) Copyright 1946, 1952, and 1971 the Division of Christian Education of the National Council of the Churches of Christ in the United States of America. Used by permission. All rights reserved.

Hebrew word definitions taken from *Hebrew-Greek Key Word Study Bible: New International Version*. Edited by Spiros Zodhiates. Chattanooga, TN: AMG, 1996.

"Dawn" © Sara Joseph from *Gently Awakened*. Sisters, OR: Deep River Books, 2013. Printed by permission of the author. All rights reserved. christian-artist-resource.com

"A Reflection...Solemn Praise" by Mandy L Gero. Copyright 2015. Printed by permission of the author. All rights reserved.

"High Places that Deceive" © Tom Graffagnino from *Wilderness to Water*. Bloomington, IN: Xlibris, 2014. Reprinted by permission of the author. All rights reserved. withoutexcusecreations.net

"Holy Saturday" by Heather Escontrías. Copyright 2016. Printed by permission of the author. All rights reserved.

"The Antique Rocking Chair" © Sarah M. Wells from *Pruning Burning Bushes*. Eugene, OR: Wipf & Stock, 2012. Reprinted by permission of the author. All rights reserved. sarahmariewells.com

"Blessing for a Whole Heart" © Jan Richardson from *The Cure for Sorrow: A Book of Blessings for Times of Grief*. Orlando, FL: Wanton Gospeller Press, 2016. Used with permission. janrichardson.com

Excerpt from "Arise" by Colleen Briggs (October 11, 2016 post on www.colleenbriggs.com). Copyright 2016. Printed by permission of the author. All rights reserved.

Coloring pages created by Pauline Mae Blankenship © 2015 and Donna Godwin © 2017.

Cover artwork by Donna Godwin © 2018. See www.donnagodwinartstudio.com

For Dad, Matt and Lynn
Meet me at The Gate.

Contents

Acknowledgments / i
As We Begin Our Journey / iii
Prelude: Call and Response / viii

one   Awakening / 11
"Awake, O sleeper, and arise from the dead, and Christ will shine on you."
             Digging Deeper into Awakening / 18

two   Resting / 39
"The one the Lord loves rests between his shoulders."
             Digging Deeper into Resting / 47

three   Confronting / 71
"I live in a high and holy place,
but also with the one who is contrite and lowly in spirit."
             Digging Deeper into Confronting / 78

four   Lamenting / 101
"I have heard your prayer; I have seen your tears. Behold, I will heal you."
             Digging Deeper into Lamenting / 111

five   Encountering / 135
"And by his wounds, we are healed…"
             Digging Deeper into Encountering / 146

six   Journeying / 169
"Be merciful, even as your Father is merciful."
             Digging Deeper into Journeying / 176

seven   Adventuring / 199
"The One who breaks open the way will go up before them;
they will break through the gate and go out."
             Digging Deeper into Adventuring / 208

Bibliography / 231

About the Author / 235

~ Acknowledgments ~

Jody Wishes to Thank...

Jesus, My Healer — I am yours. I will praise you until my last breath on earth, and then with resurrected voice and body, I will praise you through eternity.

Dale, Maddy and Evan — I love you all uniquely. You are my pride and treasure. Remember who and whose you are. Always and in all ways.

Mom — Your continued grace on this journey shines brilliantly. I love you.

Kim, my sister and friend — I could not do this without your encouragement, loyalty, and love.

Terry Wardle — Thank you for walking through the valley ahead of us and for heading the voice of The Shepherd. You are Terry, the one who Jesus loves. May your cup just keep spilling over...

Kathryn Walrath Jackson at Bible365blog.com — Thank you for guiding me in my Bible-in-a-year reading project that led to the Bible stories and verses God had in mind for this book. Your daily obedience is a vital part of this book.

Donna Godwin — Your prophetic creativity, insight, inspiration, and prayers are critical to this book. Thank you for being a creative encourager and for the Spirit-driven artwork that lends itself to the cover and interior of this project.

Laura Huntington — Thank you for your assistance with this project. More importantly, thank you for your continued faithfulness to ministering through movement and inspiring others to do the same.

Pauline Mae Blankenship, Colleen Briggs, Maria Carrasco, Susan Echard, Heather Escontrías, Randall Flinn, Mandy Gero, Susan Gizinski, Donna Godwin, Tom Graffagnino, Sara Joseph, Susie Mercer, Matthew Palfenier, Gina Pangalangan, Jan Richardson, Ruth, Sarah Wells — for allowing me to use your stories, your poetry, your words, your artwork. You inspire others to walk in their true destinies. Thank you for offering your creative gift. May you be blessed in the offering.

As We Begin Our Journey

Kintsugi is the Japanese art of repairing broken pottery with a lacquer mixed with powdered gold. When an object is broken, rather than trying to hide the cracks, the repairs are instead highlighted with gold, and the golden lines become a part of the object's history. As the artisan embraces the flaws and imperfections and repairs them with gold, it tells the story of the object. Rather than discarding the damaged and broken, the pieces are mended and cracks are filled with precious metal and, in many ways, make the object more beautiful than it was at the start. As a philosophy, it is rooted in the inherent beauty of all objects, no matter what they've endured.

And the philosophy behind *kintsugi* is the same one that drives this book.

Kintsugi is a powerful metaphor of Jesus Christ, the Master Artisan, filling and healing the shattered places in us with something more valuable. As the broken places are tenderly pieced back together, they become a beautiful place where God's glory is revealed in our weakness. This is the foundation behind *The Creator's Healing Power—Restoring the Broken to Beautiful.*

First, The Creator (big "T", big "C") has the power to heal and restore our hearts—hearts that have been broken and shattered—into something beautiful. In and through The Creator we find the grace and power necessary to turn our weakness into strength and beauty, not as the world defines it, but as something others who have experienced deep pain recognize. The Creator leads us on a healing journey of reclamation, restoration and redemption, mending the scattered into wholeness and trading ashes for beauty.

But there is more, especially for those who bring artistry, beauty, creativity, and worship to this world...

Once on a journey of healing, the creator (small "t", small "c"), as a broken object now being made beautiful, has the power to heal others, to bring restoration to a broken and hurting world so desperately in need of *kintsugi* of the soul. The Christian creator brings something very precious and valuable to this world—in the form of their creative gift—something that speaks far beyond words and explanation. Christians are the image-bearers of Christ, and as his image-bearers our role is to bring redemption, freedom, and peace to others. As we walk in our own "from-broken-to-beautiful" wholeness, we become an illuminating light in the darkness, helping others walk the path of wholeness themselves. Our own place of weakness, pain, regret, shame, and wounding becomes the very place where God now works to bring others into wholeness and redemption.

Yet we cannot lend a hand to others in the dry desert and dark valley places of life if we have not walked there ourselves and are not willing to be transparent about it. We begin to understand more fully that we cannot help others find healing if we are not on a journey of healing ourselves.

When I wrote my first book, *God's Creative Gift—Unleashing the Artist In You*, there were originally eight chapters. Only seven made it into that book. Under the wise counsel of my dear friend Dr. Terry Wardle[1], a chapter on the dual exploration of the healing journey of the artist and the artist as healer was prayerfully laid aside for another time. That time is now. What you read in the pages ahead is the story of my own healing, scriptures that led me through the dark places of my journey, and encouragement to enter a creative process that leads toward healing, wholeness, and restoration. You'll also find healing testimonies, poems, coloring pages, and inspiration from fellow travelers.

One might ask why I would write a book about healing specifically geared towards artists, creatives[2] and us otherwise right-brained souls? Although we're the only people "living in our right-mind" (as the old adage goes), artists and creatives often get a bad rap. We are labeled morose, sulky, depressed, moody, emotional, and high-maintenance. Type the phrase "artists are..." into your internet search engine and see what pops up on the list below. Mine says: "Artists are weird; artists are crazy; artists are stupid." Ouch! That hurts! No wonder we're so sensitive, so wounded, so desperately in need of God's healing touch. And yet, truthfully, aren't we all in need of his healing touch? Surely, this is a book for *all* God's children!

I would propose, alongside many others, that there is a healing nature to art, beauty, creativity, and worship, allowing one to explore and express thoughts and emotions buried deep in the spirit, uncovering them in a way that allows God's hand to touch and heal. Scientists and physicians are now confirming what we've intuitively known for years—that art, beauty, creativity, and worship have healing power. While it might be difficult to quantify and measure, the anecdotal evidence is too strong to ignore anymore. The world is in desperate need of God's healing touch, and we are the artist army called to make manifest his glory on earth. As we wield swords of beauty, we slash through the seemingly impenetrable walls of hurt that broken hearts have built to protect themselves from the pain of this world. We cannot hold back anymore. It is time to march forward into victory through Jesus Christ!

As we march forward, we want to gird ourselves with scriptural truth. Truly our healing journey does not happen apart from the ministry of Jesus Christ and the Word of God. In this book, we will dig deeply into God's Word to discover what it has to say about restoration, redemption, freedom, and healing. As such, this book is designed as an *interactive* and *in-depth* devotional Bible study that focuses on the creative healer within each of us.

This book contains seven "chapters" laid out in a workbook type format. Each chapter is comprised of two sections: the beginning of each chapter is intended as an introduction of the subject area, and the end of each chapter has a series of five "Digging Deeper" devotionals that "mine" various Bible passages related to that subject. These passages take you through a journey of healing with a focus on artistry, beauty, creativity, and worship. Each "Digging Deeper" Bible study includes *reflection questions in italics* for you to use as journaling prompts. Throughout the book you will also find movie clips, songs, and videos to use as you creatively process all you have learned and how to apply it to your healing process. I encourage you not to skip these—they are the creative gift given by others to aid you on your journey. Most songs can be found on the Internet (on YouTube, for example). In addition, each chapter concludes with a "benediction" of poetry and a coloring page—graciously shared by fellow artists on the healing journey themselves. All of them work through their creative process as a way of healing and redemption in their lives—trUly BEaUtiful men and women of God!

As we venture forward, I would also invite you to two specific spiritual practices: meditation and visualization. First, meditation. As we study Bible passages throughout this book, allow yourself to sit with any verse (or verses) that resonates with you, reading and resting with the words therein. Pay attention to passages that catch in your spirit; that you long to believe in the deepest places of your being; that are agreeing with or even grating against places within. Listen to God's voice through the reading and meditation on his Word. Second, visualization. You will also want to begin to practice picturing Jesus in scripture. As you read passages with stories of Christ, place yourself there in the scene. As you read other passages, imagine him there with you as you read.

I am deeply committed to the Word of God. In a world filled with many mixed messages, we must become dependent on the Bible as God's Word of truth. We cannot be swayed by other voices and other messages. We must rely on scripture to reveal to us the truth of who we really are, what we were created to do, where we are called to reveal his glory on this earth, and how we are to bring our lives in alignment with his good and perfect will.

This isn't just about reading the Bible for information—it's about *transformation!* It isn't about following a book of rules and regulations—it's about encounters with the Voice of Truth that leave us changed. We want to learn how to recognize the Voice of Truth and then live out of those truths in a way that brings us into empowered, abundant living. As we dig into scriptures, passages, and Bible Studies throughout this book, it is my deepest heartfelt prayer that you will find deep healing as you encounter God through his *written* Word, the Bible, and his *Living* Word, Jesus Christ.

As you move through the studies in this book, I invite you to begin to create symbols of your healing journey. You are welcome to use any medium or art form you like or work across several mediums. You can work with one symbol or medium the whole time or create something new with each meditation.

For example, if you are a painter, use the same canvas throughout the whole book, covering over things as you let old ideas go and adding layers where you've made new discoveries. If you sculpt or carve, create a series of objects that tell of your journey as you move through the studies. If you are a musician, begin to work on chord progressions, melody, and lyrics, or sing scriptures over your life in worship. If you are a writer or poet, allow your words to flow from deep within, without editing or worrying about how it reads. If you are an actor or actress, begin to write or memorize a monologue that resonates in your soul. If you are a dancer begin to work with a song that speaks to your heart or dance each day to the song selections given at the end of each meditation. If you are into photography, graphic design, or film, begin to create or capture images to reflect your heart as you travel this journey. If you are a quilter or seamstress, begin to sketch, form a pattern, and piece together. If you are an art journaler, let each passage inspire creativity in you and journal away. The possibilities are truly endless—these are simply suggestions. You have complete freedom. Experiment! Explore! Delve in!

Remember it is *the process* and not the final product that is important. I *cannot* stress that enough. What God reveals through your creative process is far more important than the final product you create. In fact, please take the word "product" out of your vocabulary as you journey through this book. Always allow the Spirit to guide your work and your process. Always listen for his gentle voice to guide and instruct. Keep the eyes and ears of your heart open as you work your creative process.

This book is not a light read. It is an *in-depth* and *interactive* study of scripture that goes *deep within* to the difficult places we'd rather keep covered. This book requires soul work, and soul work is hard work. I encourage you to move through this book *slowly*. Perhaps you might spend a week with each individual Bible study? Take your time to read the Bible passages, study and meditate on the verses provided, journal on the questions raised in each study, and work your creative process with an intentional and unhurried pace. Beloved of God, I am inviting you on a journey and into a process that needs time and nurturing. Do not feel obligated to travel at a defined pace. You know your soul—listen to it.

Before you move ahead, I must ask several things of you as a reader and as one who needs to listen closely to the needs of his or her own self. First, bathe the journey ahead in prayer. Pray as you sit down to read. Pray as you create. Pray when you put this book down to process. Pray. Pray. Pray! In addition, gather others to be praying and interceding for you over the next several months or year ahead. Second, always rely on the leading of the Holy Spirit. If the Holy Spirit presses you to move more deeply into something, press in. If the Holy Spirit gently pulls you back, draw back. If the Holy Spirit whispers, "No, not today," heed that voice. Third, healing is best done within the context of a safe community or with an empathetic witness, such as a pastor, counselor, or spiritual friend. As an artist or creative type, you might also consider a Christian expressive arts therapist to assist you. Moreover, if you have been the victim of intense trauma, I would *highly* recommend that you work through this material alongside a Christian counselor, pastor, or art therapist. Never move ahead if you feel the least bit threatened, unsafe, or strongly attacked by the enemy. Fourth, remember this is not a book to read cover to cover quickly. Pick it up, set it down, work your creative process. And finally, as previously instructed, *pray*.

If it is your desire to help bring others into healing and restoration through your art, beauty, creativity, and worship, I will include a list of books and resources for further exploration and study at the end of each chapter. If healing is a journey, as I truly believe it is, and if you want to lead others into healing, you must walk the path ahead of them or at least alongside them. These resources have helped me on my own journey—perhaps they'll help you on yours.

Remember: God is with you on this adventure. It is my fervent, heartfelt desire that the Creator's healing power will touch you in such a way that your life will be forever changed into a life of meaning, power, and abundant living. That you will hear the voice of the Faithful One who calls you by name and beckons you to follow, even in the darkest places of your journey when you cannot hear his voice or see his face. That the Great Artist will fill the cracked places of your soul with a refining gold that will radiate brilliance in the broken and weakest places of your journey; and that there you will find for yourself the miracle of his freedom and healing.

Godspeed from Your Fellow Wounded Healer,

Jody

Listen to: "Beautifully Broken" by Ashley Smith

Special note to caregivers (pastors, elders, counselors, therapists):

I suspect if you are in care-giving ministry and you now hold this book in your hand, it is because a "right-brained soul" (artist, creative, worshiper) has handed it to you to travel the road with them. This book will serve as a great resource to assist you as you travel alongside them. Creative-types are very sensitive to the world around them. They see things others may miss or pass over. They hear things that others do not pick up on. These things they see and hear touch them at very deep, profound, and sometimes very painful levels. This often makes them more susceptible to wounding and trauma. This resource will provide better understanding on how to help them reconcile their pasts and relate to the world around them in a way that brings health, freedom, and wholeness from a Christ-centered model of emotional healing. Thank you for traveling with them—may you be blessed in the journey.

Endnotes

1. Dr. Terry Wardle is the author of many books on the subject of healing, formational prayer, and spiritual formation. Dr. Wardle leads workshops and conferences through Healing Care Ministries and HCM International located in Ashland, Ohio. I am deeply indebted to Terry for leading me to much of the information found here in this book and more importantly, for starting me on my own healing journey. I would not be the person I am today without his teaching, encouragement, transparency, and obedience to the voice of the Great Physician in his own life. More information is available through www.terrywardle.org, www.hcminternational.org and www.terrywardle.com.

2. Throughout this book, I will simply use the words "creative" (singular) or "creatives" (plural) rather than using the terms "creative person" and "creative people" to describe you as the audience and reader. While many may not consider themselves an artist, they do consider themselves creative or, at the minimum, someone who enjoys art, beauty, creativity, and worship. I use this terminology in order to streamline your reading and to encompass all those who find beauty in the world around them.

Prelude: Call and Response

"In music, a call and response is a succession of two distinct phrases usually written in different parts of the music, where the second phrase is heard as a direct commentary on or in response to the first. It corresponds to the "call-and-response" pattern in human communication and is found as a basic element of musical form, such as verse-chorus form, and is used in many traditions." Wikipedia

Call	*Response*
Psalm 6, a cry of lament from David (NLT)	*Promises of healing from God's Word*

O Lord, do not rebuke me in your anger
or discipline me in your rage.

> *"I have seen their ways, but I will heal them; I will guide them and restore comfort to Israel's mourners, creating praise on their lips. Peace, peace, to those far and near," says the Lord. "And I will heal them."*
> Isaiah 57:18-19

Have compassion on me, Lord, for I am weak.

> *"Nevertheless, I will bring health and healing to it; I will heal my people and will let them enjoy abundant peace and security."*
> Jeremiah 33:6

Heal me, Lord, for my bones are in agony.
I am sick at heart.

> *"Through faith in the name of Jesus, this man was healed—and you know how crippled he was before. Faith in Jesus' name has healed him before your very eyes."*
> Acts 3:16 NLT

How long, O Lord, until you restore me?

> *"I am the Lord, your healer."*
> Exodus 15:26 ESV

Return, O Lord, and rescue me.

> *The Lord is close to the brokenhearted and saves those who are crushed in spirit.*
> Psalm 34:18

Save me because of your unfailing love.

> *Surely he took up our pain and bore our suffering,*
> *yet we considered him punished by God,*
> *stricken by him, and afflicted.*
> *But he was pierced for our transgressions,*
> *he was crushed for our iniquities;*
> *the punishment that brought us peace was on him,*
> *and by his wounds we are healed.*
> *Isaiah 53:4-5*

For the dead do not remember you.
Who can praise you from the grave?

> *Let all that I am praise the LORD;*
> *may I never forget the good things he does for me.*
> *He forgives all my sins and heals all my diseases.*
> *He redeems me from death*
> *and crowns me with love and tender mercies.*
> *He fills my life with good things.*
> *My youth is renewed like the eagle!*
> *Psalm 103:2-5 NLT*

I am worn out from sobbing.
All night I flood my bed with weeping,
drenching it with my tears.

> *The Lord God says, "My grief is beyond healing; my heart is broken.*
> *Listen to the weeping of my people; it can be heard all across the land.*
> *I hurt with the hurt of my people.*
> *I mourn and am overcome with grief.*
> *Is there no balm in Gilead?*
> *Is there no physician there?*
> *Why is there no healing for the wounds of my people?"*
> *Jeremiah 8:18-19, 21-22 NLT*

My vision is blurred by grief;
my eyes are worn out because of all my enemies.

> *He heals the brokenhearted and binds up their wounds.*
> *Psalm 147:3*

Go away, all you who do evil,
for the LORD has heard my weeping.

> *You intended to harm me, but God intended it all for good.*
> *He brought me to this position*
> *so I could save the lives of many people.*
> *Genesis 50:20 NLT*

The LORD has heard my plea;
the LORD will answer my prayer.

> *Then your light will break forth like the dawn,*
> *and your healing will quickly appear;*
> *then your righteousness will go before you,*
> *and the glory of the LORD will be your rear guard.*
> *Then you will call, and the LORD will answer;*
> *you will cry for help, and he will say: "Here am I."*
> Isaiah 58:8-9

May all my enemies be disgraced and terrified.
May they suddenly turn back in shame.

> *"But for you who fear my name,*
> *the Sun of Righteousness will rise with healing in his wings.*
> *And you will go free,*
> *leaping with joy*
> *like calves let out to pasture."*
> Malachi 4:2 NLT

1

~ Awakening ~

"Awake, O sleeper, and arise from the dead, and Christ will shine on you."

"Mama?" Cub whispers into the den's deep darkness.

"Mama? Are you awake?" he whispers more loudly.

"I am now, little one," mumbles Mama Bear, sleep heavy in her voice. "What are you doing awake?"

"I can't sleep," answers Cub, yearning touches the fringes of his words. "Tell me about Spring again," he says as he snuggles deeply into her coarse fur, letting it wrap around him like blades of grass he can just barely remember.

"Spring starts when the Snowdrops come up and push back the snow," she begins.

"How do snow drops push back snow?" he asks puzzled, remembering the early snow that came in flakes, not drops. "That doesn't make any sense, Mama." He is certain her empty stomach is causing her confusion.

Mama Bear smiles as she pictures her every word, "Snowdrops are flowers, silly bear—the very first flowers to bloom each year. They bloom so early that they must push themselves up through piles of snow that stubbornly refuse to melt. Their beautiful, white blossoms hang delicately from emerald stems and silently shout of the coming Spring."

Cub turned his head to gaze up at her—eyes filled with curiosity and wonder.

She continued, "Legend tells us that Snowdrops were birthed from a battle between the Winter Witch and Lady Spring. One year, when Lady Spring arrived to take her rightful place, the Winter Witch refused to give up her reign over the frozen earth. In the midst of the brutal battle, the Witch pierced Lady Spring's finger and a tiny drop of blood fell to the earth. The blood drop melted the bitter snow and a Snowdrop sprang up in its place, declaring Lady Spring victorious over the Winter Witch."

"I think I'm gonna like Snowdrops, Mama" said Cub, wishfully wanting winter's end. His body begins to settle into the stillness.

"After the Snowdrops come the Crocus—lavender and purple and white. Then the red tulips and yellow daffodils. And then, finally then, the trees begin to bud: new leaves forming on every branch."

"The trees grow new leaves?" questions the curious Cub.

"Yes, the Creator Spirit makes all things new," her voice echoes with knowing wisdom.

"What color are the leaves, Mama? Are they red and orange and yellow?" his voice begins to drift off as he fights back sleep.

"No, baby. They are green—the color of new life."

I believe if we are attentive enough, we all experience what I call "the awakening." If we listen closely in the silence, there's a voice. If we attune to our soul, there is a sensing. If we are in touch with the deep places within, there is a knowing. And if we have been deeply hurt, there is a pain that cannot be touched by any worldly remedy.

I remember the day of my own awakening as if it were yesterday. The days and months leading up to it had left me with a sense of "something not quite right," but "what it was" eluded me—until that day.

You see, everything in my life was fine, perfect perhaps. I was the wife of a doctor, a fine man. His position allowed me the honor of being a stay-at-home mom. I had a beautiful daughter and a bubbly son. I lived in a home that was not only comfortable, but lovely. I had many wonderful friends—close, intimate friends with whom I could share my heart—who loved me and cared for me. I was even involved in worship ministry in my local church, a vibrant church with solid Biblical teaching. Everything in my life was perfect. Or so it seemed.

Of course, I had my struggles—things that I wished I could change about my family, my husband, my life, my self. But God had continued to show his faithfulness, mercy, and love through these things, and I knew he was using them to refine me and mold me into his image. So there wasn't anything specific I could pinpoint as the source of my restlessness. Yet it was there just the same, without definition or form.

But then came *that* day, the *awakening* day…

I was at a lunch with other mothers just like me. No kids: just us moms. We sat around Patty's kitchen table; Kathy was on my right. We were all talking about our children and catching up on what was happening in our lives. We began to lament the ordeal of getting a brush through a daughter's tangled hair. Various ideas began to emerge as to how that task might be accomplished with less screaming and gnashing of teeth. At some point during that problem-solving session, an odd sensation came over me.

I looked up from my nearly empty plate, around the table at these women in conversation, and it finally hit me,

    Is this all there is to life?

        To existing… every day… day-after-day?

I was quiet as the conversation swirled around me, and thoughts overtook my mind.

These thoughts gnawed at my spirit attempting to free it from ropes of anger, dissonance, pride, and self-sufficiency. Little did I know it was this moment—the "awakening" moment—that would lead me on an unexpected journey of healing.

See, from that moment on, like a bear slowly awakening from her winter slumber, I recognized a thirst and a hunger that grew stronger each day. That thirst would not be quenched, the hunger would not be slaked, until I took the journey of deep soul work. The only thing that would bring me out of my spirit's deep slumber was a path through the dark valley and dry desert places within.

Certainly not a path I would have chosen. Not a journey I thought I even needed. My life was perfect, remember? Yet as I mined the depths of my spirit, I began to uncover wounded places long forgotten, rashly bound with soiled rags and dirty bandages. Wounded places that were keeping me from walking in the destiny God had for my life and ministry.

There were lies I believed:

"I will never be enough."

"I am too much."

"I don't do anything right."

"No one hears me."

"I am alone."

Spoken by the enemy of my soul, these lies were designed to keep me in my cave of hibernation. Looking back now, the awakening that led to my healing journey was all planned by the Master Designer, the Sculptor of my very being, the Writer of my script, the Healer of my heart. Looking back now, I wouldn't trade it for the world nor all it had to offer.

Our Awakening: from Sleeper to Seer

So, our healing journey starts with awakening. In awakening, we begin to move from "sleeper" to "seer." A "sleeper" goes through life with blinders on. They might be happy, angry or depressed, but they move through life unaware of their great need of a *Redeeming* Savior. Some sleepers even believe in Jesus, but they have yet to be awakened to his redeeming purposes in their life. A "seer" on the other hand is attentive to his or her own spirit. Seers see, not just through their eyes, but through their ears and heart. In order to see, your heart must first be awakened—awakened to your need for Jesus, not just as the one who saves you from your sins (which he most certainly does), but also as the one who reclaims, redeems, restores, renews, and reconciles the broken places within your spirit.

My friend, Dr. Terry Wardle often prays for people to awaken from winter's sleep, referring to it as a "slumbering spirit." I wrote about spiritual seasons in the life of the artist in my previous book: Spring (new beginnings), Summer (abundance), Fall (change) and Winter (death). The spiritual season of winter is one of loss and desolation. In winter, we must die to our old self and its sinful desires and rise again into our new self (Col 3:1-10). There is a sense of disorientation and disintegration that takes place in these winter seasons of our lives. As we work through our own "dark night of the soul," as described by St. John of the Cross, we must come face to face with all that holds us back from new life in Christ. When people have been in a winter season for a long period, the deep sleep of hibernation is often very difficult from which to awake. Just like the hibernating bear that hasn't eaten for months, the spirit grows weak and loses its desire to fight. Difficulties, disappointments, and wounds cause the heart to withdrawal for its own protection.

Throughout scripture, we also see many references to sleepers waking, dead rising, and those in darkness moving into the light (Isa 26:19, 51:17, 60:1; Mal 4:2; Jn 5:25; Rom 13:11). These concepts were all closely related within Jewish culture. The Greek word *egeiro* is translated "wake up" and has the dual meaning of both waking those that sleep and also to rise from death. Moreover, the word *anistemi* is translated "rise," and it means to get up, stand up, and to come back to life. Awakening and resurrection were very important to Jewish believers and had many nuances of meaning.

Like Lazarus rising from the dead, we need help removing our grave clothes so we can emerge from our sleepy tombs. Jesus is calling to us, "Come forth!" But try as we might, we still struggle to surface. Ephesians 5:14 (RSV) encourages us with a promise:

Awake, O sleeper, and arise from the dead, and Christ shall give you light.

In Psalm 57:8 the psalmist cries out, pleading with his soul to listen to his prayer and even using music to help his tired soul rise with the dawn of a new day: "Awake, my soul! Awake, harp and lyre! I will awaken the dawn." And Psalm 17:15 promises new eyesight when we fight to awaken from our slumber: "As for me, I will be vindicated and will see your face; when I awake, I will be satisfied with seeing your likeness." Beloved, we awaken to see the face of God!

As we move through this book, we want to begin to form a habit of picturing Jesus with us. Also, as we read scripture, try visualizing yourself there in the scene. Many years back, I read M. Robert Mulholland's book *Shaped by the Word*, and it revolutionized the way I read my Bible.[1] He encourages us to read not simply for information, but for *transformation*! One method he described was to picture yourself in the scene as you read the stories of Jesus' encounters with people in the Gospels. Look around. What do you see? Take a sniff. What do you smell? Listen. What do you hear? As Jesus reaches out to heal someone in the scriptures, imagine it is *your* eyes he is opening, *your* shoulder he is touching, *your* hand he is grasping, *your* face he is looking into! I will remind you several times to practice this visualization, but you are welcome to practice this whenever, wherever you'd like.

The Blessing at Daybreak

Let's continue in scripture and read about a "sleeper" who awoke one morning to "see." Take a moment to place yourself in the scene as an observer. The story of Jacob in Genesis is one filled with dysfunction and deceit. After stealing the blessing and birthright from his own brother Esau, he runs from his wrongdoing only to be tricked himself by Laban. Some would call that bad karma: we call it the principle of sowing and reaping. If you read his story from the start to finish (Gen 25—50), you see this dysfunction rise up again and again, not just in Jacob and Laban, but also in Rebekah, Rachel, and even passing onto his sons in the next generation. Deceit layering upon deceit.

At one critical part of his life, Jacob is preparing to meet his brother Esau, many years after robbing him of his birthright. He is frightened, but the angels of God meet him (Gen 32:1) reassuring him of God's blessing in his life. Jacob sends gifts, servants, and family ahead of him to Esau and stays the night at a stream where he wrestles it out with God. At daybreak, he insists on a blessing, which he receives: "Your name will no longer be Jacob, but Israel [which means struggles with God], because you have struggled with God and with humans and have overcome" (Gen 32:28).

Notice this occurred at *daybreak*—the time when one awakens from slumber! As he awakens, he finds that he has indeed overcome! He has wrestled, not just with God, but with his demons, his dysfunction, his deceit. His eyes are opened! In Genesis 32:30, he names the place Peniel, which means "face of God," as he proclaims: "I have seen God face to face, yet my life has been spared" (NLT). Jacob, once blinded by his slumber, has become a seer! He also awakens with his hip wounded. He will forever walk with a limp to remind him of his encounter with the Living God. He carries his wound with him, and the memory of his encounter, as well.

As the day awakens, his brother Esau runs to greet him with joy, and at seeing the warm smile on Esau's face, Jacob is deeply humbled. They both break down in tears, cleansing tears, washing away years of hurt and shame. In 33:10 (NLT) Jacob says to Esau, "...what a relief to see your friendly smile. It is like seeing the face of God!" In facing one of the biggest mistakes of his life, and the brother he so deeply betrayed, Jacob sees the face of God in both the joy *and* the tears. It is also a powerful story of God meeting *us* face to face, in the midst of our dysfunctions and desires, and greeting us with joy and tears.

Are you beginning to see his face, O sleeper?

Awakened to Change the World

What is your creative ministry? Fine arts, writing, music, worship, dance, photography, art journaling, acting? Repairing homes, silver-smithing, landscaping, woodcarving, sewing, sculpting? Blogging, graphic design, creating websites, social media marketing? Whatever your creative bent, if you want your creative ministry to be life-giving, world-changing, heart-healing, soul-encouraging, then you need to move from "sleeper" to "seer." The beauty you bring to this world is irreplaceable—*only you* can bring what God uniquely created you to bring, in your own individual way, place, time, and location. A single seed you plant can grow into something God uses to bring others into a healing relationship with him. All actions have ripple effects. You may never know what ripples you cause and how they change the world! Yet you must "see" to help make this happen.

I sense God has placed this book in your hands because it saddens him to see you carry the burden of the enemy's shame, humiliation, distrust, insecurity, fear, and brokenness. Christ is calling you out of the tomb in which the enemy has tried to bury you and calling you into resurrection life as *he alone* meets your needs and desires. I believe that the Holy Spirit will come and begin to meet your deepest longings as you awaken your heart and seek his face. Right now, I declare Christ's Isaiah 61 blessing over you:

The Spirit of the Sovereign Lord is on me [Jesus Christ],
because the Lord has anointed me
to proclaim good news to the poor.
He has sent me to bind up the brokenhearted,
to proclaim freedom for the captives
and release from darkness for the prisoners,
to proclaim the year of the Lord's favor and the day of vengeance of our God,
to comfort all who mourn, and provide for those who grieve in Zion—
to bestow on them a crown of beauty instead of ashes,
the oil of joy instead of mourning,
and a garment of praise instead of a spirit of despair.

> *They will be called oaks of righteousness,*
> *a planting of the Lord for the display of his splendor.*
> *They will rebuild the ancient ruins and restore the places long devastated;*
> *they will renew the ruined cities that have been devastated for generations.*
> *Strangers will shepherd your flocks;*
> *foreigners will work your fields and vineyards.*
> *And you will be called priests of the Lord,*
> *you will be named ministers of our God.*
> *You will feed on the wealth of nations, and in their riches you will boast.*
> *Instead of your shame you will receive a double portion,*
> *and instead of disgrace you will rejoice in your inheritance.*
> *And so you will inherit a double portion in your land,*
> *and everlasting joy will be yours.*

As you read this book, perhaps you can commit to speaking this over your life every day? As an artist and or creative, you often "hear" things in your spirit that others have trouble deciphering. Hear Jesus speak *each word, every day* as you read and begin to walk in the promises of scripture. Moreover, artists and creatives are often visual learners, so begin to visualize this passage as you read. Let your heart awaken from its slumber and see Jesus proclaiming, binding, releasing, bestowing, planting, rebuilding, restoring, repairing, renewing, and doubling!

Stop! Take in this moment—it is your awakening, beloved!

Role of the Holy Spirit

A brief understanding of the role of the Holy Spirit is important as we move forward. Scripture has much to say about the Spirit working in communion with the Father and Son. The Holy Spirit:

- brings revelation (Lk 2:26; I Cor 2:9-10, I Cor 12:4; II Tim 3:16; I Pet 1:12)
- sets us free from bondage to sin (Rom 8:2; Gal 5:17)
- helps us pray and sing (Jude 1:20; Rom 8:26; Col 3:16)
- empowers, equips, enables (Acts 2:4, 14-18; 4:8, 13; 19:6; Rom 15:13; I Cor 12-14)
- sustains, renews, quickens, seals (Job 33:4; Ps 104:30; Jn 3:3-5; II Cor 3:6; Eph 1:3)
- guides, comforts, advocates, teaches, reminds (Jn 12:16, 14:17, 26; Rom 8:14; Acts 8:27-29; Gal 5:16)
- heals, even raises from the dead (Mk 8:25, Jn 11:44, Acts 3:12)

Most importantly, you don't "earn" access to the Spirit—the Holy Spirit is a freely-given gift (Acts 2:17, 10:45; I Thess 5:1), and the Spirit lives in you (I Cor 3:16; Rom 8:9).

When Jesus was preparing the disciples for his departure in John 14, he promised to send a Counselor, the Spirit of Truth, the Holy Spirit, to be with them *forever*. The scripture clearly states *forever*. This isn't something that would die away. This gift was for *all disciples* of Jesus Christ, for *all time*, unto eternity. This Spirit would teach them and remind them of everything he had said while he was with them, and they in turn passed this knowledge onto all the saints through teachings captured in the New Testament. This Spirit would be sent by the Father in Jesus' name to live in us, be with us, and make his home in us. This Spirit was sent as peace, promised by Jesus, not as the world gives, but as only Christ can give (14:27).

The Holy Spirit's voice is one of truth and peace. While we will discuss this more at length later, please open your heart and mind to the Holy Spirit's presence in your life, not just as you read this book, but in everyday aspects of your life. You cannot be who God designed you to be apart from his Holy Spirit within you. The Spirit comes to teach you truth. As artists and creatives, it is especially important to balance our emotions with truth, knowledge, wisdom, and discernment. This comes through our Advocate and Counselor, the Holy Spirit. In order to live empowered lives in Christ, we must live a whole-brained life, with right and left hemispheres working together. You were created to live from a place of wholeness—wholeness of mind, of spirit, of body—in daily communion with the Holy Spirit.

As we move into our Bible studies and you begin to work through your creative process, can you trust that the Counselor, the Spirit of Truth, the Holy Spirit is with you, living in you, making his home in you? Sustaining, renewing, quickening you? Guiding, teaching, reminding you? Empowering, equipping, enabling you? Bringing you revelation and setting you free from the bondage of sin? Advocating for you? Comforting, sealing, and healing you?

If you skipped the preface, as some are inclined to do, won't you go back and read it now? It gives instructions and prepares you for the next section and for the creative process I ask you to step into over and over throughout this book. As you "dig deeper" through the devotional Bible studies here, you will discover others within scripture who were awakened—to see, to hear, to understand God more fully. You will find those awakened to see who they really are, their true identities, as they encountered Jesus in awakening. As you dig deep and mine these passages, may the Spirit guide your heart, mind, and soul. May the scriptures be opened to you with more revelation, insight, and understanding. May you begin to walk in freedom, wholeness, and restoration as you study. May your heart awaken as you move from sleeper to seer through the revelation of God's Word.

Watch on YouTube: "Whisper – Spoken Word & Dance" by Sea of Glass

Digging Deeper Into…

Numbers 22-24: Balaam's Blindness	Page 19
Acts 9: Our Vision vs. God's Vision	Page 22
Luke 19: Finding Your True Self	Page 25
John 3: Living in Mystery & Love	Page 29
Mark 8: Will you Refuse or Confess?	Page 32

Benediction of Radiant Sunrise — Page 35
Dawn by Sara Joseph

Next Steps: Resources for Your Healing Journey & Endnotes — Page 36

Coloring Page "Heaven's Paintbrush" by Donna Godwin — Page 37

Digging Deeper: Balaam's Blindness

Read: Numbers 22-24

The story of Balaam serves as both an encouragement and warning. When we first find Balaam he is referred to as a diviner (22:7), which means he would attempt to make contact with a deity for a fee. Any old god would do! You have a god? Balaam would contact it for you. It also appears from the text that Balaam was well-known for his curses as the Midianites specifically sought him out to send down curses on the Israelites. Not exactly the most reputable man of the Bible.

The story of Balaam's talking donkey found in 22:21-41 is probably the most well known story of this diviner. Scholars indicate that this section reads as a fable that serves a moral purpose. And the moral of the story is: "For all his reputed clairvoyance, Balaam is disparagingly depicted as one who could not see the angel of God standing in his path, even though his [donkey] could!"[2] I believe verse 32b is very telling in this story as the angel of the Lord says to him: "I have come here to oppose you because your path is a reckless one before me." Interestingly, the Hebrew meaning for this clause is uncertain, and while that may be, I am certain his path was indeed reckless.

So first, let's talk encouragement.

Balaam starts as a diviner but as the story unfolds we read of his awakening and find he begins to see, *truly see*, the One True God of Israel, Yahweh. After beating his poor old (and faithful, mind you) donkey, the Lord opens his eyes to see the angel of the Lord before him (22:31), and he falls facedown in submission. In Numbers 23, as the oracles begin, Balaam is on "unsure footing" with the deity called Yahweh.[3] Yet between his second and third utterances, we find a remarkable shift. In the First Oracle he simply states what he observes (see verse 23:9). In the Second Oracle he is beginning to see below the surface to something deeper (see verse 23:20-21). Finally, in the Third Oracle he is awakened to the source of his visions, and the Spirit of God, revealed through the spirit of prophecy, falls upon him:

When Balaam looked out and saw Israel encamped tribe by tribe, the Spirit of God came on him and he spoke his message:
The prophecy of Balaam son of Beor,
the prophecy of one whose eye sees clearly,
the prophecy of one who hears the words of God,
who sees a vision from the Almighty,
who falls prostrate, and whose eyes are opened:
How beautiful are your tents, Jacob,
your dwelling places, Israel! 24:2-5

In the Fourth Oracle his eyes, ears, mind, and spirit are all open to truly see:
The prophecy of Balaam son of Beor,
the prophecy of one whose eye sees clearly,
the prophecy of one who hears the words of God,
who has knowledge from the Most High,
who sees a vision from the Almighty,
who falls prostrate, and whose eyes are opened:
I see him, but not now; I behold him, but not near. 24:15-17a

Bible scholar Baruch Levine notes: "When Balaam realizes that [Yahweh] is pleased with his blessings and confident that [Yahweh] will connect with him, …Balaam sets his gaze on the desert, and the spirit of [Yahweh] alights upon him. This is an experience otherwise restricted to Israelite prophets and judges, and the fact that Balaam experiences it indicates that his status has changed."[4] Between this and the donkey, it just goes to show God will use anyone or anything. *No one* is beyond awakening!

The *Dictionary of the Old Testament Pentateuch* defines a seer as "one who is given revelation during the course of a visionary experience."[5] As we read, we find Balaam's transition from pagan diviner to seer and prophet. As one who has operated through the power of pagan gods (i.e., satan), we now discover the spirit of true revelation is upon him. He is changed by his encounter with God. And yet, there's much more to the story.

Now, let's talk warning.

Balaam's "life-changing" encounter with God *did not* have lasting effect. We quickly find him back to his old ways—still relying on and encouraging worship of pagan gods. He is believed to have been responsible for the Israelite worship of Baal at Peor (Num 25), and later he is put to death in Israel's attack on Midian (Num 31:8, 16). While his eyes were opened as he gazed upon the vast nation of Israel encamped across the deserts of Moab, they did not stay open. Oh, how quickly his spirit went back to sleep! He encountered the Living God—the Spirit of God rested upon him for that brief moment in time—and still he was lured back by the enticing ways of the enemy. In essence, he was lulled back to sleep, closing his eyes and heart to the one true God of Israel!

Balaam, for a fleeting second, saw. God opened his eyes, his ears, his heart. Yet he let the ruler of this world, satan, continue to control him. As King David so aptly states: "My sin is ever before me" (Ps 51:3). Many things can take us back from being a seer to being a sleeper once more. Do not let your spirit, once awakened, be lulled back to sleep. For when we sleep our eyes are closed—we cannot see!

We all know there is a great deal of hurt, pain, evil, and suffering in our world. We observe sin at large in our world, and we find ourselves caught up in it, overwhelmed by it, trapped by it. Other times we cope by allowing ourselves to be lulled into sleep so we can avoid it all together. Perhaps we find ourselves lured back into sin—enticed back into our old ways. Old ways of thinking. Old ways of acting. Old ways of being.

Ultimately, we cannot let Balaam's blindness be *our* blindness.

Paul tells us in II Corinthians 4:4 that the "god of this age has blinded the minds of unbelievers," but we as witnesses of Jesus in this fallen world must continually look to "the light of the gospel that displays the glory of Christ, who is the image of God." He continues in verse 18: "So we fix our eyes not on what is seen, but on what is unseen, since what is seen is temporary, but what is unseen is eternal." Despite what we see around us we must fix our eyes! Lord Jesus, help us stay focused on you!

My friend Cindy works hard to keep her eyes fixed on Christ. For her this has become both a habit and a way of being. When she is overwhelmed by life's chaos or when difficulties come her way, you will hear her say, "I just keep turning and looking into the face of Jesus!" Over and over I hear her say this. It is a habit she formed under the direction of her spiritual mentor, and now, is a part of a life awakened to the ways of the Holy Spirit. We would all be well-served to do the same.

Take a moment to consider: *how does the enemy tempt you back into blindness? What does he do to hypnotize you, to lull you, to block your vision? Have you encountered Jesus in a powerful life-changing way only to be enticed back to your old ways again? What took you back? What does the enemy use against you to cause spiritual blindness in your life?*

Now take a moment to picture Jesus there with you. Where is he? For me, he is standing behind me in this moment, hands on my shoulders, reminding me that this "study" I am writing is as much about me as it is about you. Not two minutes ago I was thinking how attacked I felt today. But now I feel the comforting touch of my Savior giving me peace and strength.

Let's stay focused, men and women of God! Join me in looking to Jesus, our Savior. Fix your eyes on his beautiful face! Keep your heart awakened to the Holy Spirit within!

Using the questions and scripture passages as your prompts as you begin to explore through creativity, won't you join me in this prayer?

Invite the Holy Spirit into this moment.
Ask the Lord Your Shepherd (Yahweh Rohi) to guide you as you pray.
Ask Jesus (God Saves) to help you remove your spiritual blinders and see his face.

Yahweh, God of Israel, be my God in this moment. Come to me and help me see. I know in my head that I need to keep my eyes fixed on you, but so often I am overcome in my heart. I confess that to you, Lord. Place your hands on my eyes and wipe away the years of spiritual blindness. Help me! You are Christ, my Savior! Save me! Send me cleansing tears to shed the scales on my eyes. I look to you and you alone. I know you are here in this moment. I use my imagination to picture you with me. I sense forgiveness, compassion, peace, love, courage, and strength. I thank you. Keep my heart awakened to you. You are mighty to save!
In the Name of Christ, who opens my eyes, Amen.

Listen to: "Tell Your Heart to Beat Again" by Danny Gokey
"My Eyes are Fixed on You" by Julie True

Digging Deeper: Our Vision vs. God's Vision

Read: Acts 9:1-19

Did you notice how many times this passage refers to eyes, sight, and vision? This is truly a passage about seeing! If you weren't paying attention the first time through, I'll give you a second to go back and read it again.

Welcome back! Did you see?

I know I'm harping on this whole "seeing thing." But it is important, once our hearts are awakened, to move from a slumbering spirit to a seeing spirit. Vision and imagination are critical for artists, creatives, and those who find beauty in this world. God is pressing this on my heart for a reason, and he will not let me move past it. So hang in there with me. You will soon know the reasons, and in the meantime, let your own heart, mind, soul, and spirit continue to awaken to God's vision for his army of artists!

Bible scholar Beverly Gaventa comments on the drama of Saul/Paul found in Acts 9. We find the drama unfolding in five specific acts:

Act 1: Early Christians are persecuted by old religious order
Act 2: Saul encounters Jesus on Damascus road
Act 3: Ananias is commanded to find Saul and he resists
Act 4: Ananias obeys and Saul's sight is restored
Act 5: Saul (now Paul) is also persecuted[6]

I love that Gaventa takes a book of the Bible titled "The Acts of the Apostles" and breaks it down in terms of dramatic acts! She goes on to say that Saul's encounter with Christ is a "major turning point in the narrative of Acts."[7] In other words, the plot hits its climax in act two. Paul encounters Christ himself and is blinded. The religious zealot is stopped in his tracks by the very Christ he has denied and persecuted. This is Paul's awakening, and it does indeed seem like the climax of this production!

But let me take this dramatic analysis another direction.

In drama and film there is a concept of five dramatic structures: introduction, rising action, climax, falling action, and conclusion or denouement. It is referred to as Freytag's Pyramid. If you analyze Paul's conversion above according to this pyramid instead, the climax would be with God's command and Ananias' refusal to go to Paul. God's command in verse 12 is important: "In a vision, [Saul] has seen a man named Ananias come and place his hands on him to restore his sight." However, to Ananias, Saul was an enemy (vs 13). Up to this point the character of Saul is portrayed as a murdering enemy of the disciples, but for God his true identity is the "chosen instrument" to spread the gospel of Jesus Christ (vs 15). Yet Paul cannot do that apart from the power of the Holy Spirit!

Saul has been zealous for God, but for all the wrong reasons! Led by the wrong vision, his mission has been to cleanse the Jewish church of these heretics—the disciples who claim Jesus as the Messiah of the Jewish nation. While God loves Saul's zealous nature (for he created him that way), Saul has been following the wrong vision in his life. God had a complete opposite vision and mission for Saul's life—he wanted him to be zealous in spreading the good news that the Messiah had come in the very person they had crucified, Jesus of Nazareth!

So let's get to the true climax of this drama. Notice Saul had specifically seen in a vision a man named Ananias come to him and restore his sight. While waiting in his own blindness, he is purposely looking for Ananias. Then Ananias shows up proclaiming, "Brother Saul, the Lord—Jesus, who appeared to you on the road as you were coming here [to persecute and kill the disciples]—has sent me [Ananias, the one you've been waiting for], so that you may see again and be filled with the Holy Spirit" (vs 17). See, the scales don't fall from Saul's eyes until Ananias follows God's commands. The Holy Spirit does not fill Saul (now Paul) until Ananias follows God's commands. Paul cannot move forward into this new vision until Ananias follows God's commands. Saul's awakening into Paul is dependent on Ananias obeying God. The good news of the gospel of Jesus Christ will not change the world until Ananias follows God's commands!

Through Ananias, God is saying to Saul, now Paul: "I have a new vision and mission for you! But you cannot do this apart from this infilling of the Holy Spirit! You must receive and be filled with the Holy Spirit to be healed and move in this new vision I am giving you! I have called you to change the world in my power. I am calling you into awakening!"

Through Ananias, God is saying to us: "Will you obey me even when it doesn't make sense? Will you be my instrument no matter where it is I call you or for what purpose? Will you be the one through which I work so that others may receive this gift of the Holy Spirit? And ultimately, will you do your part to spread the gospel of Jesus whether I call you up front or behind the scenes?"

Sometimes we're the "chosen instrument" and sometimes we're the "tuner" that tunes the instrument to follow the true vision God has placed before them! Sometimes we are the one who is changed through the beauty we create, and sometimes the beauty we create changes another.

This passage has so much to teach us. Take a moment to consider several things as we move forward today: *What is your nature, your personality? How has God created you? God wired Paul to be zealous. What is your natural wiring? What is your calling—the vision God has placed within you? Ask God if your vision has been misdirected in any way. How does your calling bring others into the saving grace and good news of the gospel of Jesus Christ? Are you working in the power of the Holy Spirit or are you working apart from God's infilling in your life? What is your true identity? How has the world seen you? How does God see you? What scales cover your eyes? What is your vision? What is God's vision?*

We don't want to awaken to "see" simply for our own sakes. We "see" to help others "see"—we awaken to awaken others. We are set free from our blindness and empowered by the Holy Spirit to share the gospel of Jesus Christ with a world desperately in need of him. As our spirits are awakened, as we are given sight, as we learn his vision for our lives, we must realize we are called to share this gift of sight to help others know the saving grace, love, and mercy of Jesus Christ. We may be "the Paul" that helps millions upon billions see. Or we may be "the Ananias" that helps *just one* see!

I will leave you with one more scripture that illustrates these same truths, and don't forget to picture it as you read. It describes the baptism of Jesus.

> The next day John the Baptist saw Jesus coming toward him and said,
> "Look [Behold! See!],
> the Lamb of God,
> who takes away the sin of the world!"

Then John gave this testimony:

> "*I saw* the Spirit come down from heaven as a dove and remain on him.
> And I myself did not know him,
> but the one who sent me to baptize with water told me,
> 'The man on whom *you see* the Spirit come down and remain
> is the one who will baptize with the Holy Spirit.'
> *I have seen and I testify*
> that this is God's Chosen One." John 1: 29, 32-34

Using the questions and scripture passages as your prompts as you begin to explore through creativity, won't you join me in this prayer?

Invite the Holy Spirit into this moment.
Ask the Lord Your Shepherd (Yahweh Rohi) to guide you as you pray.
Ask Jesus (God Saves) to help you see his vision for you.

Jesus, our Messiah and Christ, as I pray this "awakening" prayer, I want to encounter you today. I want your vision for my life and not my own vision that I have created out of my own flesh and mind. Where I have followed my own self-serving vision, help me see! I want more of your Holy Spirit filling me and abiding in me as I work alongside you to spread the good news of your gospel of peace, mercy, and love. With John the Baptist I want to proclaim, "I have seen and I testify that this is God's Chosen One." I want to walk in your identity for my life. I want to testify to your power in my life. You alone are life and light and love!
In the name of Jesus, the One Who Gives Sight, Amen.

Listen to: "Be Thou My Vision" by your favorite artist
"Beautiful Things" by Gungor

Digging Deeper: Finding Your True Self

Read: Luke 19:1-10

> Zacchaeus was a wee little man, a wee little man was he.
> He climbed up in the sycamore tree for the Lord he wanted to see!
> And when the Savior passed that way he looked up in the tree,
> And said: "Zacchaeus! You come down!
> For I'm going to your house today!
> I'm going to your house today!"

If you grew up in Sunday School, you know this song, and you probably sang it right along with me, didn't you? Poor Zacchaeus! Always known for being a "wee little man." But there is so much more to this story! Let me tell you of his true identity.

Yes, scripture tells us Zacchaeus was vertically challenged. We got that! Yet scripture also tells us he was the Chief Tax Collector, which reveals three things. First, he worked for the Roman Empire (the enemy) and therefore was hated by his fellow Jewish people. Second, tax collectors were known for skimming off the top and making their wealth by over-taxing and robbing others of their hard-earned money. Third, he was *Chief* Tax Collector, which means he was skimming profits off the other tax collectors beneath him. He was wealthy, and his wealth was made by dishonest means. Not a very popular man.

And yet there he was, one of the wealthiest men in town, still searching—for something money can't buy. I picture a short man with a bad case of Napoleon Complex. Pushing others around. Gaining wealth by robbing others. Scholar David Garland comments that a man like this "remains on the margins of society."[8] Of course he's still searching! The only things wealth had bought him were disdain, distrust, and rejection. The crowd might have parted for a more respected man, *but not Zacchaeus!*

So up he climbs into that sycamore tree looking to get a glimpse of the man named Jesus thronged by the crowds at Jericho. The Bible story right before this one is of a blind beggar (Lk 18:35-43)—one who cannot physically see but is "seen" by Christ and healed. As the story begins here in chapter 19, in some translations of verse two we find the word "Behold." It calls us as the reader to look, see, take notice. Zacchaeus, one *with sight* who *still cannot see*! Literally, because of the crowds and his short stature; and figuratively, because he cannot see the wretched man he has become!

And guess who sees *him*? Jesus!

Jesus takes note. Not of the others, but of Zacchaeus, the one who is blinded, who cannot see his true identity. Do you know what Zacchaeus means? Ironically, of all things, it means "pure." But the crowds refer to him as a sinner (see vs 7). The tax collector, the *chief* tax collector! The sinner, the *chief* of all sinners!

"Zacchaeus! You come down! For I'm going to your house today!"

Jesus says: "Zacchaeus, come down from your place of hiding, of straining, of robbing! I see you, Zacchaeus! You are the 'pure' one, but you've let the enemy rob you of your true identity. I see who you really are, and I'm calling you out of this lie into your true identity."

Garland tells us that Christ's invitation here is an act of grace and mercy. Jesus knows it wasn't just his short stature that drove him into that tree. He knows Zacchaeus was disrespected and the crowd would show no favor. In fact, they might be quite mean—shoving him aside, pushing him away, and, given his short stature, elbowing him in the nose. Fear of man drove him into that tree! Garland goes on to say that "Luke's entire gospel is driven by God's invitation in offering forgiveness and reconciliation, and Jesus' initiative with this tax collector exemplifies that divine initiative."[9] This divine initiative is one that drives Jesus' mission here on earth. His purpose is grace. He comes to redeem and reconcile all things unto himself. Christ's invitation to Zacchaeus is profound on many levels.

It is an invitation to all.

Do you hear him calling you?

Are you starting to see?

Are you moving from sleeper to seer?

Is your spirit being awakened?

Picture yourself in that tree. *What has driven you up into that tree? What are you looking for? What haven't you found? What part of your identity has been lost as you've moved through the difficulties of this world? Where has your spirit fallen asleep—closing your eyes to all that Jesus has for you?* Part of awakening is learning to see yourself as Jesus sees you. Just as Jesus saw Zacchaeus, he sees you. Picture Christ looking above the crowds and calling out to you—calling you to awaken to your true identity in Christ

Let's replace Zacchaeus with your own name and identity below:

"_____*(your name)! You come down! For I'm going to your house today!*
Come down from your place of hiding, of straining, of being an outcast!
I see you, _____*(your name)!*
You are _____*(your true identity)*
but you have let the enemy rob you of your true identity.
I see who you really are, and I'm calling you out of your false identity into this true identity."

Grab a pen and physically fill in those blanks above with your name and your true identity.

Now notice Zacchaeus' reaction to Jesus' invitation in verse 8. Right there and then he makes restitution, with interest, to all he has robbed. The NIV says "here and now"—there is an immediate repentance and repayment with fourfold interest. Several ancient documents include this fourfold restitution (four times what was owed), indicating it was the uppermost limit of the law. He is subjecting himself to the harshest penalty allowed![10] Jesus doesn't even need to instruct him to do this. Christ's simple invitation into grace calls Zacchaeus into his true self. He has moved from sleeper to seer, just like that!

As Zacchaeus walks in his true identity, Jesus walks in his and proclaims,

Today Salvation has come!

Beloved of God, in our very midst, Salvation has come and walks among us. Jesus means "God Saves." *Jesus is Salvation!* His name is Salvation—God Saves—Jesus, and he comes to seek and save that which is lost. *Have you lost your self? Your true identity? Your true calling? Have you "lost" who you really are?* Jesus has come to seek and save the very thing you have lost—to seek and save *all* that you have lost. If you grapple with what exactly you have lost, your true identity, your true calling, if you question who you really are, do not worry! Christ comes to seek and save. He comes to help you search and find and recover. As you picture Jesus with you, over and over, he will help you see! It is he who is calling out to your spirit to awaken. And as he awakens you, he will open your eyes to see.

In the fictional book *Crossroads* by Paul Young, there is a scene where God appears to the main character Tony in the form of a six-year-old girl with beautiful brown eyes and raven hair pulled back from her olive face with a garland of white flowers. In a moment of dark harassment by the enemy she comes skipping, laughing, and singing to remind him of who he really is:

> The little girl began to hop-skip around him, moving in and out of his view while touching her fingers in no particular order as if keeping a count. In a singsong voice, she declared, 'Mr. Tony, you are also a mighty warrior, you are not alone, you are someone who learns, you are a universe of wonder, you are Grandmother's boy, you are adopted by Papa God, you are not powerful enough to change that, you are a beautiful mess, you are the melody…' And with each phrase the ice chains that seemed to bind him loosened and his breathing deepened. Thoughts arose that wanted to argue and deny each statement, but as he calmed, he chose to simply watch her dance and listen to her song.
>
> What did she know? She was just a little girl. Regardless, her words carried power, of that he was certain, and they seemed to resonate in his frozen core. Her presence was like springtime unfolding, the thaw that warmed and invited new things.[11]

This is the voice of God! Speaking of our true identity, melting our hearts, making all things new! Awakening all that is asleep within.

I will leave you with one final scripture from Romans 13:11 (NIV):

And do this, understanding the present time:
The hour has already come for you to wake up from your slumber,
because our salvation is nearer now than when we first believed.
The night is nearly over; the day is almost here.

(continued next page)

Using the questions and scripture passages as your prompts as you begin to explore through creativity, won't you join me in this prayer?

Invite the Holy Spirit into this moment.
Ask the Lord Your Shepherd (Yahweh Rohi) to guide you as you pray.
Ask Jesus (God Saves) to help you see who you really are.

Jesus, our Savior and Salvation, help us find ourselves! You come to seek and save all that we have lost. Lord, we struggle to even define exactly what that is. We need your eyesight to help us see who we really are, all that we have lost, and how the enemy has kept us from walking in our true identity. As you awaken our hearts, we trust and proclaim that you are Jesus! You are Salvation! You are God Saves! Help us climb down out of our trees to accept your invitation of grace. Help us walk in true repentance as we walk in your beautiful gift of salvation. Behold! It is time for us to wake from our slumber. The night is almost over; the day is almost here. Help us to understand who we were truly created to be.

In the Name of God Who Saves, Jesus, Amen.

Listen to: "Afraid to Live" by Aaron Wardle
Watch on You Tube: "Open Up Let the Light In - Steffany Gretzinger – A Dance Testimony"

Digging Deeper: Living in Mystery & Love

Read: John 3:1-21; 7:45-52; 19:38-42

Nicodemus appears three times in the Gospel of John: at the beginning of Jesus' ministry; as talk of Jesus as Messiah grows and alarms religious leaders; and at the burial of Jesus. These passages reveal a man who grew from being confused and suspicious of this teacher from Nazareth to one who was fully devoted to Christ. Nicodemus only appears in the Gospel of John: he is never mentioned in the other gospel accounts. My suspicion is that he came forward later—that as a member of the Pharisees, he kept his growing belief to himself, and it wasn't until later that his story was known to the disciples of Christ.[12] His story stands as a beautiful example of one awakened by the Sprit of God to grow in faith and devotion.

So let's start at the beginning.

Nicodemus is a member of the Pharisee sect of Jewish religious leaders. The Pharisees were a strict, pious group that tended to view themselves as "more holy" than others. He comes to Jesus under the cover of night—he does not wish to be seen. Yet he is curious and wants to know more. He has witnessed Jesus' miracles and knows the power to perform them lies in a higher source. Jesus talks to him as an equal, yet at the same time, his words are veiled in mystery. Nicodemus struggles to keep up.

Commenting on verses seven and ten specifically, Bible scholar John Sailhamer indicates this kind of talk veiled in mysterious language shouldn't have been a surprise to Nicodemus. Nicodemus would have studied passages such as Ezekiel 36:24-27 that prophesied that God would take hearts of stone and replace them with hearts of flesh and Isaiah 26:12-19 that contains similar language to John 3. "The basic thesis put forth in this discussion [between Christ and Nicodemus] is that such an understanding of the people of God was already foretold in the Old Testament," states Sailhamer.[13] This *should have* been common knowledge to good ol' Nico! Yet Christ's talk of being born again or born from above leaves him baffled.

Jesus continues to teach of the mysteries of the Spirit and of God working through the gift of his only begotten Son. He even speaks of the manner of his own death on the cross in verse 14. At the end of this conversation (vs 21), Jesus proclaims this prophecy over Nicodemus' life: "But whoever lives by the truth comes into the light, so that it may be seen plainly that what they have done has been done in the sight of God." In the end, Nicodemus does indeed live by the truth, a truth that brings him into the light of God's saving grace. A light that awakens him to see, know, and understand.

Later, in the passage in John 7, we find Nicodemus coming to Jesus' defense as the religious leaders become increasingly intimidated and angered by Christ's ministry. Finally in John 19, we find this beautiful picture of Nicodemus accompanying Joseph of Arimathea to bury Christ. He brings an extravagant amount of myrrh and aloe, and together they prepare his body for burial. Read 19:38-42 again paying particular attention to verse 40. One can almost sense the affection and tenderness of their care as they attend to the body of the crucified Christ.

Take a moment to picture that moment. Imagine Christ's bloodied and damaged body. Imagine Joseph and Nicodemus bringing the lifeless Jesus to this garden tomb and painstakingly wiping away the dried blood, dirt, and filth. Picture them as they anoint him with precious ointments and wrap him in linen strips. I once read there would've been hundreds of yards of linen strips. This was a time consuming process as they worked with the bruised, beaten, whipped, and crucified body of Jesus. What tenderness, care, and compassion went into this process!

Now, *we* know that Christ rose three days after being laid to rest by Joseph and Nicodemus. That he shed the hundreds of yards of linen cloth in which they had painstakingly wrapped him. That he woke from a sleep that kept him deathly still in the tomb even while his spirit fought for the restoration of all that the enemy sought to destroy. That he walked through great darkness into the glorious resurrection light of salvation and that even then he carries the scars from his battle wounds.

Yes *we* know all this, but our friend Nicodemus did not. He walked in mystery and questions. Yet he found truth in the midst of his searching, and he too walked from darkness into resurrection light. Nicodemus struggled to understand Jesus—a man who spoke with mystery of the ways of the Spirit. Yet though he struggled, he still chose to defend him and eventually worship him. His belief went against conventional worldly understanding and even the "wisdom" he had gained through close study of the scriptures. Something inside Nicodemus drew him in—a tiny flame grew as the wind of God's Spirit blew gently upon it.

The fact is even though we know Christ rose again, we still walk in mystery and questions ourselves—the mystery of that resurrection, of the ways of the Holy Spirit, of fear and faith, of trusting God for restoration even in the midst all the enemy's destruction. Within each of us is a tiny spark growing until fanned into flame by the wind of His Spirit. We sometimes live in confusion and many, unanswered questions. But the story of Nicodemus calls us to live a life of awakening, of faithful seeking, of defending Christ even in our uncertainty, of worshiping him even in the dark, silent tombs of the broken, shattered places of our lives.

What questions would you bring before the Lord? What unanswered questions might you have to let go of in order to move forward in your faith and devotion? In what areas is he asking you to make a sacrifice of praise and worship, even in the midst of your pain, disappointment, grief, and mourning?

And in the midst of those questions *can you still believe?* Can you believe…

God so loved *you*
that he gave his one and only begotten Son
that if you would believe in him you will not perish
but have eternal life

And can you believe…

His resurrection life and light lives within you?

(continued next page)

Use the questions and scriptures as your prompts as you begin to create. Before you begin, one note about our prayer below. It is based on the 1917 hymn entitled, "The Love of God" by F.M. Lehman. The stanza below was originally found on the walls of a patient room in an insane asylum—left there by one considered "unsaveable" by worldly standards. Even as he faced severe rejection, deep loneliness, and eventually a solitary death, he was consoled by these beautiful words. Upon researching their origin, they were found to be the words of Jewish poet, Mier Ben Isaac Nehorai, written in the year 1050.[14] Those words are nearly 1,000 years old, and yet they still ring true to this day! Won't you join me in this hymn of praise?

Invite the Holy Spirit into this moment.
Ask the Lord Your Shepherd (Yahweh Rohi) to guide you as you pray.
Ask Jesus (God Saves) to help you understand the depths of his great love.

Lord Jesus, as we worship you through the words of this hymn, we join many others who have been comforted by its words, and we lift to you our sacrifice of praise:

> "Could we with ink the ocean fill,
> And were the skies of parchment made,
> Were every stalk on earth a quill,
> And everyone a scribe by trade,
> To write the love of God above
> Would drain the ocean dry.
> Nor could the scroll contain the whole
> Though stretched from sky to sky.
> O love of God, how rich and pure!
> How measureless and strong!
> It shall forevermore endure
> The saints' and angels' song."

In the midst of our questions, Lord, we are reassured of your great love. Help us to live in mystery. Help us to live in faith. Help us to live in your love.

In the Name of Jesus, our Resurrected Lord and Savior, Amen.

Listen to: "The Love of God" by Mercy Me or the Gaither's
"Wake Up" by All Sons & Daughters

Digging Deeper: Will you Refuse or Confess?

Read: Mark 8:1-9:1

This is a long passage with lots happening! Here's the "Cliffs-note" version with highlights from the text:

Jesus feeds 4,000 people with seven loaves (after feeding 5,000 in Mark 6)

The Pharisees came and began to question Jesus. To test him, they asked him for a sign from heaven. He sighed deeply and said, "Why does this generation ask for a sign? Truly I tell you, no sign will be given to it." 8:11-12

They leave without bread and the disciples still worry about what to eat

Aware of their discussion, Jesus asked them: "Why are you talking about having no bread? Do you still not see or understand? Are your hearts hardened? Do you have eyes but fail to see, and ears but fail to hear? And don't you remember?" 8:17-18

Jesus heals blind man at Bethsaida

Once more Jesus put his hands on the man's eyes. Then his eyes were opened, his sight was restored, and he saw everything clearly. 8:25

Peter confesses Jesus as Christ, the Messiah

"But what about you?" Jesus asked. "Who do you say I am?"

Peter answered, "You are the Messiah." 8:29

Jesus predicts his death

"Whoever wants to be my disciple must deny themselves and take up their cross and follow me. For whoever wants to save their life will lose it, but whoever loses their life for me and for the gospel will save it." 8:34-35

There is so much going on here. I will be relying heavily on Bible scholar David Garland in this study as he lends some powerful thoughts on this beautiful passage.

Thousands of people are traveling long distances to see and hear Jesus teach. After three days, any food they brought with them is gone, and Jesus refuses to send them home hungry for fear they will collapse. Even though Jesus has just fed 5,000 a short time ago, the disciples still wonder what to do. Garland states: "The disciples are slow on the uptake and grope for answers in the dark, expecting nothing miraculous from Jesus again. Jesus patiently has the disciples go through their inventory and provisions. They do not realize that even with their scanty supplies, they have in Jesus enough to feed the entire world."[15]

Jesus performed the exact same miracle just a short time ago. Moreover, in the meantime, he's walked on water! He's healed the demon possessed and the deaf and mute! Yet they are still blinded by the trivial: "[The disciples] consistently fret about insignificant resources. ...Their anxiety over such things keeps them from looking up and seeing what Jesus has done in their midst."[16] They are with him, witnessing everything, and yet they cannot see! Their slumbering spirits have yet to awaken to the Spirit of God in Christ. Garland continues: "They are mired in their own little world, with its petty alarms, and cannot see God's reign breaking into their midst.[17] As he meets their physical hunger, he is also declaring that he can feed their spiritual hunger. Jesus proclaims, "I am the bread of life. Whoever comes to me will never go hungry, and whoever believes in me will never be thirsty" (Jn 6:35).

The Pharisees fail to see, as well. Filled with suspicion they ask for a sign, not from God, but from heaven. This indicates that they are looking for an apocalyptic sign, a sign that Jesus came to deliver Israel from the cursed rule of Rome. "But Jesus will offer this generation no noisy sign from heaven, only the wind whistling through an empty tomb after his crucifixion," says Garland.[18] They cannot see because they are caught up in their own preconceived notion of what the Messiah should do. They expect a man to cause an uprising against the tyranny of Roman rule, but their plan is not God's plan. *This* Messiah will go all the way to the grave to demonstrate God's faithfulness to his people.

In response to both the disciples and the Pharisees, Jesus opens the eyes of the blind man of Bethsaida in a two-step healing, suggesting that like the disciples and the Pharisees, this "blindness is stubborn and hard to cure."[19] With Jesus' persistence however, the man's sight is restored and, as the text says, "He saw everything clearly" (vs 25). While it took effort, in the end all is clear again. Just as Jesus promised—sight to the blind! He goes on to restore not just physical sight, but spiritual sight. Peter understands and proclaims that Jesus is the Christ, the Messiah, the Anointed One of Israel. *Finally!* Hearts awakened, they are beginning to see.

Are you? Miraculous signs are all around us and yet we often fail to see. Over and over God has demonstrated his faithfulness to us—in big and small ways, every day miracles, grand miracles. And yet, our spirits have fallen asleep. We walk through life with blinders on. Our ears cannot hear the still, small voice over the loud din of worldly noise. Caught up in the everyday hassles and concerns of life, we fail to look up and see Jesus at work, in our very midst. We are blinded, asleep, deaf. Preconceived notions of how God should act and what he should do in our lives, leave us with unmet expectations and worse, doubt and fear. We are afraid to awaken because this world has caused us pain, hurt, and disappointment.

At the end of this passage, Jesus begins to tell them how the Messiah would die and be raised again, and they argue against God's redemptive plan. Once more, preconceived notions of how Christ was to restore God's kingdom on earth get in the way, blinding them to the events they'll soon witness as he travels the Way of the Cross. And he is not the only one who would have to carry a cross—all that follow him are called to deny themselves and carry the cross of the Anointed One who would go before. All! That includes you and me!

One of my favorite songs my mother, a beautiful pianist, has played is "Via Dolorosa" by Sandi Patty. The Via Dolorosa is Latin for "Way of Suffering" or "Way of Grief," and it is the name of the path that Jesus walked through Jerusalem to the hill of Golgotha outside town. The lyrics of the chorus are touching:

> *Down the Via Dolorosa called the way of suffering*
> *Like a lamb came the Messiah, Christ the King!*
> *But He chose to walk that road*
> *out of His love for you and me.*
> *Down the Via Dolorosa, all the way to Calvary.*[20]

The Way of Suffering is all well and good for Jesus, but *what about for us? Do our own preconceived notions include the following thoughts?*

Now that I've found Jesus, everything will be perfect!
    Jesus will take all my worries and troubles far away!
        From here on out, it will be blessing after blessing!
            God makes everything great!

While there is some truth mixed in with these statements, they all fall short of the life Jesus demonstrated to us. We want to be like Jesus, but often all we want is the glory and perhaps, if we're honest, the wave-your-magic-wand miracles. However, that is not the whole truth of the life Christ calls us to emulate. This passage here in 8:34-9:1 is quite the opposite.

Take a moment to reflect on the miracles of God's faithfulness in your life and the lives of those around you. *Where has Jesus shown up and worked a miracle? Where has the Bread of Life fed you and nourished you?* Take time to remember. Not just today, in this moment, but *every day!* Reflect on his goodness and mercy and provision in your life and in the lives of others. Let it serve as a reminder of the miracles he has worked. Now take a moment to reflect on your own preconceived notions. *What are the ways in which you try to put God in a box? What "rules" or "statements" have you lived by that might contain an element of truth but go against what Jesus is saying in Mark 8? Where have you been blind? Where have you refused to see?*

Using the questions and scripture passages as your prompts as you begin to explore through creativity, won't you join me in this prayer?

Invite the Holy Spirit into this moment.
Ask the Lord Your Shepherd (Yahweh Rohi) to guide you as you pray.
Ask Jesus (God Saves) to help you follow him wherever he leads.

Jesus Messiah, as I come to you with all I have, you take my loaves and fishes and leave me standing before you empty-handed. Yet I know once I have handed everything over to you, the miracles can begin. Christ, multiply my meager offering to feed not only my own hungry spirit, but also the spirits of those around me. I confess that I come with pre-conceived notions of how I think you should be and how life should be with you. I surrender those expectations to you now. Pierce my heart. Make it your own. Awaken me to the possibilities of all that you intend for me. I join Peter and proclaim: "You are the Christ!" Help me speak it out in faith and hope. And as I do, may it pierce others' hearts with its power and transform multitudes with its powerful truth.

In the name of Jehovah Jireh, My Provider, Amen.

Listen to: "Via Dolorosa" by Sandi Patty
"Slumber" by NEEDTOBREATHE

A Benediction of Radiant Sunrise

Dawn
by Sara Joseph

Faint blush of salmon stains the sky
Inky night bids a swift good-bye
Color spilled, relentless flow
The dawn of day a forceful glow

No man can bottle this fuchsia hue
Day once begun will stride on through
Dimming darkness and gaining strength
The day must live its destined length

Quiet whisper bids me learn
A lesson from the gleam of dawn
"You walk a path, O Righteous One,
Which like first radiant beam of sun

"Dispels darkness and welcomes Me
Though faint at first, with little to see
Shining brighter till full force of day
Destined for glory though fashioned of clay."

What joy to know that once begun
No turning back the blazing sun
My way will march the way of dawn
Until my time on earth is done

Brighter, sharper, erasing night
No taint of ink, no dimming sight
From glory to glory, ever bold
From blush to fuchsia and then to gold.

Next Steps: Resources for Your Healing Journey

The Healing Presence by Leanne Payne

When the Heart Waits by Sue Monk Kidd

Gently Awakened: the Influence of Faith on Your Artistic Journey by Sara Joseph

God's Creative Gift—Unleashing the Artist in You by Jody Thomae, as well as www.jodythomae.com for creative spiritual practices, resources, and devotionals.

www.12tribesministries.com is the ministry of Cindy Fort. Healing art prompts, resources, support, and practical application of God's word to encourage and bring restoration. Explore "Paths of Healing" and "Paths of Creativity" tabs.

"The Awakening" is a 4-day seminar where you discover what it means to be defined by Jesus and live out of your true identity. See: www.healingcare.org

Endnotes
1. Mulholland, *Shaped by the Word.*
2. Levine, *Numbers 21—36*, 137.
3. Ibid., 235.
4. Ibid.
5. Buller, "Prophets, Prophecy," 664.
6. Gaventa, *Acts of the Apostles*, 146.
7. Ibid., 149.
8. Garland, *Luke*, 747.
9. Ibid., 751.
10. Butler, *Luke*, 315.
11. Young, *Crossroads*, 199-200.
12. My suspicion here holds no basis in scholarly research. John was written later than the other synoptic Gospel accounts, and relied heavily on oral tradition. I believe that as the stories of Jesus' ministry were told among believers, the story of Nicodemus came out as a beautiful story of growing in discipleship and devotion to Christ.
13. Sailhamer, *NIV Compact Commentary*, 487.
14. Accessed February 2, 2016 at www.ministrymagazine.org/archive/1950/09/the-story-of-the-love-of-god
15. Garland, *Mark*, 307.
16. Ibid., 311.
17. Ibid.
18. Ibid., 309.
19. Ibid., 312.
20. Patty, *Via Dolorosa*, 1990.

The Creator's Healing Power—Restoring the Broken to Beautiful

2

Resting

"The one the Lord loves rests between his shoulders."

At the start of the movie *The Legend of Bagger Vance,*[1] we find Rannulph Junuh, the character played by Matt Damon, struggling to get his golf swing back as he hacks one ball after another into the defying darkness surrounding his home. Bagger Vance, played by Will Smith, mysteriously appears out of that same darkness—his only explanation being he was "taking in some of God's glories." Junuh was once a promising golfer, but after a harrowing World War I experience where his entire unit, save Junuh, was killed in battle, he returned with what we would now label Post Traumatic Stress Disorder. He has flashbacks, drinks to alleviate pain and erase memories, and suffers from severe depression. The struggle to get his golf swing back is merely a metaphor for the very real struggle to get his life back.

Junuh "hires" Bagger to be his caddy for a mere $5, and Bagger sets to correcting his "swing." What I love about this movie is the underlying spiritual themes that remind us that the Holy Spirit journeys with us in our struggles. Take a moment to watch two scenes from the movie on YouTube titled: "The Legend of Bagger Vance Clip 1 Authentic Swing" and "The Legend of Bagger Vance Clip 2 Seeing the Field."[2] They both reveal a great deal about the presence of the Holy Spirit with you and the way the Spirit speaks truth into your life.

What is the Holy Spirit saying to you in these lines from the movie?

"Well, you lost your swing. We got to go find it.
Now it's somewhere... in the harmony of all that is, all that was, all that will be."

Have you lost your swing? Your life? Your self? Your identity? It's in Christ—who was, and is, and is to come. And he will help you find it.

"Inside each and every one of us is one true authentic swing.
Somethin' we was born with. Somethin' that's ours and ours alone.
Somethin' that can't be taught to ya or learned. Somethin' that got to be remembered.
Over time the world can rob us of that swing.
It gets buried inside us under all our wouldas and couldas and shouldas."

Inside you is your one true self, your real identity, your true destiny and calling in life. You were born with it–it's yours and yours alone. Do not let the world, the enemy, your shame or regret rob you of it.

And as Bagger Vance has Junuh set his eyes on his calm competitor, Bobby Jones:

"Put your eyes on Bobby Jones. Look at his practice swing, almost like he's searchin' for something.
Then he finds it. Watch how he settle hisself right into the middle of it.
Feel that focus. He got a lot of shots he could choose from:
…but there's only one shot that's in perfect harmony with the field.
One shot that's his authentic shot, and that shot is gonna choose him.
There's a perfect shot out there tryin' to find each and every one of us.
All we got to do is get ourselves out of its way, to let it choose us. Can't see that flag as some dragon you got to slay. You got to look with soft eyes. See the place where the tides and the seasons and the turnin' of the Earth, all come together—where everything that is, becomes one.
You got to seek that place with your soul, Junuh.
Seek it with your hands. Don't think about it—feel it.
Your hands is wiser than your head ever gonna be.
Now I can't take you there, Junuh. Just hope I can help you find a way."

Beloved, push your pride and ego out of the way. Look with heavenly eyesight for the place where the tides and the seasons and the turning of the Earth all come together within the deepest places of your soul. As an artist, seek it with your hands—hands that hold paint brushes, mold clay, and are covered in charcoal; hands that play instruments and write stories, poems and scripts; hands that hold cameras and design graphics; hands that reach, grasp and hold while you dance. Those hands are wiser than your head is ever going to be. Artists of God, let your hands help you find the way.

This chapter is all about resting in the Presence of the One who is always with you, who has never left your side, who is with you, around you, in you. In that rest you find your true identity in the Presence of the One who created you to be who you are. The One who has placed a destiny and calling within you.

I have already been encouraging you to picture the presence of Jesus with you as we've been working our way through this healing journey together. This "presence thing" is pretty important! In fact, it is difficult, dare I say impossible, to move forward in healing and using the creative process as an avenue of healing without an understanding deep in your spirit that God's presence is with you.

Resting in God's presence is where you discover and nurture your own "authentic swing." God alone is your true center, consistently calling you back to your destiny and design—your true identity. When you rest in God's presence, you will learn that you are protected and provided for. It doesn't matter what's going on around you or what chaos the enemy is heaping on you. God is with you, protecting you and bringing provision to you. When you rest in God's presence, you will find power for ministry to others. Creativity for creativity's sake is wonderful, but creativity in the presence of God will take you and your ministry to a new place with a front row seat to the workings of the kingdom of God and the power of the Holy Spirit.

It truly is all about resting in His Presence!

Resting Between His Shoulders

Let's start in God's Word.

As Moses prepares to die, he blesses each tribe of Israel. For Benjamin, the blessing is simple:

> *"Let the beloved of the Lord rest secure in him, for he shields him all day long, and the one the Lord loves rests between his shoulders."* Deut 33:12

The phrase "between his shoulders" is a poetic way of saying that the tribe of Benjamin occupied the land between Mount Zion (the City of David where the Ark of the Covenant would come to rest) and Mount Moriah (where Solomon would one day build the Temple). This is sacred land in Israel—a place where God's holy presence resided. Due to the geography of the land, with these mountains shielding either side, it is a physical place of protection.

The English Standard Version translates it differently:

> *"The beloved of the Lord dwells in safety. The High God surrounds him all day long and dwells between his shoulders."*

In this translation, God both surrounds Benjamin *and also dwells between* Benjamin's shoulders—which is quite different in its meaning. God is found *both* surrounding him and in the midst of him, in his heart. These two interpretations disclose two truths. Like Benjamin, when we rest in his presence, we rest between the shoulders of God, protected and secure in a love that shields us. We lay our heads back against him and hear God's sacred heartbeat. Furthermore, we are both *surrounded* by God and *indwelt* by God. God's Holy Temple is in us. His presence finds its rest in our hearts. God is "resting" in us! Are we "resting" in him?

Another truth we find in this passage is that we are secure, shielded, safe, and surrounded. For some, "resting" is difficult because we don't feel secure or shielded, safe or surrounded. This is especially true for those who are affected by physical trauma, neglect, or abuse. Physically your body seldom feels safe. We will talk more about this in a bit. For now, can you simply believe in your head, even if not in your bones, that you are safe, that the Bible is true, and trust the Lord at his word?

Let's practice this a moment: I invite you to find Rita Springer's song *Between Your Shoulders*, find a comfortable place, and rest in God's presence as you listen.

Mindfulness and the Body

Dr. Curt Thompson is a psychiatrist who studies the effect of spiritual practices on the brain and body and is a great proponent of present moment practices. He first explains the mind/body connection:

> The mind is embodied, which means it is housed in your physical self and depends on your body to function. Of course, the mind includes the brain, but other parts of the body play a role in the flow of energy and information. For example, you become aware that you are anxious in part because you sense your pulse rate increasing and feel your heart pounding in your chest.[3]

Thompson goes on to state:

> I suggest that many elements of our mind/body matrix are means by which God is trying to get our attention, but we have not had much practice reflecting on them. We...often don't focus on our feelings, memories, what our bodies are telling us, or the depth and meaning of our narratives. The more we pay attention to these things—what our brains are telling us—the more we are ultimately paying attention to God. ...By paying attention to our mind-body experience, we are paying attention to what the Holy Spirit is telling us.[4]

Thompson starts by simply asking clients to start paying attention to what they are paying attention to. What events, information, situations, etc. are you paying attention to and what emotions and feelings are arising as a result? It's amazing what we attend to every day, all day. When we start paying attention to what we're paying attention to, we find that we are often caught up in negativity, hectic-ness, busy-ness, anxiousness, worry, and/or boredom. We find our hearts and minds disconnected from the heart and mind of God, that we are *not* taking every thought captive, and that we are worrying about the things God asked us to place in *his* hands. Spiritual practices that help us attend to the presence of God in the present moment are the first step in rising above all this.

Thompson goes on to propose that when we come before him, God often begins by asking:

What are you doing here?

Read I Kings 19, paying attention to verse 9. Elijah is hiding out in a cave, when God shows up and asks him this question. He asks similar questions of others in scripture as well (see Gen 16:8). In the words of Thompson:

> He does this with all of us. First, he comes to our deserts and lonely mountains. He asks us questions, sometimes difficult ones that may initially drive us deep into caves of our own minds, into the recesses of old neural pathways and ancient, repetitive memories. His probing may leave us exhausted, famished, and terrified. His queries may even elicit the very feelings we try so hard to avoid. Often the question is simply, *What are you doing here?* He never asks with scorn or derision but always with hope and anticipation. He asks with the tone of a God who is eager for us to retrace our neural pathways, to eventually take a different route and create a new end to our story. To "remember" our future differently.[5]

So, take a moment to be still and know that he is God. Tend to your soul for a moment. See if God is asking you, "What are you doing here?"

Somatic Memory

Related to and complimenting Thompson's ideas of embodied mindfulness, is the idea of somatic memory. In *The Body Remembers* by Babette Rothschild and *The Body Keeps the Score* by Bessel van der Kolk, the authors discuss somatic memory and its effect on victims of trauma.[6] *Soma* means body, so somatic memory is basically the idea that the body remembers sensory images and stores them for later recall. Let me give you an example. Near the end of the Disney movie *Ratatouille*, the food critic Anton is taken back in time to a wonderful memory of his mother's cooking by Remy the Rat's ratatouille dish. All of his senses are overwhelmed as he takes in the sight, smell, and taste of the dish, and those sensations take him back to a special place in time. In essence, his body remembered. However, in some cases, memories don't get filed away correctly and fail to integrate into our life story. Have you ever smelled something that took you back somewhere but you couldn't quite recall where? The body remembers, even when the mind doesn't.

This is true for both positive and negative experiences. Even when our mind fails to translate our sensory input and experiences into memories we can recall, our body still remembers. That is why unprocessed, negative experiences and emotions can reveal themselves through disease and illness. We see this most vividly in stress and its negative effect on our health. While we might want to separate physical healing from emotional, spiritual, and psychological healing, we simply can't. We must see ourselves as a total being, not separate parts—all subject to brokenness and disease.

This is especially true for those who are affected by trauma and abuse. For many, the body does not feel like a safe place, and they might find spiritual practices involving the body or stillness very difficult. It is important to understand the concept of embodiment, as well as the mind/body connection, in order to begin to reclaim our bodies. Rev. Marcia Shoop has studied and written about embodiment and spirituality, particularly as it relates to trauma. She writes:

> Tragedy and suffering, and the pain and loss that come with it, condition all of us and the way we live as bodies in this world. The way that the body holds and is marked by harm…is the nature of the body itself. We, as bodies, are conditioned on a cellular level by experience. Experiences that harm have particular power to affect our embodied life. Tragic experiences are those of unrecoverable loss and intense suffering that are part of all human experience.[7]

There are many practices that help reclaim a sense of embodiment, including: visual imagery to scan the body, movement exercises like yoga and tai chi, deep breathing, and massage. I have taught in the area of embodied prayer, creative worship, and moving with mindfulness for years, and have seen the miracle of people reconnecting to their bodies time after time. Shoop states: "These practices can, over time, begin to coax feeling into stretching out and flowing more freely. These practices tap into the body's story and invite the body into a place where it re-members, integrates, rejuvenates."[8]

Shoop invites us into embodiment informed by the words of Christ found in John 6:56: "Those who eat my flesh and drink my blood abide in me, and I in them." Christ comes and makes his dwelling not only among us, but in us:

> Transformation is the core promise of Christian life. …Our bodies change in an incarnational faith—our individual bodies and our corporate bodies. Jesus is asking to be ingested so that he can dwell in us; and we are changed in form when Deity inhabits us this way. Where sin and suffering distort us, that affliction is healed in a deep and profound way. A path is cleared for us to learn to function and feel anew. …We are transformed bodies, not simply transformed minds and hearts.
>
> Living into these embodied gifts of God takes practice. Like a creek bed slowly changing course, practice is the trickling current that creates transformation in time. Practice is the wind, the push in the current. Practice nourishes our embodied competency for redemption. The body can become more and more available for redemption by nurturing itself.[9]

Creative spiritual practices help us find ourselves: heart, mind, soul, and body. They help us connect the fragmented, bifurcated pieces of our wounded selves and begin, with God's healing presence, to put them back together.

So, pause, and take a moment to take in God's presence with you now.

Safe Place

One way to rest in God's presence is called "Safe Place," a spiritual practice developed by Dr. Terry Wardle, who works in the area of healing and formational prayer. Wardle explains, "When I am helping a person experience Christ in a wounded past, I always spend time helping the person find a safe place within where he or she can meet Jesus."[10] Safe Place is like a "home base" within the soul. Did you ever play hide and seek or tag? There was always a "home base" to return to where we were out of harm, so to speak. Where we couldn't be tagged or where we returned safely from our hiding places. Safe Place is similar to this in many ways.

There are several points that are critical here. Wardle states: "Traumatic events have conditioned the wounded to anticipate sudden disaster at any moment. Pathways have formed in the brain and when something the least bit threatening occurs, fight, flight, or freeze responses automatically kick into gear."[11] When we create a place of "safety" within the heart and mind, it doesn't mean that all risk is eliminated, however "it does mean that an environment is created to eliminate all unnecessary risk."[12] Wardle also states:

> Communicating truth by creating word pictures is employed all through scripture. …Creating a safe place within is a way that the Spirit communicates truth through a surrendered and sanctified imagination. …For some people it takes time to develop this skill. Many believers accustomed to a more cognitive expression of the Christian life, have never experienced the Lord in this way. The idea of giving the Lord access to their "creative imagination" will seem like a foreign concept.[13]

For many it is helpful to be guided through this by a friend, mentor, caregiver, counselor, or pastor at first. This is especially true if you are the victim of trauma, deep emotional pain, or have been involved in the occult, any type of ritualistic abuse, or new age philosophies and mystic practice.[14] Having someone by your side to both guide you through this practice and to keep you covered from spiritual attack is important. It may be necessary for you to put this book aside until you have found someone to be by your side for this practice. Remember: the enemy does not want you to find healing, freedom, and restoration, so he directly wars against any attempt to find liberty. In addition, your body has been programmed to respond to perceived threat and will do whatever it takes to protect you. This will often get in the way of freedom in your life. Also, for some the word "safe" in "Safe Place" may cause great difficulty. You can replace it with peaceful, restful, or calm.

Here are the steps in the practice of Safe Place:[15]
- Sit quietly in a comfortable position.
- Take several deep breaths, letting them out slowly.
- Begin to whisper words of thanks and praise to the Lord.
- After a few moments, invite the Holy Spirit to take over your imagination.
- Ask the Spirit to create within your mind a safe place where you can meet the Lord. It may be an imaginary place or somewhere you have been before that is special, like a cabin, beach, or spot along a quiet stream. It can also simply be a color or a ray of light if imagery is difficult for you.

- Rest there for as long as you like, enjoying all the surroundings. If you experience some dissonance or distraction, ask the Holy Spirit to take it away in the name of Jesus.
- When ready, invite the Lord to join you in that place. If that frightens you, ask him to come as the Lamb, or to simply allow you to feel his presence.
- Once there, notice the warmth of his love. Let it soak into your being. If you are allowing Christ to be there, notice his posture, eyes, and extended arms. Draw close to him if you desire.
- When ready, tell Jesus how you feel about him. Then ask how he feels about you. He may respond with words or maybe actions. Either way, experience his acceptance and delight.
- If you are ready to conclude the exercise, simply spend a few moments in thanks and praise.
- Take a few deep breaths, letting them out slowly. Amen.

Please know that some people will find this extremely easy and fulfilling; others will struggle and find it very frustrating and perhaps frightening. If you struggle, be patient with yourself. Also note that some people may not be able to sit quietly for Safe Place: they may instead need to stand and gently walk circles, sway, or go on a walk. I am very kinesthetically oriented so learning to sit quietly was a process.

In my own experience with Safe Place, I can tell you several things. First, my Safe Place has changed over time. The changing scenery is often reflective of the changing seasons in my spiritual life. I have learned to "take in the view" and be attentive to the ways my Safe Place environment might be changing. Second, Jesus shows up in many different ways. Sometimes he appears as "typical" Jesus—white robe, blue sash, and all. He showed up for a friend of mine in a red and black flannel shirt and looked like a mountain man. He will occasionally appear as an animal for me. Sometimes, a park ranger. For a season in my life, Jesus showed up as a blond-haired, blue-eyed little boy about the age of six who wore a striped shirt and blue jeans. At first I didn't even know it was Jesus! That was one of my favorite images of Jesus, appearing after a season of deep, difficult soul-searching—calling me out to play. Remember: you are creative. There's no telling how Jesus might show up for you. Be open.

Some Christians can be suspect of using imagination. Leanne Payne is the author of *Healing Presence*. Let her wisdom lend counsel: "Symbol is the key for the fusion of thought with feeling. The symbolic mind, working properly, brings together head and heart."[16] And with gentle warning, she adds they should "always to be interpreted through and by sound interpretation of the Word, the Scriptures."[17] For the artist, imagination, visualization and symbols are the tools with which we work. It is how we reveal beauty in this world. We intuitively understand that symbols bring heart and mind together. For the creative Christian, we should also keep in mind that we need to work with scriptural integrity.

Now, take a moment, and rest in God's presence.

Resting in God's Presence with Creativity

As we move forward in our Bible studies, we will begin to use the Safe Place spiritual practice, to be mindful of God's presence with us, and to rest in the presence of God with us. And lest you fear you'll have to spend hours sitting around trying to sense God's presence, let's not forget as artists and creatives, we can add creativity to practice the presence of God. As you approach your easel or wheel, walk toward it with intention and prayer, asking God to be with you as you create. As you sit down to write, art journal, sing, play, craft, or sew, take several deep breaths and remember that the Creator sits down with you. Invite him to help you, to enter your creative process or worship with you. As you work through a dance or a drama, picture Christ there with you as a part of the choreography or scene. Perhaps you might want to create something that is representative of your Safe Place?

I will leave you with one last video to watch from *The Legend of Bagger Vance*—find it on YouTube as "The Legend of Bagger Vance Clip 3 In the Woods." Sense God's presence as you watch.[18]

Beloved, there's no one on the earth that doesn't have a burden to carry that they don't understand. But it's time to lay that burden down. You have a choice—a choice to stop right where you are or to start walking back to where you've always been and to wait there. Be still, real still. And remember—remember who you really are. The Holy Spirit is telling you it's time to come out of the shadows. It's time for you to choose. You are not alone—God is right there with you. You have a purpose, one that was given to you when you came into this world. You ready? Don't hold back. Let yourself remember. Now is the time.

Take a deep breath.

It's time to remember.

Listen to: "Be Still My Soul (In You I Rest)" by Kari Jobe

Digging Deeper Into…

Psalm 91: Protection of His Wings	Page 48
Psalm 57: Music in our Silent Caves	Page 52
II Samuel 9: Safe in the King's Presence	Page 55
I Kings 17—19: Provision in God's Presence	Page 59
Mark 4: Jesus Calms the Storm	Page 63

Benediction of Heartbeat — Page 67
    A Reflection… Solemn Praise by Mandy L Gero

Next Steps: Resources for Your Healing Journey & Endnotes — Page 68

Coloring Page "Hidden" by Donna Godwin — Page 69

Digging Deeper: Protection of His Wings

Read: Psalm 91

Psalm 91 is a beautiful psalm of encouragement, instruction, and reassurance from God. I return to it often, especially when I am feeling attacked. It reminds me of his faithful protection in times of trouble. There are several images in this passage worth noting. Remember as an artist, creative, worshiper, or one who appreciates beauty: imagery is very important. We often understand images and symbols more deeply than others around us. Exploring and understanding imagery in scripture is often a calling of the creative Christian as we help uncover and interpret these images and symbols for others around us. With that critical calling in our minds, let's begin.

Observe with me the beginning of verse four from the Amplified Bible:

He will cover you and completely protect you with his pinions,
And under his wings you will find refuge.

Reminiscent of Ruth 2:12 and Matthew 23:37, it reveals a feminine, nurturing image of God: a protective mother hen gathering her chicks under the shelter of her feathery wings.

Let's read the remaining part of that verse in the English Standard Translation:

His faithfulness is a shield and buckler.

Like Psalm 62:2 and Proverbs 18:10, it illustrates a strong, masculine image of God. A buckler is a small round shield that attached to a soldier's arm. This image depicts a warrior ready to go to battle to protect the person or city he is duty-bound and trained to defend.

These feminine and masculine images open our eyes to see God as mother *and* father. Now, I recognize that many did not grow up with mothers that nurtured or fathers that protected. Core longings and basic childhood needs were not met through our parents in a way that made us feel safe, secure, or cared for. In fact, it was quite the opposite, and we now live fractured lives as a result. However, as difficult as it might be to imagine, God *is* the *perfect* mother and father. God is *your* mother and father! No matter what your *earthly* parents did, your *heavenly parent will never fail you*—he is the one perfect source of all you need. He protects you, nurtures you, covers you.

Read on through the imagery of verses 5-10. A great battle encircles you, but you stand firm. You will "only observe with your eyes" (vs 8) not experience the death and destruction of those around you. But only *if* you make God your refuge and strong tower (vs 9)—the place you rest. As you read on in 11-13, we find more beautiful imagery—of being lifted by angels so as not to bruise your foot. In fact, that very foot, the one that is protected, will be the very foot that treads and tramples the lion and the serpent! Think on that image a moment! Imagine his angels lifting you out of your current circumstance or trouble. Look down at your feet and see that they are whole and strong, without bruise or injury. Now imagine those feet coming down and trampling upon your circumstance with powerful victory!

Next, note how this psalm changes "voice" in verses 14-16. Bible Scholar Beth Tanner notes that the psalmist has previously asked the following questions of desperate pain back in Psalm 88:14 and 89:46:[19]

> *Why do you reject me?*
> *Why do you hide your face from me?*
> *Will you hide yourself forever?*
> *How long will your wrath burn?*

Perhaps you feel like that? Like God has forgotten you, rejected you, and hidden his face from you? Perhaps much like your earthly parents? I know there have been many times in my own journey when I've asked those very questions of God. Yet he is so faithful! In our questioning, God answers, reassuring us of his faithfulness:

> *Because you hold fast to me in love, I will deliver you;*
> *I will protect you, because you know my name.*
> *When you call to me, I will answer you;*
> *I will be with you in trouble; I will rescue you and honor you.*
> *With long life I will satisfy you and show you my salvation.*
> Ps 91:14-16 (ESV, translation altered)

This picture of God as one who directly answers our questions is a powerful image, helping our meager faith rise to the surface. We feel like God is hiding his face from us, but Tanner offers this encouraging interpretation: "God is not hiding, but is instead providing a hiding place for the faithful one."[20] Turn that image around in your mind for a moment.

Now, the question is this: will you be faithful? Faith-full?

It is very easy to get trapped in the downward spiral of the "questioning whys:"
Why have you gone silent?
Why wasn't I born into a more loving family?
Why did this happen to me?

There are a million "whys" we could ask ourselves. Most of those whys contain the unspoken belief that God has gone missing or wasn't there for us when we needed him. We might know, as a fact in our head, that God is with us, but there in the deepest recesses of our hearts and souls, we believe he is not. That he has somehow removed himself from us. This is when we must call up our faith, a faith that believes and trusts amidst the questions and pain.

Brother Lawrence also speaks to these questions:

> What can we do when we no longer find the Lord? The key is found in the word *faith*. Faith is the one thing, perhaps the only thing, which will not fail you in such a time. Let faith be your support. The very foundation of your confidence must be your faith. At a time like that, when God seems to have forsaken you, you must exercise your faith in him.[21]

Over and over I have found this to be true. My own testimony of healing and wholeness rests on faith. Faith is the bedrock upon which our foundation must rest. We must hold fast to him in love. Moreover, Tanner goes on to say that this faith is a mystery without answers, much like God himself:

> We too know that in times of doubt, with questions of [God] hanging in the air, the answers that finally come never provide a definitive explanation of why these things happen in the first place. As these ancient people knew, God and our faith in God is a mystery, and for that mystery there are no definitive answers, rational or otherwise, that suffice.[22]

The writer of Psalm 91 speaks from a place of deep faith, but it is a deep faith that comes from resting with God as Father. We might feel as if we will never have that kind of faith. We doubt, we fear, we still ask why he hides. We may not feel his protection. We may still struggle because we want answers to the whys of our life. *Can we allow the faith of this psalmist here to stand in for our faith? Can we say we believe and yet ask God to help our unbelief (Mk 9:24)? Can we trust that God protects us, covers us, encircles us, even when we feel exposed, uncovered?* If this psalm is one of encouragement and instruction, *then can we take courage and learn from its teaching?*

Meditate on Isaiah 26:3 for a moment:

You will keep in perfect peace
those whose minds are steadfast,
because they trust in you.

Now take a deep breath. Remember.

(continued next page)

Using the questions and scripture passages as your prompts as you begin to explore through creativity, won't you join me in this prayer?

Invite the Holy Spirit into this moment.
Ask the Lord Your Shepherd (Yahweh Rohi) to guide you as you pray.
Ask the Lord of Hosts (Jehovah Sabaoth) to protect you from the enemy.
Ask the Lord Your Peace (Yahweh Shalom) to quiet your heart before him.

Yahweh Shalom, I want to stay in your perfect peace, yet I fear that is an impossibility. And if truth be told, I have a great many fears as this battle rages around me. Help me to look to you, as the God who covers me under the protection of your wings. Help me to look to you, as the God who is a shield about me. Help me to look to you as the one who sends his angels to keep me from even stubbing my toe. Help me to look to you as the one who helps me trample the lion and serpent under my feet! I believe, Lord, but help my unbelief! In all the places where I fear you cannot be. In all the places where others have failed me. In all the places where I won't let you in so you can offer me what they couldn't give. In all the circumstances, problems, pain, and whys. In faith, I believe! And where my faith still wanes, let the psalmist's words of faith above speak for my weary heart. Help me hold fast to you in love.
In the name of God my Heavenly Father and Mother I pray, Amen.

Listen to: "Steal Me Away" by Jody Thomae
"Psalm 91" by Lincoln Brewster

Digging Deeper: Music in our Silent Caves

Read: Psalm 57

There is much to unearth in this Psalm! So grab your pickaxe and let's get mining!

First, let's set the context. In Psalm 57, the anointed but not yet appointed King David is found hiding out in a cave, trying to escape the current King Saul, who has gone mad with jealousy and fear. You might want to take a moment and also read I Samuel 22—24 to give you an idea of what is happening in David's life as he writes this song found in Psalm 57.

Now, let's begin to excavate the layers.

Even though *physically* David is taking refuge in a cave, in verse one we find that *spiritually and emotionally* David is taking refuge in God. The "I" here should be more appropriately translated "my whole self" as in:

> *My whole self takes refuge in the shadow of your wings.*

And where do we find him? Under the shelter of the feathery wings of God. This is no accident! David often uses this image and these words to remind himself of God's protection: it has become both a visual and verbal symbol of remembrance. Payne relates this truth about God and the way he uses symbols in this way:

> God sends us pictures and he sends us words. Pictures—that is, metaphor, symbol, myth, dreams, and visions—are a vital part of the language of the heart. We need to understand this symbolic language. But one can think imaginatively without images. Knowledge, wisdom, understanding come to us as *word* (i.e., more nearly concept) as well as in picture form.[23]

The words and the image it creates have become deep "soul-truth" for David, even when he is in doubt, hiding in the dark recesses of desert caves. This is why imagery and symbol are so important to creative Christians.

In verses 2—3, David "cries out" to God. The Hebrew here is *qara* and it means: "to cry out, call, name, proclaim, pronounce, preach." I love that this is not a cry of whining or weakness, but of proclamation and strength. And what is he boldly proclaiming? That God will rebuke Saul, fulfill his purpose for David, and "send out" his love and faithfulness.

In verses 4—7, he alternates between explaining the difficulty of his situation and then praising God. He ends with a declaration of a steadfast heart that proclaims God's faithfulness through song. Bible scholar Beth Tanner lends wisdom to the composition of this psalm: "[This is] a literary structure where the problem with the enemies is literally surrounded by the confident statements of trust."[24] Through this chorus of praise, Tanner sees "a musical crescendo [that] moves from the evocation of a bent and bruised soul to the twice-stated declaration of a steadfast heart."[25] She also points out that David has turned his whole self towards praise of God. As he does so, he gathers instruments and others in praise of the Faithful One in verses 8—11: "The one praying is now leading the chorus that rings through the heavens."[26] David's place of fearful hiding has now become a sanctuary of praise under the shelter of God's protective wing. This cave is now a temple, and David calls on his instruments of praise to raise a song to awaken the dawning of a new day. He proclaims:

> *For great is your love, O Lord, reaching to the heavens;*
> *Your faithfulness reaches to the sky.*

If we see David's cave as a place of withdrawal and hiding, we might think it a negative place. But sometimes, in the midst of withdrawal and hiding, we actually find quite the opposite. Henri Nouwen explains:

> Human withdrawal is a very painful and lonely process, because it forces us to face directly our own condition in all its beauty as well as misery. When we are not afraid to enter into our own center and to concentrate on the stirrings of our own soul, we come to know that being alive means being loved. This experience tells us that we can only love because we are born out of love, that we can only give because our life is a gift, and that we can only make others free because we are set free by him whose heart is greater than ours. When we have found the anchor places for our lives in our own center, we can be free to let others enter into the space created for them and allow them to dance their own dance, sing their own song, and speak their own language without fear.[27]

This is all very evident in Psalm 57.

When I was first digging into this passage for this study, I was struggling. My church, which once had a thriving creative arts ministry, was now apathetic towards creativity and the arts. I was scheduled to lead worship and felt surrounded on many sides. The lion and the serpent were biting at my heels! The *Prophet* in me wanted to call out the church on its apathy, but the *Priest* in me had a worship order to plan.[28] All day long I was receiving "words" from God: "Break the chains!" and from God's people: "Press into Jesus and His Word." But I was distracted, letting the lion and the serpent keep me from what God had called me to do.

Finally I sat down with my guitar and simply began to worship. I received the breakthrough I needed to not only plan for worship, but to deal with this issue at church with which I was struggling, as well. As I pressed into Jesus and worshiped, it broke the chains on my spirit!

I *then* went to the library to study this passage and realized all I had been experiencing aligned with what God's Word was revealing to me. Worship breaks chains. God answers as we cry out and proclaim that he is holy and sovereign over all. As we tell him of our difficulties and lament the pain they are causing us, we break free from the enemy's strongholds on our hearts and souls. With our whole self, we can enter into the hidden caves of sanctuary and shelter and find that all of heaven joins in our praise. There we can rest in God's presence.

David knew that music could not only soothe but also heal the broken places of the soul. As he rested under the shelter of God's wings, he called out to his spirit to lift a song of praise to God. *Can you remember a time when your praise brought break-through in a situation in your life? Recall this time in your mind. Did the praise change the situation or simply change your attitude about the situation? In what current situations in your life is God calling you to sing? To sing from the sanctuary of your cave of praise?*

(continued next page)

Using the questions and scripture passages as your prompts as you begin to explore through creativity, won't you join me in this prayer?

Invite the Holy Spirit into this moment.
Ask the Lord Your Shepherd (Yahweh Rohi) to guide you as you pray.
Ask the Lord Who Sees (El Roi) to look upon his child as you cry out to him.

Lord Jesus, our Savior and Christ, I choose in this moment, in this situation, to lift my song of praise to you. Let it echo through the cavernous empty spaces and places within, filling me with songs of deliverance and freedom. Let it ring out and reverberate against the walls of my heart and soul, and as it does may it bring healing to the deepest recesses within. Search my heart. Fill it with praise. You are worthy. You are holy. I praise you. For great is your love, O Lord, reaching to the heavens; your faithfulness reaches to the sky. I rest in you.

In the Name of Him Who is Seated on the Throne and Reigns Forever, Amen.

Listen to: "Break Every Chain" by Tasha Cobbs
"I Will Sing" by The Brilliance

Digging Deeper: Safe in the King's Presence

Read: II Samuel 9

The story of David and Mephibosheth is a beautiful story of loyalty, love, and restoration. In this story, David has now rightfully taken the throne in Jerusalem. As he goes about the proper actions to establish his reign over Israel, one of those actions would be to kill any remaining heirs of Saul as they might try to lay claim to the throne. However, David has taken an oath with both Saul and his son Jonathan, and here we find David is a man of his word.

David's first oath was with Jonathan (I Sam 20). David and Jonathan loved each other like brothers, and their relationship was one of loyalty and love. This covenant was rooted in this loyalty and love for one another. David's second oath was with Saul (I Sam 24). David had been in the service of Saul since he was young, and he was also loyal to Saul. However, this loyalty was rooted in respect and honor for the one God had appointed as ruler and king. Interestingly, when David becomes king and goes about finding any remaining descendants of Saul and Jonathan, he recalls and honors his oath *to Jonathan* not Saul: "Is there anyone still left of the house of Saul to whom I can show kindness *for Jonathan's sake*?" (vs 1, *emphasis added*). He isn't seeking out Saul's descendants out of duty-bound respect for Saul, but out of his deep love for Jonathan. In his seeking he finds Mephibosheth, the son of his dear friend Jonathan.

Mephibosheth comes, falling at David's feet in fear, for he fully expects to be killed at this point. While Mephibosheth is crippled in both feet, which precluded him from ruling as king, he had a son named Mica (which interestingly means "Who is like Yahweh?") who *would be* entitled to the throne. Yet David takes them in regardless of the potential threat to his reign as king. Instead of killing them both, David shows them mercy. Going against cultural expectations, he restores Saul's property to his descendants and invites Mephibosheth to live under his protection and dine at his table. Mephibosheth falls at his feet again—this time in humble respect for the great kindness David has shown. In both verses 6 and 8, the English translations use the words "bowed down." In spite of this similarity, in the Hebrew they have very different meanings. In verse 6 what is translated "bowed down" means "to fall down before the face of" and implies fear and trepidation. Basically, Mephibosheth is throwing himself with trembling at the mercy of David. However, in verse 8 what is translated "bowed down" means "to prostrate oneself in homage" and implies deep respect and worship. As the story unfolds, we find Mephibosheth moving from fear to respect. David's kindness, compassion, loyalty, and love for Jonathan and his son begins to break down the walls of fear and terror Mephibosheth has built to protect himself from the wrath of the king.

Inviting Mephibosheth to the king's table spoke volumes—it was a privilege not offered to many. Despite his deformity, he was welcomed and honored by the king in the presence of others. Despite his possible threat to David's reign, he is given protection as an ally and friend. In returning Saul's property and appointing Ziba as a caretaker, David was making provision for Mephibosheth and his family for generations. David's every act is an act of mercy, kindness, loyalty, and restoration.

This story points to the same relationship we have with Christ and also reveals the kindness he extends to each of us. We are crippled, traumatized by life lived in this world and by the actions of others. In the presence of Our Mighty King, we truthfully deserve death. Instead, Christ invites us to his table of protection, provision, love, and mercy. We are welcomed and honored by the King in the presence of others, given a seat of honor. In II Samuel 19:28, Mephibosheth says to David:

> *For all my father's house were but men doomed to death before my lord the king,*
> *but you set your servant among those who eat at your table.*

We too were doomed to death, but Jesus, out of covenant with God and out of his great love for his brothers and sisters, sets us among those who eat at the King's table. We are invited to sit, to dwell, to stay, *to rest* at the Lord's Table of provision and protection.

Leeland has written a remarkable song called *Carried to the Table* based on this passage. It so beautifully captures not only the story of David and Mephibosheth, but of Jesus and each of us. Take a moment to listen to it now, paying careful attention to the lyrics. I have twice had the opportunity to co-create and dance to this song as part of regional worship services. Both times the part of Jesus was danced by Robert "Bobby" Wesner, Artistic Director of Neos Dance Theatre. The other dancers included women who were *not* professional dancers. Together, we worked creatively as a group to choreograph our movements.

We started by asking the dancers to scatter across the stage in various postures of deformity, wounding, and brokenness. As the song progressed, Jesus came to each one, lifting them out of their brokenness and literally carrying them to the "Table of the Lord," which was represented by a large cross draped in flowing red fabric. As they gathered with the others at the cross, they joined in a unison dance of worship and praise. One by one, each was healed and brought, imperfections and all, to a place of honor as they knelt in worship before their Savior.

The dance was a powerful representation of love's restoration. The part of Jesus was danced by a classically trained dancer—Bobby danced with strength and might, every movement one of perfection and mastery. Moreover, the parts of those "carried to the table" were *not* professionally trained. While they moved with grace and beauty, they didn't have the same mastery and perfection as the character of Jesus. In the same way, our perfect Savior works with us despite our imperfections and flaws. He pulls us up out of our broken and wounded "postures" and helps us move with grace and beauty. He is a wonderful redeemer!

I can also tell you that the creative process of developing this piece with those involved became a healing creative process for many. Assuming a physical posture of their own woundedness allowed them to embody their own pain and brokenness. Each depicted her wounds differently—some bent, some prostrate, some deformed, some defiant. Then as Bobby, representing Jesus, came to each one he worked with them individually to bind their wounds and pull them from brokenness to wholeness. Watching this unfold in the choreography process was remarkable to say the least!

He carried each one differently—Lindsay was pulled, like Mephibosheth unable to walk, dragging her feet behind her, until she was at last made whole when she took her place at the table. Emma was lifted quickly out of her backward bent posture and raised high and straight into the air. Angela turned away struggling to accept the generous love of the Savior. Kim ran with Jesus in a grand, sweeping motion around the stage and to the cross as she was "swept away by his love." Laurie somersaulted forward and onto her feet, caught up in the river of his mercy. Lindsey Jo stumbled clumsily, trying to come to grips with the nature of his kindness. Amy danced her way *all the way* to the cross. I was gently carried, cradled in the loving arms of Christ.

Near the end of the song, Bobby went out to the audience where he began to gather others to join those who worshiped at the foot of the cross. As Jesus, he brought couples, children, men, and women, inviting them to join in the feast of worship at the Lord's Table. He tells the story of one woman at the edge of her seat looking up hopefully at him, eager to be invited. As soon as he extended the invitation, she jumped out of her seat and ran to the cross. Bobby smiles as he remembers, "I could barely keep up!"

And isn't that how it should be?
That we should be so eager at Christ's invitation
that we jump at the chance and run freely into his welcoming presence?

Picture that for a moment: you are running to his banqueting table so fast that Jesus can't even keep up with you. He comes up behind you, breathless at your overwhelming excitement!

Many people commented on the tremendous power of this dance. They could see their own wounded selves in the dance, in the various postures, and in the way Christ lifted each one from brokenness to wholeness. Read again (above) about the different postures and how he carried each dancer uniquely. *With which do you most relate? Imagine each one as Jesus lifts them up and carries them to the table of his grace, mercy, and love. How do you see your own pain and woundedness? What would it look like embodied in a posture? How do you see yourself reacting to Christ's hand reaching, extending, pulling, lifting, as he carries you to the cross where his forgiveness flows?*

Allow Jesus, your Savior, to carry you to the cross and to seat you at this table he has readied for you:

You prepare a table before me in the presence of my enemies.
You anoint my head with oil; my cup overflows.
Surely your goodness and love will follow me all the days of my life,
and I will dwell in the house of the Lord forever. Ps 23:5-6

(continued next page)

Using the questions and scripture passages as your prompts as you begin to explore through creativity, won't you join me in this prayer?

Invite the Holy Spirit into this moment.
Ask the Lord Your Shepherd (Yahweh Rohi) to guide you as you pray.
Ask the Lord Who Sanctifies (Yahweh M'Kaddesh) to purify your imagination.
Ask the Lord Your Provider (Jehovah Jireh) to help you picture yourself seated at his table of protection, provision, safety, and love.

Lord Jesus, Carrier of My Wounds, help me see myself as I truly am—broken and in need of your grace and mercy. I know that I am dead without you, that I cannot live until you extend your hand of kindness towards me. I know that I am crippled and in need of your redemptive love for me. Help me see you come to me and lift me from my broken posture to a place of restoration. Help me see you carry me to the table, carry me to your cross where your mercy flows down in mighty torrents of your love. Help me run boldly into your presence. Help me to join in the dance around your throne. Help me dance with grace and beauty.
       In the Name of Jesus, My Redeemer and Restorer, I pray, Amen.

Listen to: "Carried to the Table" by Leeland
"Feast of the Lord/At the Table" by Richard Smallwood & Vision

Digging Deeper: Provision in God's Presence

Read: I Kings 17—19

There is much to be learned from the life of Elijah. I will focus on two main ideas: 1) the difficulties of following God's call and 2) God's provision amidst the difficulties.

Elijah emerges onto the Israelite scene during the reign of King Ahab and Queen Jezebel. This is a critical time in Israel's history—they have fallen far, far away from God's commands, worshiping idols. And not just any idols, but Baal and Asherah. These are the gods of great sin—impurity, lust, greed, child sacrifice, temple prostitution, and rampant perverted sexual sin. To say that things were *not good* for the Israelites is a gross understatement! In the midst of their great sin, Elijah pronounces a great drought.

In the midst of this terrible drought and resulting famine, God provides for Elijah through desert ravens and a Gentile widow. And the provision of unending oil is nothing compared to the miracle of bringing this widow's son back to life. God's spirit flows through this prophet's very being, and he is recognized throughout the Hebrew nation as a prophet of power. Soon we find him on Mount Caramel calling down fire on a water-soaked sacrifice, all to demonstrate that the Lord God was "turning their hearts back" to him (18:37). All of Israel falls to their knees proclaiming, "The Lord—He is God!" (18:39). He puts all the prophets of Baal to death by the sword, and then, of all things, takes off running in fear of Queen Jezebel.

This has always puzzled me. The Lord works through him in great power to put these rotten false prophets to death and a woman sends him running into the desert afraid for his life? This Queen Jezebel must have appeared mighty powerful in the eyes of Elijah! Finally at the end of his marathon run, he collapses beneath a broom tree and calls on God to take his "miserable" life.

Comparing Elijah to Moses and Jeremiah, Bible Scholar Lissa Wray Beal reveals this truth about the difficulties of ministry:

> [Yahweh] does not allow these individuals to settle into their self-pity or perpetuate their desire for death and release. He meets them there and engages them at their point of discouragement. Through that encounter they are enabled to return to minister—under circumstances no less onerous or non-responsive. Something much larger than their own understanding or ease is at stake, to which they have been called.[29]

As we know from the story of Esther, if we fail to walk in God's calling and will for our lives, God's deliverance will rise up from another place (Esth 4:14); another means will be provided to accomplish God's plan. In Elijah's story, his successor Elisha rises up to finish what God had started through Elijah.

Many of you as Christian artists, creatives, and worshipers have been called into prophetic and priestly ministries in your churches and communities. Let's be truthful, prophetic and priestly ministries are demanding. God never promised it would be easy. If you are further called into healing ministry, then consider trial and testing to be a given. The enemy wars against all of this. He does not want God's priests, prophets, or healers to walk in their divine destiny. The gods of Baal and Asherah, the same gods that ruled the evil heart of Jezebel, will chase you down in an attempt to kill you and, not succeeding, will hound you until you are left defeated and exhausted under a broom tree in the desert places of your life.

But there is another truth more powerful than any "truth" the enemy can toss at you: God's perfect plan *will be* accomplished—nothing can thwart it. Now, for every plan in which you play a part, it is God's desire that it be accomplished through you. *But* if not through you, then by another. So I ask you this question: *Do you want to finish what God has started in you or do you want another to step up and fulfill your role in his kingdom here on earth?* I know this is a hard pill to swallow, for, in fact, I swallow it right along with you. The difficulties of ministry can leave us exhausted on many levels. We might find that we cannot go on. Like Elijah, you might choose to let another come alongside you and that person might rise up to take your place. That is okay! Elijah is still considered among the great prophets in the Bible and even appears at the transfiguration of Christ (Matt 17). He still continues in prophetic ministry next to Elisha and trains him up in power and strength, and God's will is accomplished through Elisha instead.

There is another truth this story speaks to, and that is this: while following God's call on your life might be difficult, God will always provide. Throughout the story of Elijah, we see God provide for him over and over. However, it's not always in the way Elijah might have preferred:

- Bread from *unclean* ravens
- Housing, bread, oil through a *Gentile* widow
- Powerful ministry that came with *hatred* from Jezebel
- Instead of death, an angel with food to nourish him and *more tasks* to complete
- Completion of calling, but *through another*

God always provides for Elijah, but in ways that were very contrary to his own thoughts, plans, and preferences. Even as he asked for God to take his life, God instead sends an angel to nourish and provide for him, keeping him alive. God's provision helps prepare Elijah for ministry (ch 17) and to recover from ministry (ch 19). In I Kings 19, the angel's first meal provides for Elijah's past and the second for his future.[30] In the place of God's presence, Elijah receives sustenance for a lifetime of ministry—past, present, and future. Eventually, God *did* answer Elijah's prayer to "take" his earthly life and provided Elijah a ride straight to heaven in a fiery chariot (II Kng 2:1-14). Again and again we see God's hand of provision for Elijah.

The same is true for each and every one of us. God will provide for you. He will provide in unexpected ways, if you will only have eyes to see it. His provision might go against all we think we know about God and the plans we have worked out in our own minds. God will provide for a lifetime of ministry—for all the difficulties of the past and the worries of the future. This is why resting in God's presence is so important.

God's provision, equipping power, care, and compassion are all revealed *in his presence!* Our strength is renewed *in his presence!* God's healing, restoration, and redemption come *in his presence!* We cannot fool ourselves into believing that any of this can happen apart from his beautiful presence. If you continue to struggle with this idea of resting in God's presence, I hope this will convince you. Use your creative process as a way to spend time in God's presence. If you enjoy being creative, if you enjoy worship, if you enjoy beauty, consider this a wonderful gift from the Father. He has given you a way into his presence, if only you will allow it. Imagine he is there with you at your studio, your writing desk, your potter's wheel, your theater, your music room, your favorite nature trail.

Sara Joseph is the author of *Gently Awakened: The Influence of Faith on Your Artistic Journey*. Over and over, she speaks of her utter reliance on the Holy Spirit in her artistic calling. When she was in need of direction and guidance, God provided. When she was in need of studio space, God provided. When she needed inspiration, God provided. She even tells the story of a time when she was low on supplies and God asked her to use the money she had saved to buy supplies for *someone else*! Despite great hesitancy, she obeyed, and God has provided her supplies ever since. Her book is a beautiful testimony to the faithful provision of God. She writes about relying on the Godly currency of faith versus the earthly currency of money:

> If you open your heart to the possibility of a life that is a pulsing, growing, cell-by-cell increase, like a magnificent tree planted by living waters, then you are on your way to learning how to garner the rich supply intended to anticipate and supply all your needs as they arise. Act on that belief by trusting God to provide when tackling whatever he leads you to do. Soon you will recognize that you are dwelling in your wealthy place as you find yourself not lacking in any resource pertaining to your life and calling. The Holy Spirit will guide you, if invited, and teach and empower you to tap into that boundless supply as needed.[31]

She is very clear that this provision comes through spending time in God's presence, reading his word, and following the Father's voice in all decisions. Her life is a testament to the fact that God will indeed provide as you rely on him as your Living Water, the only water that will satisfy.

Ultimately, provision is just a by-product of time in his presence. His presence should take precedence as the utmost need in your life. In his last writing here on earth, Brother Lawrence wrote:

> I am sure you know that most people's love for the Lord stops at a very shallow stage. Most love God for the tangible things he gives them. They love him because of this favor to them. You must not stop on such a level, no matter how rich his mercies have been to you. Many outward blessings can never bring you as close to God as can one simple act of faith.
>
> So seek him often by faith.
>
> Oh, dear friend, the Lord is not outside of you, pouring down favors. The Lord is within you. Seek him there, within…and nowhere else.
>
> Let the Lord be the one, the only, love of your life.[32]

Where have you grown weary in your calling and ministry? Where have you seen God work in mighty ways only to turn and run from the threat of the enemy chasing you down? Where have you cried out for death in your life? Won't you at this very moment turn those areas over the God? Allow him to send his ministering angels to nourish you, to feed you, for the journey behind and the journey ahead. *Where have you seen his provision in unexpected ways? Ways that you have refused to acknowledge as gifts from God because they didn't come as you expected? In what areas of your life have you sought after earthly currency rather than God's currency of faith?*

Let these verses from Psalm 27:4-5 call your heart back to its "True Center." Take a deep breath, allow them to resonate in your spirit, and remember.

One thing I ask from the Lord, this only do I seek:
that I may dwell in the house of the Lord all the days of my life,
to gaze on the beauty of the Lord and to seek him in his temple.
For in the day of trouble he will keep me safe in his dwelling;
he will hide me in the shelter of his sacred tent and set me high upon a rock.

Using the questions and scripture passages as your prompts as you begin to explore through creativity, won't you join me in this prayer?

Invite the Holy Spirit into this moment.
Ask the Lord Your Shepherd (Yahweh Rohi) to guide you as you pray.
Ask the Lord Who Sanctifies (Yahweh M'Kaddesh) to purify your imagination.
Ask the Lord Your Provider (Jehovah Jireh) to help you begin to picture, sense, or create a place of protection and provision around you.

Oh Lord God, you are Jehovah Jireh, my Provider. Yet, how often I have failed to recognize your provision and protection over my life. In my frailty and weakness, I have run into the desert and fallen beneath a broom tree of my own making. I confess that to you now, Oh Lord, and ask you to send your angels to come and nourish me as I rest in your presence. Feed me, for I am weary from my journey. Feed me, for I have miles yet to travel on the path you have laid before me. You alone are my Sustenance and Living Water. I trade all my earthly currencies of wealth, fame, and comfort for the Godly currency of faith.
In the Name of Jehovah Jireh, My Provider, I pray, Amen.

Listen to: "Resting" by Rita Springer
"I Shall Not Want" by Audrey Assad
Spend some time in healing worship today. If available, find the YouTube video of this song entitled
"Audrey Assad // I Shall Not Want (Live @ OneThing 2015)"
It is 26 minutes of powerful, soaking worship that includes a prayerful song for healing.

Digging Deeper: Jesus Calms the Storm

Read: Mark 4:35-41

This is a short passage but there are several keys things you must understand about its context and what it is saying about Christ to fully grasp its depth of meaning.

The Jewish people believed that the sea was the place where God and evil collided.[33] The story of the "crossing of the sea" in Exodus 14 was a critical part of their oral history and as well as their very identity as a people.[34] Here in Mark, the fact that Jesus calls them to cross over to the other side in the evening also casts a foreboding shadow over the story. Many of the disciples were experienced fisherman, so as the storm clouds gather they are aware of the eminent danger and threat of possible death. Bible scholar Kent Bower indicates "the storm is symbolic of opposition to God and his rule."[35] In terms of Christ bringing God's kingdom rule here on earth, everything is at stake. And Jesus is sleeping. Yes, you know the story—sleeping.

Not ironically, this story in Mark follows the Parable of the Mustard Seed: i.e., "The Kingdom of God is like a mustard seed" (4:30-32). From this tiny mustard seed grows a massive plant where birds and animals are safe in its shade. Jesus seems to be saying, "If you will just believe that this tiny thing will grow into something large enough to protect and shield, you will see God's kingdom here on earth." But now, here in the midst of the storm, the mustard seed story seems a world away.

Moreover, the passage immediately following the calming of the storm is the healing of the demon-possessed man. After calming the mighty sea and proving his might over nature, Jesus proves his might over demons. He is walking in his true destiny not only as the Son of Man, but as the Son of God.

But for now…

in this moment…

Jesus is sleeping.

I love the way the disciples come to him saying, "Don't you care?!" And yet, isn't that how *we ourselves* often come to him? How many times do we say to God…

Don't you care?!?!

In the face of death or injustice or evil…

Don't you care?!?!

When we ourselves believe he is sleeping on the job…

Don't you care?!?!

A question rooted in our deep-seated fear…

Don't you care?!?!

…I know. For I've asked it myself.
And how does Christ react? He doesn't even answer them directly with words. He responds with action, and the words he does speak are to creation itself:

Peace! Be still!

The Greek for "peace" here is *siopao*, and it is a direct command. If someone asks you to be quiet, you can voluntarily choose to be quiet. However, this is *not* voluntary—it *must* be obeyed! Christ rises from his apparent disinterest in their frightful situation, and with one word he silences the wind and the waves. His words are forceful and filled with divine power and strength. The storm obeys because it has no choice. Jesus commands the very thing he had a hand in creating, and it instantly obeys.

He then turns his attention to their original question of "Don't you care?" He says:

Why are you so afraid? Do you still have no faith?

Do you think he might be asking the same question of us? *Why are we so afraid? Why do we struggle with our faith?* Jesus responds to us:

Why are you so afraid?
A mustard seed is all I ask.
That's all you need, and I'll do all the rest.
Don't you see? I command the wind and the waves!
I command the very world I created! I even command the demons!
All of creation and every power above and below must *obey my command!*

St. Augustine speaks this beautiful reminder to all of us: "When we allow temptations to overcome us, Christ sleeps in us. We forget Christ at such times. Let us, then, remember him. Let us awake him. He will speak. He will rebuke the tempest of the soul, and there will be great calm." Think on that a moment: *Christ sleeping in you.* Christ, sleeping in you, and at the slightest arousal, he is awakened to command nature, his angels, and even demons. Let us, indeed, remember!

There are other times in scripture where Jesus offers "peace:"

Peace I leave with you; my peace I give you. I do not give to you as the world gives. Do not let your hearts be troubled and do not be afraid. Jn 14:27

On the evening of that first day of the week, when the disciples were together, with the doors locked for fear of the Jewish leaders, Jesus came and stood among them and said, "Peace be with you!" After he said this, he showed them his hands and side. The disciples were overjoyed when they saw the Lord. Again Jesus said, "Peace be with you! As the Father has sent me, I am sending you." Jn 20:19-21

But the peace he offers here is a different peace than his command to the sea. This is the Greek *eirene*, which is an untroubled state of serene calm. According to the *Hebrew-Greek Key Word Study Bible* definition, "Such a state of peace is the object of divine promise and is brought about by God's mercy, granting deliverance from all the distresses that are experienced as a result of sin."[36]

We must begin to understand more and more:

Through Jesus Christ, peace is a position of power.

It is not complacency or surrender or admitting defeat. The peace Jesus offers is a promise of deliverance. Romans 16:20 says, "The God of peace will soon crush Satan under your feet." That is not defeat or surrender—it is strength, power, and might! Peace as a position of power does several things:

- Provides clarity and a clear mind
- Provides security, comfort, and calm
- Increases creativity, ideas, insights, and solutions
- Contributes to our sense of well-being, reducing anxiety and stress

- Contributes to our health, lowering the risk of diseases resulting from anxiety and stress and improving sleep and rest
- And most importantly, defeats the enemy, crushing satan under Christ's feet

Resting in the presence of God positions you to experience the power of peace.

There is a painting entitled *Peace, Be Still* by artist Stephen Gjertson that was originally commissioned for the United Church of Christ in Sandstone, Minnesota. The original work still hangs there in memorial to the artist's grandparents who had a combined 85 years of service to the church's music ministry. I understand he actually painted five different versions of the same painting.[37] I once read a fascinating article about his creative process and how the different versions were altered over 25 years of working with the same original vision for the painting. However, the primary thing that drew me to this painting in the first place is that the water is completely still, with absolutely no indication of the great turmoil that preceded it.

We live in a home by a lake. I've seen my fair share of storms sweeping in across the water. We've even been out on our small boat as the ominous wall of rain marches in like a massive army. One thing that never happens is water going to complete stillness *as* the storm recedes! Often it goes still *after* the storm has passed, but not *as* the storm is retreating. In *Peace, Be Still* the water is calm and still *even as Christ's arms are still raised overhead*. This is not a natural calming that comes after a storm, but a supernatural calm in the midst of the storm. In the painting you can still see the wall of rain and lightening in the background—Jesus' mighty arms raised, pushing back the very heavens in obedience to his command.

I think my favorite version of the painting is the 1996 version. In this version the brilliant light of heaven is reflected on the water, drawing your eye back to another boat in the distance—they too are the benefactors of this divine miracle! The same is true for us in the divine miracles of our lives. Christ calms us in the midst of our storms, and still others find peace as we radiate heaven's light where there were once dark, menacing clouds. His brilliance pushes back the destructive army that advances against us all!

Today as we enter into prayer, you might want to refer back to the Safe Place exercise on page 44, remembering to change the word safe to peaceful, restful, or calm, if necessary. *Today I want you to be purposeful to enter into Safe Place. Allow his peace and rest to come over you today. As you do this, as much as you are willing, ask Christ to enter into your Safe Place. As you picture Jesus there with you, spend some time asking him about your authentic swing, your true self, your destiny and callings. Ask him to help you identify the giftings, talents, abilities, and passions he placed in you. Ask him how your own calm in the midst of the storm might affect others. Ask him how you can partner with him to push back the evil that attempts to advance against us all.*

If you continue to struggle, perhaps you can picture yourself in this Bible story—in a small boat on the sea. Imagine Jesus there beside you. Perhaps he lies on the floor of the boat asleep until you wake him? Picture him commanding the wind and waves. Witness all falling calm in obedience to his command. See him turn to you and ask:

Why are you so afraid?
Do you still have no faith?

And even as you struggle to answer, know that he is there with you…

Always.

Allow these different translations of Psalm 16:8 take you into Jesus' presence:

I keep my eyes always on the Lord.
With him at my right hand, I will not be shaken. NIV

I am always aware of the Lord's presence;
he is near, and nothing can shake me. GNT

I know the Lord is always with me.
I will not be shaken, for he is right beside me. NLT

Using the ideas for spending time with Jesus in your Safe Place, as well as the questions and scriptures above as your prompts as you begin to explore through creativity, won't you join me in this prayer?

Invite the Holy Spirit into this moment.
Ask the Lord Your Shepherd (Yahweh Rohi) to guide you as you pray.
Ask the Lord Who Sanctifies (Yahweh M'Kaddesh) to purify your imagination.
Ask the Lord Your Provider (Jehovah Jireh) to help you picture, sense, or create a place of protection and provision around you.
Ask the Lord Who Is There (Yahweh Shammah) to join you in that place.

Yahweh Shammah, The Lord Who Is There, although I sometimes struggle to believe this truth, I declare and proclaim that you are indeed with me, always. Help me take my strength and courage from you. Increase my faith, exponentially, from a tiny seed to a thriving tree that gives light and life to others. The enemy tells me you are asleep, that you don't care. But I call on the truth that you are always there, within me, next to me, afore and behind me. That you stand ready to calm the raging sea about me. That with a single word, all is perfectly at peace. And in that perfect peace, may I find your power. I want to radiate your peace to a world so often in confusion and chaos. Lord, I keep my eyes on you, aware of your presence, knowing you are always with me. I will trust that you stand right beside me. I will not be moved. I will not be shaken.
In Jesus name, the Name of Perfect Peace, I pray, Amen.

Listen to: "Just Be Held" by Casting Crowns
"Eye of the Storm" by Ryan Stevenson

﹏ A Benediction of Heartbeat ﹏

A Reflection… Solemn Praise
by Mandy L Gero

Sacred Heart, Ever Holy Beat
Now Echoes in this soul,
Jesus at Home in the depths,
A heart exposed, abandoned
to Glories and Grace,
No longer ashamed or blamed,
Just Beating in Peace,
A Song that began life,
the song that breathes,
Deep unto night,
All fears put to flight,
Love Magnificence Delights
Redeeming shadows and valleys,
Kindly bowing mountains,
Dawning Eternal Joys,
Hearing ever beating Heart of Jesus…

Next Steps: Resources for Your Healing Journey

Essential Practices of the Faith (SDG Publishing, Ashland, Ohio) is a study resource that explains some of the spiritual practices modeled by Jesus. Volume 1 includes: praise, hearing God's voice, relinquishment, forgiveness, listening prayer, and lament. See www.essentialpractices.com.

Every Breath We Take: Living in the Presence, Love, and Generosity of God by Terry Wardle

Strong Winds & Crashing Waves by Terry Wardle

The Depths of God: Walking Ancient Paths Into His Presence by Pat Chen

Endnotes

1. *The Legend of Bagger Vance*, directed by Robert Redford, based on a book by the same title by Steven Pressfield, 2000.
2. If clips are no longer available, they can be found at movie time markers 50:23—52:08 and 1:14:08—1:18:30, respectively.
3. Thompson, *Anatomy of the Soul*, 29.
4. Ibid., 59.
5. Ibid., 87.
6. Rothschild, *Body Remembers*, and van der Kolk, *Body Keeps the Score*.
7. Shoop, *Let the Bones*, 62.
8. Ibid., 51.
9. Ibid., 129.
10. Wardle, *Strong Winds*, 83.
11. Ibid., 80.
12. Ibid., 82.
13. Ibid., 83 & 85.
14. Ibid.
15. Ibid., 84-5. This steps here are quoted directly: quotation marks eliminated for readability.
16. Payne, *Healing Presence*, 172.
17. Ibid., 139.
18. If clip is no longer available on YouTube, it can be found at movie time marker 1:38:40—1:42:40.
19. Tanner, "Psalm 91," 700.
20. Ibid.
21. Lawrence, *Practicing His Presence*, 92.
22. Tanner, 701.
23. Payne, 171.
24. Tanner, 486.
25. Ibid., 437.
26. Ibid., 490.
27. Nouwen, *Wounded Healer*, 91-92.
28. In *God's Creative Gift*, I devote a chapter on the *Prophetic* role of the artist and another on the *Priestly* role of the artist. Understanding both of these roles is critical if you are involved in creative/worship arts ministry.
29. Beal, *1 & 2 Kings*, 256.
30. Cogan, *I Kings*, 452.
31. Joseph, *Gently Awakened*, 174. Find out more about Sara and her valuable resources at christian-artist-resource.com.
32. Lawrence, 106.
33. Garland, *Mark*, 190.
34. Brower, *Mark*, 138.
35. Ibid., 140-141.
36. *Hebrew-Greek Study Bible*, 1615.
37. A PBS article about Stephen Gjertson's creative process, as well as the different commissions of this painting, were originally found at www.stephengjertsonstudios.com/pbsarticle.html (accessed April 14, 2016). Unfortunately, this article is no longer available online.

3

~ Confronting ~

*"I live in a high and holy place,
but also with the one who is contrite and lowly in spirit."*

The following is a personal healing testimony from Maria, Creative Arts Director at a church in Northern California:

"When I say Jesus is awesome, amazing, sweet, loving, and faithful, those words do not even seem to describe him fully. There's an event that has changed the course of my walk with him. I was with my good friend Toni who has an amazing Christian counseling practice called 'In the Potter's Hands' (I love that the name is even 'artsy'). She and I were discussing a traumatic event in my life. At the age of four, I had a really high fever—almost 105. My parents rushed me to the hospital emergency room where the doctors put me in a tub of ice. I remember the event well for being only four at the time. What stood out was how my mother stood there doing nothing. How can a four-year-old understand that what was happening was for her good? But I kept thinking, 'Why is she letting this happen?' I wanted her to rescue me.

This memory has come up often during my adult life. But it wasn't until my friend Toni said, 'Let's see what Jesus has to say about it,' that I truly processed the memory. So we prayed. I closed my eyes, and Jesus showed me how he was there with me. He circled the tub I was sitting in a few times, and then he came and put his hands on my face. He showed me that he was comforting me when I felt all alone and that his touch brought my fever down. The joy and love I experienced by him revealing this to me is beyond my natural comprehension. He's amazing!

Now sometimes we can start to question God and his goodness and over-think things. Or the enemy can come in and start lying to you. I started asking myself, 'Did that really happen?' As I drove home that day, I started praying for a confirmation that it wasn't just my imagination running away with me. I said a quick prayer in my head asking him to confirm what happened. I shared with no one else the incident of the trauma or my prayer time with Toni and what the Lord showed me that day.

Later the next day a good friend sent me a picture of a piece of artwork, saying, 'I thought you'd like this.' The drawing was a little girl with her eyes closed and two hands touching her face. This was my confirmation! He was with me—he consoled me, comforted me, and healed me of a traumatic memory.

As an artist myself, he used art to confirm my moment of healing. How sweet and personal is that? I matter to him. We matter to our Lord. He is a loving and relational God that wants to heal our hurts and remove our pain. By his stripes, we are healed.

This beautiful event has sky rocketed my faith and trust in him. I am now creating a drawing that will remind me of that day and his faithful and amazing love. When the Lord said, 'Behold, I am with you always…' that is a promise that we can stand upon. My testimony has also been an encouragement to my friend Toni with her counseling practice—a wonderful reminder that he is with her, her ministry, and that he's in the healing business."

This chapter is about confronting all the things that hold us back: our pasts, our trauma, our wounds. Confronting our dysfunctional behaviors, our demons, our sins. Confronting the lies in our heads that hold us back and keep us from being who God created us to be. Some might wonder why we just can't get over it? Let bygones be bygones! Leave well-enough alone! Truth is, we struggle to forgive and forget. We combat lies we believe as a result of our pasts. We wrestle with guilt, regret, and shame. We fight to be free from our pasts. Good Christians shouldn't feel like this, we assume. But truth is, we do. Let's explore another movie for insight.

In *The Lion King* the young lion cub Simba is involved in a tragedy that takes the life of his father. His Uncle Scar (who actually caused the tragedy to take over rule of the African plain) fills him with shameful lies and tells him to run away and never return. He shortly runs into a warthog and a meerkat, and they become his unlikely friends. As Simba tries to shake off the memory of his father's death, Pumbaa, the wacky warthog, tells him, "Leave your past in the behind." Of course, Timon the cheeky meerkat quickly corrects him: "Leave your past behind you." Yet, as the movie unfolds, we find that advice impossible for Simba to follow. Eventually the past catches up with him—his father's voice echoes in his spirit and reminds him of whom he was really meant to be. Is it any wonder that the lies he's believed all his life came from the mouth of his aptly named uncle, *Scar*?

The same is true for us—eventually our past has a way of catching up with us. Our own emotional scars leave behind lies, holding us back from who we were created to be. Yet somewhere deep inside, if we choose to listen, the Father's voice calls to us, reminding us of these truths:

    Who we really are,

        all we are meant to be,

            our destiny and calling.

In the same way Simba wrestles with the guilt and lies of his past, we too mull over our painful memories, regret, shame, and the things that have been said and done to us over the years. Yet, in the end do we listen to the lies? Or do we listen to the voice of the Father? Simba chooses to walk in his true identity, confronts the lies of his past, and brings restoration to the African plain. He takes his rightful place as king and leads those that creation has entrusted to him. As he walks in his true identity and rightful inheritance, he brings balance, restoration, and wholeness where there was once evil, famine, despair, and brokenness.

Confronting our past can be frightening. Some of us have been deeply hurt. Some of us carry great burdens of guilt and shame. Some of us have sunk so deep we cannot see the light of sky above us. Yet, I promise you, when we've reached the end of ourselves, God is there. God is with us. God is for us. God is in us. All we need to do is *reach* for him and *keep reaching* for him. It takes courage and perseverance. It isn't easy, but God's word promises us: "To the one who is victorious, I will give the right to sit with me on my throne, just as I was victorious and sat down with my Father on his throne" (Rev 3:21). Just like Simba, we can choose to take our rightful place as sons and daughters of the Living God and as wounded healers guiding others into wholeness and restoration as we walk in the footsteps of Jesus.

Let God's truth speak encouragement to us:

He is the Lord who heals. (Ex 15:26)
He promises to heal and bring abundant life. (Jer 33:6)
We cannot do it apart from Jesus Christ. (Acts 3:16)
Awesome power is found in his radiant scars. (Hab 3:4)
By his stripes we are healed. (Isa 53:5)
He binds our wounds and heals our broken hearts. (Ps 147:3)
He takes up our pain and bears our suffering. (Isa 53:4)
He forgives all our sins and heals our diseases. (Ps 103:3)

Author, prophetic minster, and pastor Pat Chen, offers this wisdom: "Finding genuine healing in God may require coming to the edge of uncertainty. But if we keep our eyes on the ocean of Christ's mighty love for us, we'll be cleansed by the waves of his presence."[1] Do you have the courage to walk to the edge? Are you ready to jump in?

First the Bad News

In life, we get knocked around—sometimes a little, sometimes a lot. Some of us got something we didn't need or deserve, as in abuse. Some of us did *not* get something we needed and deserved, as in neglect. Some got both. We were all created with God-given longings, such as the need for safety, security, nurture, significance, purpose, understanding, acceptance, belonging, and love.[2] When these core longings are not met in loving and caring ways, we are hurt, often at deep, developmental levels.

Consider physical wounds for a moment. My brother had a young colt at his farm that got tangled up with a manure spreader. The resulting gash was deep, however, the vet recommended only a few small stitches. He wanted the wound to stay mostly open so it could heal from the inside out and so resulting infection from the manure wouldn't get trapped under the skin. Emotional, psychological, and spiritual wounds are no different. If we cover them up without cleaning them up and letting them heal from the inside out, we will one day find poisonous infection trapped beneath the surface.

As we can see from the example from *The Lion King*, wounds left unchecked will leave us believing lies about ourselves, our world, and even God. These lies are not based on truth, yet we subconsciously embrace these distortions as truth. Many lies we know in our heads as false, but yet we still live as though they are true.

Many of the lies we believe are rooted in our God-given core longings:
- Safety – I am not safe. The world is very dangerous.
- Security – Everyone I care about abandons me.
- Nurture – No one truly cares for me. I do not feel compassion from the people around me.
- Significance – Nothing I do is of any worth. I am a mistake.
- Purpose – I have no real purpose in this world. My life has no meaning.
- Understanding – No one understands me. No one listens to me. Nothing I say makes a difference.
- Acceptance – I am not accepted for who I am. I do not fit in.
- Belonging – I am alone. I am always left out. No one includes me.
- Love – I am not loved. If they really knew me, they wouldn't like me.

If we are truthful, many of these lies have crossed our minds—some, every day. And these lies leave us with feelings of fear, shame, guilt, pain, and anger. It often feels like an emotional storm within.

Left unaddressed and unhealed, these wounds and the resulting lies we believe lead to dysfunctional behaviors, i.e., improper behavioral choices aimed at meeting a need or killing emotional pain.[3] This is the negative "fruit"—behaviors we use to cope with the pain inside of us. If left unchecked they can easily become addictions. In Biblical terms, this is sin. These are behaviors that "miss the mark" of all God would have for us if we lived fulfilled, abundant lives. Also note that even "good" things can be sin. For example, exercise if done to excess and used to mask pain, can become an addiction whereby a person cannot take one day off of the regimen to rest, even when injured. Perfectionism, people-pleasing, and any type of "–holic" (workaholic, alcoholic, shopaholic, etc.) are other examples of behaviors that are outside the good and perfect will of God.

So it is the wound that must heal, from the inside out. Simply stopping dysfunctional behavior by self-control, self-will, and determination never really gets to the heart of the matter. And often, it simply leads to different dysfunctional behaviors still aimed at alleviating the pain from the original wound. Dysfunctional behaviors are symptoms of unaddressed wounds and emotional upheaval—coping mechanisms that help you deal with the pain. Eliminating them does not cure or heal you. So we want to get the root of the wound and "confront" it in the loving, grace-filled presence of Jesus.

Now the Good News

So, here's the good news. In fact, this good news is indeed *the very gospel message of Jesus Christ!* Jesus came and paid for our sin, once and for all. All God's wrath was poured out on Christ as he suffered on the cross for the sins of all humankind. As he paid this debt, it cancelled the old law of sin and death and replaced it with a new law of grace, mercy, forgiveness, and love. Jesus came to bring good news to the poor in spirit, bind up the brokenhearted, and free the captives!

Ephesians 1—3 is filled with the good news of Jesus Christ. We are: chosen before the creation of the world to be holy and blameless; adopted as sons and daughters; redeemed by his blood; lavished with the riches of God's grace; marked with a seal, the Holy Spirit, our guarantee of our inheritance; and given the spirit of wisdom and revelation to know him better. We are alive in Christ; raised up with Christ; saved by grace, not works; and brought near through the blood of Christ. We are no longer foreigners and aliens, but fellow citizens and members of God's household. We can live lives rooted and established in Jesus' love.

Through Christ there is no separation. Ephesians 2:14-18 says that Christ "destroyed the barrier, the dividing wall of hostility, by abolishing in his flesh the law with its commandments and regulations." In the Jewish Temple, there was literally a dividing wall between Jew and Gentile, separating Gentiles from worship. For us, sin is the barrier—the dividing wall—that separates us from worship of God. But Jesus came to break down that wall of separation so we can enter into God's Holy Temple of worship. This is the beautiful, glorious good news of Jesus Christ of Nazareth, our Savior and Messiah! Won't you take a moment in his presence, thanking and worshiping him? He alone is worthy of our praise!

Now, in that place of presence, imagine coming before the cross of Christ. Beloved, there is such grace, love, and mercy found at the foot of the cross of Jesus! Perhaps you could ask Jesus if there's a specific sin he would like to address now, in this moment.

Once he has identified that sin for you, join me in this process called the Six R's of Repentance, developed by Dr. Terry Wardle:

- Recognize – confess that sin to him
- Repent – turn away from that place of separation
- Renounce – any level of demonization that has occurred as a result
- Receive – freedom, forgiveness, and cleansing from Christ Jesus
- Realign – your life and will with the Lord
- Rejoice – praising him for his grace, mercy, and love

In Jesus name, Amen![4]

I invite you to use this practice again and again in your life as you seek to align yourself with God and all that he has for you. It is a simple, yet effective way to deal with the issue of sin in your life, and will help you walk in agreement with his Spirit.

At the same time, begin to dig beneath the surface of that sin asking the Lord to reveal wounds that are at the heart of this dysfunctional behavior. As you address each one, ask the Lord to bring you "wisdom and revelation so that you may know him better" (Eph 1:17). It's not enough, nor will it work, to simply change the behavior. That is not the "key to wholeness."[5] Doing this in your own strength will not bring lasting change in your life. Redemption, freedom, and true healing are ours through the miraculous, wonder-working power of Jesus Christ. Recognizing and repenting of our sin and renouncing (i.e., confronting) the hold it has on our lives are critical steps on the healing journey. Through the Holy Spirit's gentle yet firm guidance, we can begin to uncover the deep places within that drive us away from his perfect embrace.

Jesus, Our Creative Healer

Let's refer back to Maria's testimony that opened this chapter. In her memory, the four-year-old Maria never got closure on the traumatic event in her life. Although the "adult Maria" understood cognitively that the ice treatment most likely saved her life, the "child Maria" deep inside her could not reconcile the event. Even knowing her mother was most likely experiencing her own trauma—watching helplessly as her child was "tortured" in ice—still doesn't help the child within her understand why this happened to her. Even though her mother might love her and care for her, the enemy will use that event to form lies that are difficult to "out-think" because her heart, soul, and body still hurt with the pain from that wounding event.

For example, Maria may grow to believe that her mother did not love her or that she stood by watching without compassion or that she is incapable or ineffective in parenting. As she grows, she may develop misplaced distrust for motherly figures in her life, assuming they are all incapable of helping her when she is in trouble. This may affect her own mothering skills in varied ways, as well. It can also affect Maria's picture of God in that she would struggle with the motherly, nurturing side of God. Left unconfronted, these types of lies can cut so deeply, they dominate and destroy our lives, allowing dysfunctional behaviors develop to alleviate the pain.

Maria might know in her head that God is loving, caring, and nurturing, but her heart tells her a different story. The enemy does not want her to believe that God is good. He wants to separate her from God in any and every possible way. He will use this event and the lies that formed as a result to keep Maria alienated and distrustful of him and others around her. Instead, as her friend Toni prompts her to go to Jesus with this trauma, and then, as she lets Jesus minister to her while she lies in the horrifying tub of ice, she is comforted. In allowing the "child Maria" to be comforted, the "adult Maria" realizes the truth: the Lord is always with her and his healing touch brought down her temperature that day. She experiences this in a very real, visceral way—not simply in her head, but also in her heart, soul, and body. As Maria allowed Christ into the traumatic memory of that event, she found that God is undeniably loving, caring, nurturing, and protecting. She now knows this in her head *and* in her heart. Lest you think every "confrontation" is violent or negative, let Maria's story serve as an illustration that "confrontation" while resting in the safe arms of Jesus can be a beautiful, comforting experience.

Of course, as soon as she began to experience freedom, the enemy still tried to get inside her head and tell her it wasn't real. But God already knew that was going to happen, didn't he? Through the Holy Spirit, he prompted her friend to send her the picture of the child being comforted, reinforcing the truth that he was with her, consoling her, and healing her. I love that God used art to speak into this artist's life! He is so specific in how he deals with each of us. He is such a good God!

Walking in Truth

Once we confront our wounded pasts, our dysfunction, and the lies we believe, in a loving encounter with Jesus, we need to walk it out in faith. As Maria's story illustrates, the enemy will immediately confront you again with more lies. We need to walk in truth! Walking in truth means we're secure in the truth that his love is real, immense, immeasurable, over-flowing, and unending. It is always enough! Nothing we do or don't do, nothing we say or don't say, makes a difference in the way he loves us. No way we perform or don't perform or get things "right" or "wrong" makes him love us any more or any less. Walking in the truth means we daily live that out as perfect truth. While on occasion we may doubt or fall back into old habits or thoughts, we choose to believe and live out our lives in a way that reflects the truth that his love is enough. To live in any other way is to call him a liar, and I refuse to do that.

Consider that thought a moment: to live in a way that opposes the truth of God's word is to call God a liar. Many times I doubt, but as soon as I recognize my thoughts as doubts and fears, I want to instead proclaim his truth. This is a habit, a discipline, of taking every thought captive (II Cor 10), of letting his word go forth and accomplish what God has willed it to accomplish (Isa 55), and of walking in the freedom of Christ through the truth he so freely gives (Jn 8). As a discipline, it takes work and effort until it becomes a natural habit, a natural re-wiring of the brain. We have to re-wire our brains to believe the truth—and re-wire it in such a way that this is not just what we believe in our heads, but what we believe in our hearts.

For me, I know, that I know, *that I know* his love is and will always be... enough! Glory to God! All praise to my Savior! Thank you Holy Spirit! And his love is enough for you, as well. It will always be enough. No matter where you've been or what you've done, his love is always enough. Trust him at his word.

Recently, Wardle was teaching on the love and acceptance of Christ. He posed this question...

> *What if for the next sixty days you simply focused on Christ; not your faults or your sin or your problems or your pain, but on Christ, letting him be the center of your attention?* [6]

Think on that a moment, what if you did that? Sixty days of focusing on the beautiful face of Jesus? Nothing about your own self, only him? Do you think many of these issues would simply take care of themselves as you did? I believe they would. That is why, again and again, we turn our focus to Christ and his healing power and love.

This is why we also press forward in our deep study of his Word, why time and again we will focus on the scripture as the Word of God—his Voice of Truth. Over and over I will remind you to spend time resting in his beautiful presence and to picture Jesus there with you or to picture yourself in our scripture passages. Artist and author Sara Joseph brings us this poignant reminder:

> God does communicate with us in innumerable languages through various media: music, art, science, and literature, through inspiration, dreams, and ideas. His voice is in the very air about us! It tells us about his ingenuity, humor, creativity, care, subtlety. ...However, none of those ways of speaking gives us specific direction, insight that is unique to our lives, or warnings that must be heeded. None of them tells us about our future or deal with our past. They allude to his presence but leave us hungry for more. And that is why we possess a foolproof, although often ignored, language of communication in the Bible. ...My life changes when I grasp that the Bible holds the secrets of all that I ever want to know about God—not just in an academic sense, but experientially if I chose to act on what I read.[6]

Focus on the face of Christ, the Living Word of God. Focus on his holy presence. Focus on the Holy Bible, the Written Word of God, not academically, but experientially.

As we move into our Digging Deeper Bible Studies and as you bring more of your pain and false beliefs into the Saving Light of His Beautiful Presence, I want to leave you with this prayer from Ephesians 1:18-23 (NLT). It is my prayer over your heart, mind, spirit, and body:

I pray that your hearts will be flooded with light so that you can understand the confident hope he has given to those he called—his holy people who are his rich and glorious inheritance. I also pray that you will understand the incredible greatness of God's power for us who believe him. This is the same mighty power that raised Christ from the dead and seated him in the place of honor at God's right hand in the heavenly realms. Now he is far above any ruler or authority or power or leader or anything else—not only in this world but also in the world to come. God has put all things under the authority of Christ and has made him head over all things for the benefit of the church. And the church is his body; it is made full and complete by Christ, who fills all things everywhere with himself.

In the Powerful Name of Jesus Christ, Amen.

Listen to: "Reckless Love" by Cory Asbury

Digging Deeper Into...

II Samuel 13—15: Dysfunction in the House of David	Page 79
Zechariah 3: Clean Garments for His Priests	Page 82
II Chronicles 14—16: Repentance and Rest	Page 86
John 8 & 10: Voices in Our Heads	Page 90
II Corinthians 7: Sorrow Leads to Repentance	Page 94

Benediction of The Good Shepherd — Page 97
High Places that Deceive by Tom Graffagnino

Next Steps: Resources for Your Healing Journey & Endnotes — Page 98

Coloring Page "Royal Redeemer" by Pauline Mae Blankenship — Page 99

Digging Deeper: Dysfunction in the House of David

Read: II Samuel 13—15

Keep your Bible by your side. You will need it to dig through this study. It's packed! Also note this study may take you a bit more time to work through with many scripture passages. No need to rush—take as much time as you need. Now, let's jump right in. Feet first!

I can't even begin to explain all the dysfunction we find in the house of King David. For being a "man after God's own heart," I am often so perplexed by his actions and decisions.

Let me step back a moment and give you some background.

David was anointed as the future king of Israel in I Samuel 16 but he does not take the throne until it was clear that God (not David) had routed Saul, opening up the throne for David. In the II Samuel 7, David has finally taken power, and God makes this covenantal promise to him: God will establish his house, offspring, throne and kingdom; David's house and kingdom "will endure forever" before God; and his "throne will be established forever" (vs 16). There is obviously something very special about David that God would make this *covenantal promise* to him and to his future generations. Take some time to read David's heartfelt response in II Samuel 7:18-29.

Despite his moving response, David soon finds himself in a pickle with the lovely Bathsheba in II Samuel 11, and as a result, David's house is now cursed by God. The "love child" of David and Bathsheba, conceived in lust and deceit, is taken from them, dying as an infant. Read II Samuel 12:9-12, taking note of verse 11:

> *Out of your own household I am going to bring calamity on you.*

It's not but one chapter later before we see the curse begin to unfold, taking more victims, one by one.

The story of Amnon and Tamar has always deeply disturbed me. We will spend more time addressing the tortured Tamar in our next chapter, but for now I will focus on the men in this story: Amnon, Absalom, and David.

Let's start with Amnon, the firstborn son of King David by his wife Ahinoam. Who wants to reach through the pages of scripture and strangle that man? I do! But the thing about Amnon is that he is simply carrying on the actions of his father. David took what was not his out of greed, desire, and lust (Bathsheba). Amnon does no different (Tamar). While David killed Uriah and seemingly gets away with it, Amnon "kills" Tamar and also seemingly gets away with it. What about "Thou shall not steal," "Thou shall not covet," "Thou shall not commit adultery," and "Thou shall not murder" do these men not understand? Although David is deeply angered about the rape of his daughter by her half-brother, he does nothing about it. Another I might like to strangle!

Second: Absalom. Because David does nothing, Tamar's full-brother Absalom takes matters into his own hands. Because David will not dispense justice, Absalom will. Two years he plots and plans. And when David delivers Amnon into Absalom's hands at the sheep shearing, in his attempt to seek justice, he physically kills the man who emotionally and culturally "killed" his sister Tamar and takes off running for his own life. Of course, his revenge is not enough to assuage his angry heart, and eventually he rises up against his father, the one who did not come to his sister's rescue and defense. As Absalom returns to Jerusalem, it's David's turn to flee. Absalom "lays" with David's concubines in full site of everyone, just as the curse predicted. This action was known in that culture as a statement of power and indicated that a new king is rising up and taking all that belonged to the now fallen king.

Third: David. Somewhere along the way the shepherd boy who created and sang songs in the wilderness to Yahweh, has wandered far from God. In the midst of his trials caused by Saul, he clung to God, crying out for protection, provision, and mercy. Then he took power, and something came over him. He saw Bathsheba and, despite having the pick of any young virgin in the land, he chose her. As a result of his sin, dysfunction enters the house of David, and while he is contrite, he never quite figures out how to deal with the generational dysfunction his actions have caused. I believe a piece of David died with the first son conceived by him and Bathsheba, and he never quite knew how to address the despair within.

Instead, his life falls into destruction, division, and decay. Read Psalm 38 by David. Somewhere along the way, his dysfunction and despair have caught up with him. In this passage we see how the emotional, psychological, and spiritual illness has ended in physical illness. Continue reading Psalms 39 and 40 also by David. God's Word reveals a different path. Many choose to wallow in the pain and sorrow of the past, their mistakes, and the terrible things that have happened, but God calls us to repentance. These three Psalms move from sorrow through repentance and into refreshment in the presence of a forgiving and loving God.

When I first began to study these passages and the dysfunction of David's house, I wasn't certain where it would lead us. I just kept reading and uncovering more and more dysfunction. "How could David be a man after God's own heart with all this dysfunction?" I asked myself. "When will it end?"

There is a telling passage in I Kings 1—2. Near the end of David's life, as his son Adonijah was positioning himself as the next king, David declares Solomon as king, finally setting things right, *according to God's will*. Of course, sneaky Adonijah tries one last attempt at the throne by manipulating Bathsheba to convince Solomon to give him David's concubine Abishag. Again, this is an attempt to demonstrate his power over Solomon. But Solomon will have none of it! He cuts off the generational dysfunction once and for all. It will no longer have any rule over the house of David! God's covenant remains strong as Solomon lives out of God's blessing over David's house from generation to generation until the time of Jesus of Nazareth.

The Old Testament stories reveal that God's covenants come with conditions—we accept those conditions or God can remove his promise over us. The good news, in fact the *great news*, is that Jesus offered a *new covenant* of the bread of his presence and the new wine of his over-flowing provision. His body was broken and his blood was shed in our place. He became our sacrificial lamb, the lamb that was slain to cover the sins of his children, the sons and daughters of God. But this new covenant comes with a condition as well: that we accept this new covenant and consider his gift of love as we "do this in remembrance." Every time we take communion we are reminded of his covenant. We remember, and in calling it to remembrance, we walk in this covenant of love—a love that is poured out continuously over us.

Think about taking communion, especially as one who is moved by symbolism, worship, and beauty. First, think of all the times you've taken communion with little or no consideration to the beautiful depth of its meaning and significance for you. Now instead imagine being in the Upper Room with Jesus and his disciples. Picture him lifting the bread, blessing and breaking it. Visualize him holding up the cup, blessing and drinking from it. As you go back in time, remember that the words that accompanied these actions would seem puzzling to you, just as it was for the disciples. Only later would it make sense. Imagine what it was like for the disciples to eventually come to the full realization of those previous actions of Jesus.

After his resurrection, he comes again and dines with them, and as he is breaking the bread, their eyes are opened and they see! Read Luke 24:30-32. Watch as all the pieces fall together into a New Covenant of love, grace, and mercy. Understanding floods your heart and mind as you see him as the final sacrificial lamb:

Behold! The Lamb of God who takes away the sins of the world!

Next time you have the opportunity to take communion, remember! *Won't you consider taking it as if for the very first time? Taste the bread, as if for the first time. Drink the wine, as if for the first time.* As you swallow, consider the pride and pain Jesus swallowed to bring you into loving, covenantal relationship with God. Imagine the love of Christ that drove him to the cross with *you* as his prize (Heb 12:2)!

Using the exercise of imagination and scripture as your prompts as you begin to explore through creativity, won't you join me in this prayer?

Invite the Holy Spirit into this moment.
Ask the Lord Your Shepherd (Yahweh Rohi) to guide you as you pray.
Ask the Lord Who Sanctifies (Yahweh M'Kaddesh) to purify your imagination and help you picture, sense or create a place of protection and provision around you.
Ask the God of Forgiveness (Elohim Selichot) to join you in that place and remind you of his covenant of mercy, grace, and love.

Jesus Christ, our Final Sacrifice, we are moved in your presence. We watch the truth unfold as you take the bread and the cup and lift them up. Broken and poured out for our sins, you are the only covenant we will ever need. As we begin to repent and release our dysfunction and sin before you, we are overwhelmed with the knowledge that your covenant is one of grace and love and mercy. Over and over, you shower it out upon us. We ask, "Lord, how can it be that you, my God, would die for me?" and your response is this, "I have loved you with an everlasting love." Lord we thank you and praise you for amazing love! We rejoice in your great love for each of us.

In the name of Jesus, the name of Love and Grace and Mercy, Amen.

Listen to: "Adulteress Heart" (based on John 8) by Jody Thomae
"How Can It Be?" by Lauren Daigle
"My Victory" by Crowder

Digging Deeper: Clean Garments for His Priests

Read: Zechariah 3

The Book of Zechariah, contains visions from the prophet whose name means "the Lord remembers," and is filled with great symbolism. This passage is very powerful. Let's picture the drama as it unfolds.

In the opening scene, we find Joshua, the High Priest, standing before the Angel of the Lord, with satan at his right. Our main character is Joshua, and he stands as one accused. As High Priest, Joshua stood before God on behalf of the people (including you and me). The Angel of the Lord is a mysterious character. Many scholars believe the phrase "angel of the Lord" used here in Zechariah identified the pre-incarnate Christ. For dramatic purposes, let's assume he does represent Jesus. Our third character is satan. In Hebrew *satan* meant "accuser"—he is there to give an indictment or accusation against Joshua.

Imagine a courtroom drama: dark brown wood adorns the walls, and the lighting is poor. The Judge sits above all, surveying the scene from his lofty position. Joshua stands in filthy rags, apparently guilty of the crimes of the entire nation. There is no way out of this. Satan is jeering and looking upon Joshua in disgust and contempt, as he takes a deep breath to begin his denunciation.

But... before the accuser has a chance to even open his mouth in condemnation, Christ rebukes him, and Joshua is snatched from the fire! Jesus takes Joshua's filthy rags and exchanges them for a robe of righteousness, in full view of both Judge and accuser. He also places a clean white turban on his head, clearing his mind of guilt and shame. What a beautiful picture of salvation! We find it several other places in scripture, both previous to this one here in Zechariah, and again through the parables of Christ. Meditate on these a moment:

I put on righteousness as my clothing;
justice was my robe and my turban. Job 29:14

I delight greatly in the Lord; my soul rejoices in my God.
For he has clothed me with garments of salvation
and arrayed me in a robe of his righteousness,
as a bridegroom adorns his head like a priest,
and as a bride adorns herself with her jewels. Isa 61:10

But the father said to his servants, "Quick! Bring the best robe and put it on him.
Put a ring on his finger and sandals on his feet. For this son of mine was dead
and is alive again; he was lost and is found." Lk 15:22, 24

As the scene continues, the Angel of the Lord addresses Joshua and the others with him (vs 8)—those whom Christ calls a sign or symbol of things to come. In storytelling, we know this as foreshadowing. Often times in movies, the musical score and the way the scene is shot alerts you to pay attention, and we sense this information will be helpful to unravel an otherwise twisted plot. In Zechariah this is one of those scenes.

Zechariah prophesies that a Branch or Shoot, a servant of the Lord Almighty, will grow up. This imagery is found several other places (Isa 11:1; Jer 23:5-6; 33:14-18; Ezk 17:3-6, 22-23), and according to Bible Scholar Anthony Petterson, paints three symbolic pictures for us:

> The 'new growth' or 'Shoot' is a Davidic king of humble origins, who is associated with the coming kingdom of God with all its blessings. The metaphor of a 'shoot' captures three important ideas: first, it expresses the idea of something new springing from what had been cut down; …secondly, it expresses the idea of some measure of continuity between the old and the new; …and thirdly, it captures the idea of small of humble beginnings of the new growth, which at the same time will grow to produce something magnificent.[7]

At the time this scripture was written, Israel was in enemy exile. They needed to know that something new would spring from their place of captivity; that this new thing would still somehow be connected to the old; and that that new thing would grow into something magnificent. This gave them hope despite their circumstances. Does it bring *you* hope? It should! For this foreshadowing is for *your* own life, as well.

Of course Petterson then points to the end of verse nine: *"I will remove the sin of this land in a single day."* The most important foreshadowing of things to come! He states:

> Christians know the single day Zechariah foresaw—the day when the Messiah ('Shoot') Jesus hung up on a cross outside Jerusalem, suffering the judgment of God and taking sin on himself. As the great high priest he offered the superior sacrifice, the once-for-all sacrifice of his own body. If the cleansing of Joshua fitted him for service, 'How much more, then will the blood of Christ, who through the eternal Spirit offered himself unblemished to God, cleanse our consciences from acts that lead to death, so that we may serve the living God!' (Heb 9:14)[8]

We know how the movie ends, so when we read Zechariah we can see the beautiful symbolism it holds. We watch this courtroom scene and see the critical evidence that points to a verdict of *"Not guilty!"* for everyone who believes. That verdict still stands to this day!

Note the way in which this scene deals with Joshua, the High Priest who represents all of us. He is:

    called out,

        cleansed,

            clothed,

                and commissioned.[9]

In the same way, we are called out of the filthy rags of our guilt and shame. We are cleansed by the blood of Jesus. We are clothed in white robes of righteousness. We are commissioned to serve God as his priests *in this day!* Take a moment to picture that for yourself! Consider verses 6—7 as Joshua's (and our) commission. Instead of being charged with the death penalty, we are charged to walk in God's ways and keep his requirements in order to have a place of standing among God's priestly tribe. This is true for all of us, not just preachers and leaders. We are equally called into the priesthood of *all* believers (I Pet 2:9). We are called out, cleansed, clothed, and commissioned to be his priests and prophets in this present age![10]

I recently saw a video of a small boat of snorkelers that stumbled upon a young, female humpback whale floating on the surface of the water. There was absolutely no movement when they first found her. They feared she was dead, but a short blast of air a few minutes later revealed she was not. One of the snorkelers ventured cautiously into the water to find her entangled in a large fishing net. They set about to free her with a small pocketknife and were able to free one pectoral fin within a few minutes. However, it took another hour of pain-staking work to finish the job. After working diligently to free her, they cut the last piece of net from her tail. She swam away, but stopped about 500 yards from the boat and began an hour-long show of breaching, tail slaps, tail wags, and pectoral fin slaps.

Having been freed by the helping hands around her, she was able to celebrate her freedom with a powerful display of leaps and breaches. Over and over she propelled herself into the air, demonstrating her great liberty and joyous delight at having been freed from the entanglement of that which threatened to drag her under the water to her death.

In my own work in embodied prayer and healing movement, I have seen the children of God move in much the same way. As they are freed from the entanglement of sin and shame, they are released to leap and bound into the air with great liberty and release. Their entire being speaks of their freedom and joy as they celebrate! Hebrews 12:1 says: "Let us throw off everything that hinders and the sin that so easily entangles."

What is entangling you? Your past? Your pain? Your problems? An addiction? An affair? An abortion? What dysfunction, disbelief, and disease needs confronted? What lies, shame, and guilt enmesh, ensnare, and entrap you? It is time to throw it off! For many, these entanglements have become a habit. It's time to create a new habit! Refer back again to the Six R's of Repentance found on page 75. Return to the Lord over and over. Keep your eyes fixed on Jesus! If you fall, stand up and start over, again and again, until a new habit of repentance and renewal is formed in your life.

Just as Zechariah prophesied thousands of years ago, it is time for a *new thing* to grow up from the old things that have been cut down! This new thing will look back to the old, but with a whole new vision of freedom, joy, and celebration! This new thing might have humble beginnings but it will grow up into something magnificent!

Behold, I am doing a new thing;
now it springs forth, do you not perceive it?
I will make a way in the wilderness and rivers in the desert;
to give drink to my chosen people, the people whom I formed for myself
that they might declare my praise. Isa 43:19-21

(continued next page)

Using the questions and scripture passages as your prompts as you begin to explore through creativity, won't you join me in this prayer?

Invite the Holy Spirit into this moment.
Ask the Lord Your Shepherd (Yahweh Rohi) to guide you as you pray.
Ask the Lord of Hosts (Jehovah Sabaoth) to protect you from the enemy.
Ask the Lord Who Sanctifies (Yahweh M'Kaddesh) to purify your imagination and help you picture, sense or create a place of protection and provision around you.
Ask the God of Forgiveness (Elohim Selichot) to join you in that place and speak words of forgiveness and freedom to your spirit.

Angel of the Lord, the One who stands beside us and rebukes the accuser, I trust in you and in your power to silence the lies of the enemy. He seeks to bring me guilt and shame, but you seek to cleanse and clothe me in righteousness. Lord, in this moment I picture you taking my filthy rags and cleansing me with the waters of your forgiveness. I picture you clothing me in a pure white robe. I accept your unfailing love, grace, and mercy. I declare that I am called out, cleansed, clothed, and commissioned as your servant. I declare a new thing from the old broken places of my past. I declare it will be more magnificent than I can even imagine! I bow at your feet in awe and worship.

In the Name of the One Who Silences My Accuser, Jesus, Amen.

Listen to: "Clean" by Natalie Grant
"Before the Throne of God Above" by your favorite artist
"Oh What Love" by The City Harmonic

Digging Deeper: Repentance and Rest

Read: II Chronicles 14—16

I once met a man named Asa. He knew all about his Biblical name—he was named after a king obedient to God's commands, who had smashed all the places detestable by God and commanded the people of Judah to follow God's ways, and was granted rest for his obedience. I couldn't help but think his mother was a God-fearing woman who named her son Asa for good reason. But sadly this Asa was walking far away from his identity and destiny as one who sought after the Lord. For this prodigal son was staggering drunk and on his way to a strip club. Instead, he was following the later years of Asa's reign, when the king was stubbornly refusing to call on the Lord who saves.

Initially, King Asa was a king of reform—and not just any reform, *worship* reform. When Asa took power he went throughout the land and destroyed all the places of pagan worship. As a result of this "spiritual house-cleaning," God blessed him with peace and "rest on every side" (14:7). According to Biblical scholar Steven McKenzie, "Not since Solomon (I Chr 22:9) has rest been noted as a characteristic of a king's reign."[11] And here within this rest, Asa took on the task of sweeping reforms and numerous building projects.[12]

In verse 14:9 we see the Cushite army marching out against Judah, but King Asa calls out to the Lord:

> *"Lord, there is no one like you to help the powerless against the mighty.*
> *Help us, Lord our God, for we rely on you, and in your name we have come against this vast army.*
> *Lord, you are our God; do not let mere mortals prevail against you." (14:11)*

The Hebrew word translated "called" in verse 11 is *qara* and it "denotes the enunciation of a specific message which is usually addressed to a specific recipient and intended to elicit a specific response."[13] Asa wasn't simply shouting a haphazard message to a random god in order to garner any kind of response. It was a *specific* request, and God delivers a *specific* response: he not only struck down the Cushites, he *crushed* them (14:13). The Hebrew word here is *sabar*, and it means to break into pieces or smash. God was not about to let Asa down!

As they return to Jerusalem, the prophet Azariah comes out to meet them saying:

> *The Lord is with you when you are with him. If you seek him, he will be found by you,*
> *but if you forsake him, he will forsake you. For a long time Israel was without the true God,*
> *without a priest to teach and without the law. But in their distress they turned to the Lord,*
> *the God of Israel, and sought him, and he was found by them.*
> *Be strong and do not give up, for your work will be rewarded. (15:2-4, 7)*

So King Asa took courage and took his reforms even further—this king was on a mission! And after all was accomplished, he organized a massive worship service. Read verses 15:11-15 again. Asa's courage is contagious. Together, the people of Judah repent and turn back to the Lord wholeheartedly, seeking after him eagerly until "he was found by them," and they were "given rest on every side" (15:15).

In chapter 16 however, Asa's reign takes a disappointing turn. As neighboring King Baasha mounts up against him, Asa relies on his political ties and the wealth of the temple treasury (instead of God) to secure his position. What happened to the king who called out to the God who smashes the enemy to pieces? Within four years of his extravagant worship service, Asa is inflicted with a disease, and again, instead of relying on God, he relies on physicians and eventually dies. In his pride, he refused to cry out to the God who rescues. It is a sad end to a man once so determined to rely on God for his very survival.

There are many things we can apply here to our own journey. We must be fully reliant on God. We must cry out to him. We must not rely on our own strength, intelligence, or resources, but seek after the Lord in all things. It doesn't matter how insurmountable your battle looks, the Lord is fully capable of crushing the enemy. A God of might and power, he can *and will* crush the enemy—if you will let him! Cry out to him with specific requests in specific situations in your life, and be willing to do the work required of the Lord. Rest comes with repentance—we must repent and turn away from the detestable ways of evil idol worship. In ancient times, idols were made of wood and precious metals. Today, our idols are much more deceptive: self-reliance, pride, envy, greed, slothfulness, entitlement, lust, hatred, negativity, comparison, self-loathing, and our own needful reliance on others for our sense of worth, importance, and identity.

Do you want to be made whole? That is a critical question. Some would rather stay the way they are because soul work is hard work. Or in some cases, there's some secondary gain to being hurt or broken (attention, identity, definition). Again:

Do you want to be made whole?

In John 5:1-15, we find a man who has been lame for 38 years by the Pool of Bethesda, a pool believed to have special healing powers. Jesus has come to celebrate a feast in Jerusalem, and as he passes this pool he finds this man and asks him,

"Do you want to be healed?"

At first that seems like a strange question: he's been lame for 38 years and lies by a pool with healing powers. Of course he wants to be healed! But if Christ asked the question, there must be a reason. I believe Jesus wants us to answer the question for ourselves, as well. Some of us have lived in our wounding for so long it has become our very identity. If we aren't ready to step out of that identity, then certainly we are not ready to be healed. *So beloved, I ask you, in the depths of your being, do you want healing and restoration? Or do you want to hang onto your victim-hood? Do you want to bring your sin into his light or do you want to remain in the darkness?*

Wardle states: "One principle must be followed to experience wholeness: whatever is in the darkness must be brought into the light of Christ."[14] He also encourages us to let the Holy Spirit be our guide as the one who is given to lead us into all truth (Jn 16:13):

> You are allowing the Holy Spirit to shine light upon the dark, painful, hidden events of your life. The purpose: to reveal those events that are at the very core of your feelings of shame, unworthiness, and anger.
>
> If you let him, the Holy Spirit will unveil the secret and shameful ways of your past. Why? That you might renounce Satan's claim to that part of your life and move on to wholeness in Christ Jesus. Instead of denial that leads to dysfunction, what results is healing that brings freedom and newness of life.[15]

No need to go on a witch-hunt—let the Holy Spirit reveal the dark places within. God already knows all the sinful and broken places in you, and frankly, has already forgiven you for those things. However, in order for God to go about the business of sanctifying you and setting you apart for his service, he needs you to work through these broken places in your life.

The word "sanctification" is often regarded with a negative connotation in modern churches. People think it is about following all the rules, but it is so much more! Wardle teaches: "Sanctification is a Holy Spirit driven process that shapes us into the image of Christ, empowering us to live out of who we now truly are in him."[16] This is not about turning you into something you are not—it's about becoming who you truly are! Remember the picture of the Japanese *kintsugi*? Return to the preface if you don't! God needs to repair all the broken places in order for his light and beauty to shine through you.

> *Be strong and do not give up for your work will be rewarded! (II Chron 15:7)*

Our God is a jealous God. He wants us to be fully committed to him and him alone. We must worship and seek after him wholeheartedly. As we sift through the broken places within, we find the ashes that need to be offered up to him in repentance so that he can trade our ashes for something beautiful. As we do so, it becomes an extravagant sacrifice of worship. Verse 16:9 says:

> *For the eyes of the Lord range throughout the earth*
> *to strengthen those whose hearts are fully committed to him.*

I believe that is still true today. And if the eyes of the Lord are looking for fully-committed hearts, then I want his eyes to seek and find *me*. I don't know about you, but I want to be the kind of worshiper that catches the eye of God! I want to offer up the broken pieces of my life so God can transform them into a beautiful masterpiece—*kintsugi* of the soul! I am seeking the strength that only he can give through his life-giving, resurrection power!

Consider this verse from Isaiah 30:15:

> *This is what the Sovereign Lord, the Holy One of Israel, says:*
> *"In repentance and rest is your salvation, in quietness and trust is your strength,*
> *but you would have none of it."*

What do you think God might be saying to you through this scripture? Are you seeking God in repentance and rest? In quietness and trust? Or are you having none of it? What areas of your life is the Holy Spirit prompting you to examine? What "heart work" is the Lord asking of you?

(continued next page)

Using the questions and scripture passages as your prompts as you begin to explore through creativity, won't you join me in this prayer?

Invite the Holy Spirit into this moment.
Ask the Lord Your Shepherd (Yahweh Rohi) to guide you as you pray.
Ask the Lord Who Sees (El Roi) to look upon his child as you cry out to him.
Ask the Lord Who Sanctifies (Yahweh M'Kaddesh) to purify your imagination and help you picture, sense or create a place of protection and provision around you.
Ask the God of Forgiveness (Elohim Selichot) to join you in that place and speak his words of forgiveness and truth deep into your spirit.

Lord God, strong and mighty, I trust you to crush the enemy before me. I trust you to help me find the idolatrous places within that are in need of your forgiving embrace. I trust you to shine your light upon the dark and hidden places within me and illuminate the idols I worship instead of you. I trust the guidance of your Holy Spirit to help me. I know I withhold parts of myself from you, but I want to give you my whole heart. Reveal places in me in need of repentance so I can enter your rest. I am in need of your protection, forgiveness, and healing. Lord, as your eyes roam the earth, may I catch your eye.
In the Name of the He Who Brings Light to the Darkness, Amen.

Listen to: "Sing to Jesus" by Fernando Ortega
"Repentance & Rest" by Aaron Wardle

Digging Deeper: Voices in Our Heads

Read: John 8:42-47; 10:1-6 & 10:25-30

I find these words of Christ to be very cutting. Christ, as the Living Word of God made flesh (Jn 1:1, 14), is using his spoken words to divide the wolves from the sheep in these passages. His words are indeed sharper than a double-edged sword, penetrating and dividing soul and spirit, judging thoughts and attitude of the heart (Heb 4:12).

Let's examine the John 8 passage first. In this we see satan as the "father" or originator of lies. Lies are his "native language"—meaning they are out of his very character or nature—so *out of* and *consistent with* his very nature, he speaks. Your native language is learned from the community into which you were born, but satan is the originator of this language: from the beginning of time he speaks falsely. Verse 44 says he was a murderer from the beginning. When he appeared on the scene in Genesis 3, his intent was not simply to deceive Adam and Eve, but to destroy them and take them to the grave. You must understand that: 1) the enemy is real, and 2) his intent is to kill you. Plain and simple, that's his mission, from the very beginning of time, to this very moment in time, until he is chained forever in the pit of hell.

I have often heard people say, "Satan cannot create," and I believe that to be true. However, here we read that he "created" this language of lies. I would call him "crafty" instead. He doesn't *create* anything new—he simply states the exact opposite of all he knew as God's truth—that is crafty, not creative. In Genesis 3 (Temptation and Fall of Man) we see that he uses the truth but he twists it into a falsehood to propagate a lie. In Matthew 4 (Temptation and Victory of Christ) we find him misusing and misquoting scriptures to deceive Jesus in his weakened state. In this sense, you must understand all evil in the world has its source in satan. Anything bad in your life did not come from God. It came from the enemy of your soul.

> Don't ask why God did "this" to you: ask why the enemy did!
> And in that answer you might possibly find your purpose, calling, and identity!

Now let's turn to the John 10 passage. I love how it starts with Jesus saying, "I tell you the truth." It's as if he's saying, "The enemy's been lying to you, my friend, but *I am here to tell you the truth.*" That makes me want to listen to what he has to say! And he starts by saying that the man who comes any other way than through the front gate is a thief, but the Good Shepherd Jesus comes in through the front gate and calls to us. We as his sheep don't just listen: we heed, we respond, we follow. In ancient times, all the sheep of the village were kept together in a community pen or fold for protection at night. Every morning the shepherds would come and call out with a distinct call or whistle, and the sheep belonging to that shepherd would respond and follow him—*they knew his voice* (vs 4). In this sense, it takes discernment to hear the voice of the One True Shepherd. There was more than one voice calling to them each morning: they had to discern or distinguish their own shepherd's personal voice or call.[17]

In the same way, it takes discernment on our part to distinguish the Voice of Truth over all the other voices in our heads. So let's talk about these 'voices'—both the ones that lie and the ones that speak truth. The voices in your heads can include: your own thoughts; significant others who impacted you; the enemy; and the Holy Spirit. Note that both our own thoughts and the voices we hear of significant others who have impacted our lives can be 1) negative or bad (lies); 2) positive or good (truth); or 3) neutral. Also note that the voice of the enemy will always be lies and the voice of the Holy Spirit will always be truth.

Sometimes it's hard to distinguish God's voice from all the other voices in our mind: it is frankly very difficult to tell the truth from the lies because the enemy wraps his lies in false truths and half-truths (remember Gen 3 and Matt 4). While we struggle to hear the Father of Love over the Father of Lies, the following might prove helpful in discerning whose voice we are actually hearing:

Father of Love	**Father of Lies**
peace/comfort	worry/anxiousness
power	control
positive	negative
quiet/still/soft	loud/obnoxious
subtle	overpowering
courage	fear
encourages	discourages
builds up	tears down
redeems/restores	discards/destroys
gentle correction	cruel punishment
calm, clear mind	confusion
call to action	forced to reaction
gentles guides	promptly pushes

In my own experience, any time I feel immediate pressure to react rather than measured peace to act, I can attribute it to the enemy. When I am anxious or fearful or distressed, I confront the Father of Lies. When I am settled or calm or assured, I am confronted by the Father of Love.

Additionally, the Holy Spirit will often speak through a variety of sources including nature, simple objects or pictures, art, music, people he's placed in your path, and, of course, God's written Word, the Bible, and the Living Word, his Son Jesus Christ. If a voice does not align with scripture or Biblical truth, then I am forced to dismiss it as a lie. In times like that, it is often helpful to call on the wisdom of others further along on the journey than me. This is especially true of the enemy's crafty deception—when he is talking in half-truths or false truths.

Now, what to do with those nasty lies that like to make a habit of roaming around in our heads? When you hear something that is a lie, speak the direct opposite as truth. For example, if you hear: "I am stupid," speak instead: "I am filled with wisdom." Or if you hear: "I am not worthy of love," speak instead: "I am worthy and loved." I know this might sound like a trite exercise or elementary solution, and at first, as if it might not work. Persevere! The enemy has been filling your head with lies for a very long time. So long, in fact, that many of these lies have set up camp in your heart and mind. It takes time to re-wire your brain to think differently. Take yourself into the presence of Jesus and begin to speak the truth over your heart and mind (whether you believe it yet or not). As he speaks his truth into your heart, repeat those truths over and over, again and again. Every time you speak truth in the presence of the Father of Love, it is like a broom sweeping out the lies of the past. Let him do the cleaning. He's happy and beyond willing to do it.

The following is a rather lengthy quote from Bible scholar Rodney Whitacre, but it speaks directly to the heart of what this book is about. He is writing about the Jewish followers of Jesus who were questioning Jesus in John 8 and 10. He is also speaking to us in this day. Lend your ear to his wisdom:

> The Great Physician is diagnosing their disease, and they are not happy about it. They have put their faith in Jesus, yet they rebel as he tries to help them become true disciples. When confronted with their inner disease they should have accepted his assessment and repented. This is what each of us must do as a disciple of Jesus, for each of us has inner disease that he desires to cure and that must be cured. His diagnosis is perfect, and he knows how to heal us. He does not have to leave us waiting while he goes in the next room to consult his medical books. Nor does he lack the resources to effect [sic] our cure. He lacks nothing except our signature on the permission slip to get on with the process. Discipleship includes allowing Jesus to deal with our inner brokenness and deadness. He will not be satisfied until we come out entirely clean and whole, a fact that is part of the good news. To be a disciple one needs not only the humility to receive what Jesus reveals about himself but also the ability to receive what he reveals about oneself. He always reveals in order to redeem. The judgment the light brings is meant to lead us to salvation, not condemnation. The sin is condemned in order to reveal it as sin and lead us to repentance. If we reject the diagnosis or the cure, then the light does indeed bring condemnation, for we have chosen to remain in our state of alienation from God, who is the one source of life.[18]

Did you hear that?

His diagnosis is perfect, and he knows how to heal us!

Whitacre brings up an important note here. If you are sensing condemnation in your soul as we talk about repentance, ask the Lord to move your soul from condemnation to conviction. If something in you is rising up against this, then it is rising up against the truth of God's word, and it is not of God. I will be brutally honest here: if it's not of God, then it is of the enemy.

Read this verse from Hebrews 4:12 in two translations:

For the word of God is alive and powerful. It is sharper than the sharpest two-edged sword, cutting between soul and spirit, between joint and marrow. It exposes our innermost thoughts and desires. NLT

For the word of God is living and active, sharper than any two-edged sword, piercing to the division of soul and of spirit, of joints and of marrow, and discerning the thoughts and intentions of the heart. ESV

Could it be that his sword is penetrating the depths of your soul and exposing and confronting your thoughts and intentions? Instead of rising up against this, press into it and allow Jesus to bring conviction (not condemnation) to your heart. If you need to wrestle this out with God, that is okay. He can handle it. Simply allow your spirit to be open to what he might be teaching you in this.

In the final season of *American Idol*, contestant La'Porsha Renae shared her story as a mother going through divorce and as a survivor of domestic abuse. In one episode she took the stage to sing *No More Drama* by Mary J. Blige, and by the end of the song she had brought down the house with her beautiful, transparent performance. As I watched her perform, I was struck by the deep sense of an artist using her creativity to break free from the chains that had held her captive to lies.

Take a moment to consider the lies that have been spoken over her. And yet here in this performance, she embraces the words of the song and begins to declare the truth:

> Now you're free from all the pain
> Free from all the games; free from all the stress
> So find your happiness…
> Only God knows where the story ends for me
> But I know where the story begins
> It's up to us to choose whether we win or lose, and I choose to win![20]

As the final lyric rings out she looks right into the camera and sings, "No more!" Then she begins to shake her arms, as if she is literally shaking off the chains that have bound her. It is obvious to all that this moment of artistic expression has been a break-through moment for her. The audience cheers as she walks into her newfound freedom. Ryan Seacrest and the judges recognize there are no words for what she's just experienced. Her own experience on the stage, and the shouts of those around her, speak volumes. She is free! She has confronted the lies of the enemy!

Pause and return to Whitacre's quote above, and ponder what the Great Physician might be diagnosing in you. *What might Jesus be revealing in order to redeem in your life? What is he bringing into the Light, and how are you reacting to the "Son exposure" as he does? What lies have you believed, and how can you begin to speak the truth into those lies? How might being in the safety and provision of his Sweet Presence help sweep away the lies that you have lived with? And will you allow him to do so?*

Using the questions, quote, and scripture passages as your prompts as you begin to explore through creativity, won't you join me in this prayer?

Invite the Holy Spirit into this moment.
Ask the Lord Your Shepherd (Yahweh Rohi) to guide you as you pray.
Ask the Lord Your Peace (Yahweh Shalom) to quiet your heart before him.
Ask the Lord Who Sanctifies (Yahweh M'Kaddesh) to purify your imagination and help you picture, sense or create a place of protection and provision around you.
Ask the God of Forgiveness (Elohim Selichot) to join you in that place and speak his words of truth over you.

Holy Spirit, you are the one who holds the broom. Sweep away the lies that I have believed about myself, others, and you. Shine your exposing light on the lies the enemy has used to keep me in bondage to sin and misery. Help me see them for what they are: lies used by the enemy of my soul to destroy me and send me to my grave. Your word says in Psalm 16:10 that you will not abandon my soul to Sheol, the grave, or let your holy one see corruption. So, therefore, I will declare the truth that I am worthy. I am forgiven. I am beautiful. I am strong. I am significant. I am your beloved child. I am your prince. I am your princess. I am loved by the God of all Creation! He created me in his BEaUtiful image! I choose to believe and walk in the truth!
In the Name of He Who Speaks Truth, My Good Shepherd, Amen.

Listen to: "Brokenness Aside" by All Sons & Daughters
"Beloved" by Jordan Feliz

Digging Deeper: Sorrow Leads to Repentance

Read: II Corinthians 7:8-11

The Apostle Paul wrote at least two letters to the church in Corinth. Paul's first letter to the Corinthians was very direct: Paul did not mince words. Here in Second Corinthians we find, despite his clear instruction, the people still had some issues to resolve. It also appears from the text there was someone discrediting Paul and many had fallen prey to his lies. It seems both Paul and Titus had visited Corinth and set them straight. As a result they had fallen into a state of sorrow, but as we will soon see it was a Godly sorrow, not a worldly sorrow.

So the remorse felt by the church at Corinth is a result of Paul's rebuke and their having fallen for this accuser's lies. At first it seems Paul considered his correction too harsh. But we see here that he no longer regrets it, for it produced a Godly sorrow that led to repentance among his fellow believers. Paul's first letter had caused a stir, and justly so, but also a subsequent change of heart. The church at Corinth was now back on track after Paul's admonishment. We must realize this wasn't just a guilt trip, but an avenue of God's blessing and grace.

Our last four studies in repentance are much the same way. We are not studying repentance to put us all on a great big guilt trip, but to move us to the kind of Godly sorrow that brings about a change of heart and mind, a true repentance leading to greater wholeness, redemption, and restoration. Read James 5:13-16. I believe our sin makes us sick—at all levels: emotionally, physically, and spiritually. When we hold onto those things that God has asked us to release to him, we hold onto defiance, disease, and death. God is calling us out of that life into new life in him! All regret is to be left behind so that new life can rise to the surface—one that seeks earnestness, justice, and refreshment in the Lord's presence.

Verse 10 is clear that there is a difference between Godly sorrow and worldly sorrow: Godly sorrow brings repentance that leads to salvation and leaves no regret, but worldly sorrow brings death, guilt, and shame. Bible scholar Scott Hafemann expounds on the difference:

> Paul is aware... not all experiences of "feeling bad" lead to repentance. People feel guilty for all kinds of reasons. The reason the Corinthians' remorse led to repentance was because they had "become sorrowful as God intended"—that is, experiencing the kind of genuine remorse that leads to a real change in one's way of life. Being sorrowful as God intended is feeling the deep grief that comes from knowing that our attitudes and actions have harmed our relationship with God. "Godly sorrow" feels bad because it is missing out on God.
>
> ...Their repentance toward Paul leads to salvation because it was not a death-producing "worldly sorrow." Worldly sorrow is the grief that comes about because one's actions result in missing out on something the world has to offer. Worldly sorrow feels bad because it wants more of the world. Such sorrow causes us to focus even more on how hurt we are, thereby helping to bring about the death that comes from living for self rather than for Christ.[20]

Take a moment to examine your own remorse, regret, and sorrow. In the list of questions below the first is Godly repentance, and the second is worldly in nature. Are you:
- *convicted* by the Holy Spirit or *convinced* you can never change?
- *contrite* over your sin or *condemning* yourself for failing again?
- *grieving* separation from God or *granting* yourself a pity party?
- *identifying* God's will for your life or *idealizing* yourself as a victim?
- *returning* to God's plan for you or *turning* to your own plan?

In verse 11 we see that godly sorrow produces fruit: earnestness, indignation, alarm, longing, concern, and readiness to see justice done. Is your repentance going to produce fruit or just smell-up the world with self-pity? Godly sorrow brings redemption. It is productive and aligns with his good and perfect will. A worldly sorrow would be the opposite of that—void of redemption and out of sync with his will.

In another vein, Bible scholar Mark Seifrid proposes the idea that God brings sorrow as a kind of gentle wounding in our life in order to bring us into full healing and wholeness. This is a sting of conscience that comes from God's correction. It is a deep conviction of the heart through the Holy Spirit's wisdom that runs counter to the dysfunctional ways in which we behave. He states:

> [The Corinthians'] grief was worked by God and rested in his hand. It had its time, but that time came to an end in their change of heart. ...The healing that God works through wounding is complete and whole. God wills to restore us, not destroy us. Even though he must perform the latter in order to accomplish the former. That is the essence of salvation: we must be stripped of our idols and given the true God.[21]

Many have made an idol of their wounds, using victimization as an identifier of self instead of their true God-given identity. They identify themselves *first* as a victim or a survivor instead of *first* as a child of God who has overcome though his power and grace.

Sometimes one may say something that's difficult for us to hear, but it's spoken out of love. The essence of speaking the truth in love is to bring one another into maturity in Christ (Eph 4:14-16). I suspect that some of the things I have written in this chapter have been difficult to hear. Please know that they are written with great love and with desire that we *all together* might be brought into greater maturity, deeper healing, and complete wholeness. I am on this journey *with* you.

Wardle teaches that when you turn from your dysfunctional behavior (or repent), it will often get worse before it gets better. Because now, instead of killing the pain, you have to deal with the pain. You have to face it head on. But in the end, this is a good thing as it helps us also come face to face with our Savior, Redeemer, and Friend, Jesus Christ, who walks us into freedom! Wardle writes of this journey:

> First, there is a recognition of sin and admission of brokenness, followed by godly sorrow that leads to repentance. Realizing one is powerless to change, the door is opened to the only One who can bring transformation. From here the season of recovery begins. Wounds are brought into the light for healing and distortions replaced by the truth of God's living Word. What eventually results is freedom and the fruits of righteousness.[22]

Sometimes you simply have to walk through the sorrow, moving through the valley of repentance, out into the saving light of his love!

Ponder this promise of repentance from Acts 3:19-20 in several translations:

Now repent of your sins and turn to God, so that your sins may be wiped away. Then times of refreshment will come from the presence of the Lord, and he will again send you Jesus, your appointed Messiah. NLT

Repent therefore, and turn back, that your sins may be blotted out, that times of refreshing may come from the presence of the Lord, and that he may send the Christ appointed for you, Jesus. ESV

Now it's time to change your ways! Turn to face God so he can wipe away your sins, pour out showers of blessing to refresh you, and send you the Messiah he prepared for you, namely, Jesus. MSG

Do you hear that, men and women of the Living God? It is time to repent and change your ways. Let God wipe away your tears of sorrow. Your time of refreshment in his presence is here! Jesus has been sent to meet you as you seek him! Let go of the past and turn to your future in Jesus Christ!

Using the scripture passages as your prompts as you begin to explore through creativity, won't you join me in this prayer?

Invite the Holy Spirit into this moment.
Ask the Lord Your Shepherd (Yahweh Rohi) to guide you as you pray.
Ask the Lord Who Sanctifies (Yahweh M'Kaddesh) to purify your imagination and help you picture, sense or create a place of protection and provision around you.
Ask the God of Forgiveness (Elohim Selichot) to join you in that place and speak his words of forgiveness over your life.

Jesus Messiah, pour out your showers of blessing to refresh me. I am standing with arms and heart wide open before you. I turn from my past, from my dysfunction, from the lies I have believed. Wash me clean in the rivers of your grace, love, and mercy. I choose to walk in your future for me. I choose to walk in your salvation and wholeness. I choose to walk in the truth of your word over my life. You are good, oh Lord, and all that you do is good. Lord, help me to treasure your correction in my life. Help my sorrow to be Godly sorrow that leads my heart into true repentance. I lay down my idols. I worship you alone.

In the Name of My Redeemer, Jesus, Amen.

Listen to: "O Come to the Altar" by Elevation Worship
And watch: "Clear the Stage" by Jimmy Needham – A Dance Testimony
(Video on YouTube posted by CherieAmour: take note of her testimony below the video)

☙ A Benediction of The Good Shepherd ❧

High Places that Deceive
by Tom Graffagnino

Now if Doeg's your head shepherd,
Rest assured, you'll find no peace.
"*No Shalom*" will be your pasture,
And confusion will not cease.

His Anxieties will lead you
To 'high places' that deceive...
And where idols tempt... then taunt you,
And where sin and ill's conceived.

It's where Mammon may consume you...
And indulgences are sold.
It's where Asherah seduces,
It's where Baal collects his toll.

It's where grace and rest elude you;
It's where *busy*-ness prevails...
Where the din of rebel chatter
Is a cliff you cannot scale.

It's a pit that has no bottom...
It's a night that has no dawn.
It's a never-ending treadmill...
It goes on... and on... and on...

But there is *another* Shepherd...
One who's good and kind and true;
And a high place in his presence
He's preparing now for you!

Yes, his voice is calm and gentle
Like a brook that gently falls...
Living water for the dying,
Like a soothing harp... He calls.

This Good Shepherd knows high pastures
Where the skies are clear and rare,
And His springs provide still water...
If you ask... He'll take you there.

Next Steps: Resources for Your Healing Journey

The Broken Way: a Daring Path into the Abundant Life by Ann Voskamp

Wounded: How to Find Wholeness and Inner Healing in Christ by Terry Wardle

Endnotes
1. Chen, *Depths of God*, 143.
2. Wardle, "Dysfunctional Behaviors," 7-77.
3. Ibid.
4. Wardle, *Healing Care*, 163-164.
5. Wardle, *Wounded*, 29.
6. Joseph, *Gently Awakened*, 77-78.
7. Petterson, *Haggai, Zechariah & Malachi*, 143.
8. Ibid., 146.
9. Ibid.
10. I wrote a great deal about the priestly and prophetic roles of the artist in *God's Creative Gift—Unleashing the Artist in You*. These are two critical roles for artists and creatives as we move forward as an army of artists called to bring forth God's glory and praise.
11. McKenzie, *1–2 Chronicles*, 276.
12. Ibid., 277.
13. *Hebrew-Greek Study Bible*, 1549.
14. Wardle, *Wounded*, 26.
15. Ibid., 31.
16. Wardle, "People of the Presence," 32.
17. Whitacre, *John*, 256.
18. Ibid., 221-222.
19. Mary J. Blige, *No More Drama*, MCA Records, 2001.
20. Hafemann, *2 Corinthians*, 312.
21. Seifrid, *Second Corinthians*, 309.
22. Wardle, *Wounded*, 193.

4

Lamenting

"I have heard your prayer; I have seen your tears. Behold, I will heal you."

I'm a big fan of old episodes of TLC's *What Not to Wear*. Viewing a 2012 episode, I watch Stacy and Clinton help a woman named Dolly. Dolly is loved by her friends, and together they often go out dancing. Dolly shares that she relishes the freedom of it. But Dolly also insists on hiding under disheveled, over-sized clothing. As they stand in the '360 Room' Dolly confesses that she was the victim of childhood sexual abuse. As is the case with many victims of sexual trauma, it has affected the way she dresses, her self-confidence, and sense of self-worth. If you've not watched the show, the '360 Room' is a circular room of mirrors that enables you to see yourself in 360 degrees, from every angle and perspective. It's a very revealing room, in more ways than one.

As she confesses the crime against her, we the viewers realize that the reflection surrounding her reveals much more than simply an image in a mirror. In Dolly's mind, her image is fractured beyond recognition. She fails to see what everyone around her already sees: Dolly is a remarkable woman of beauty and joy despite her pain. Stacy and Clinton remind her of the little girl within who wants to dance.

"Let's go in and get her out," says Stacy with more truth than she could possibly realize. I often wonder if they both don't have a degree in psychology or counseling.

What I love about Stacy and Clinton is that through the "art" of fashion, they walk her through a process of repairing the fractured pieces of the mirror of her self-image into a healed image of her true self. Later in the episode, as she struggles to stand in front of a mirror in a fantastic dress, Stacy and Clinton encourage her, "You have to keep looking at her to get to know her, because you've forgotten about her for a long time."

As Dolly cries, they asked if they've upset her. She shakes her head no, as she discloses, "It's a release!"

As she cries, her tears help her let go of the agony of her painful past, and as she lets go, the fractured mirror of her heart is made whole once again—*kintsugi* of the soul! A beautiful image to behold!

The heart cannot let go of what it has not grieved.

I believe this with all my heart, because I have lived this out in my own life, and because I have seen this played out in the lives of many others I have encountered on my healing journey. There is indeed pain in our lives, and in order to let go of that pain and move forward into all God has called us, we have to mourn our losses. We must allow our hearts to feel and express the fullness of our pain. In this chapter we will explore grief and lament. Hopefully by the end of this chapter, you will discover that tears are a natural part of God's intricate and caring design of you as his beautiful creation; that every tear has reason and purpose; and that tears of lament are a natural and necessary part of our spiritual journey.

As we begin, consider Psalm 56:8 in several translations:

You keep track of all my sorrows.
You have collected all my tears in your bottle.
You have recorded each one in your book. NLT

You have kept count of my tossings;
put my tears in your bottle.
Are they not in your book? ESV

You've kept track of my every toss and turn
through the sleepless nights.
Each tear entered in your ledger,
each ache written in your book. MSG

Every tear we cry is precious to the Lord. Every. Single. One. No tear is ever wasted or unnoticed by God. Take a moment to meditate on the image above: God collecting your every tear. Imagine him writing down every tear—taking account of your pain and sorrow. This should give you great comfort knowing God cares so deeply about you that he records *every* tear you cry. What an amazing thought!

Tears, Grief & Lament

Sharon and her family were active members of our church community. When God called them to the other side of the United States, we were all deeply saddened. What always stood out to me in that season were the tears that streamed down Sharon's face most of the time. She would explain why they were moving, teaching us about obeying God's voice despite fear or sadness, assuring us of God's call on their lives, laughing about the beautiful memories we had all made together, dancing with us at our ministry rehearsals—all the while, tears streaming down her face. I have always greatly admired Sharon for her transparent courage in that season of her life. She wore her tears like a badge of honor! Through smiles, laughter, great sorrow, and worship, tears coursed their way down her beautiful face.

Interestingly, tears caused by intense emotion are chemically different in nature than the tears that keep your eyes lubricated or the tears produced when you chop an onion. They contain specific hormones and painkillers, produced by the body when you are under high levels of emotion, stress and/or pain and are believed to be ridding the body of these chemicals in order to help return you to a more relaxed state (*homeostasis* in scientific terms). God has created our bodies in a myriad of amazingly intricate ways. Everything about our body has specific purpose and is designed to keep it functioning in a healthy, productive way. Tears are no different. Your body produces chemicals under intense emotion. In order to process those chemicals, God made tears. So the next time you are holding back tears, let them flow instead—you'll be healthier as a result.

God says he has heard our prayers, seen our tears, and he will heal us (II Kgs 20:5); that those who sow with tears will reap with songs of joy (Ps 126:5-6); and that one day he will wipe every tear from our eyes (Rev 7:17, 21:3). The Bible reminds us over and over that God is with us, especially when we mourn. Consider these truths found in scripture:

- ❖ **He is a God of all comfort:**
    Blessed be the God and Father of our Lord Jesus Christ,
    the Father of mercies and God of all comfort, who comforts us in all our affliction,
    so that we may be able to comfort those who are in any affliction,
    with the comfort with which we ourselves are comforted by God. II Cor 1:3-4 ESV

- ❖ **God calls on his people to cry out in lament:**
    This is what the Lord Almighty says:
    "Consider now! Call for the wailing women to come; send for the most skillful of them.
    Let them come quickly and wail over us
    till our eyes overflow with tears and water streams from our eyelids.
    Teach your daughters how to wail; teach one another a lament." Jer 9:17-18, 20b

- ❖ **God cries with his people:**
    Let my eyes overflow with tears night and day without ceasing;
    for the Virgin Daughter, my people,
    has suffered a grievous wound, a crushing blow. Jer 14:17

- ❖ **And two of the most powerful words of scripture:**

Jesus—the very man who will in the *next* moment step in and work with resurrection power—in *this* moment joins you in your tears (Jn 11:35). Feeling and understanding your pain, he weeps with you. As we move forward, let us be assured of the presence of the One who sees, the One who comforts those who mourn, the One who weeps with us, the One who wipes every tear from our eyes.

While we will do much exploration about lament, Wardle offers this succinct explanation to start.

Lament is:
> the act of taking our disappointment and pain
> > in an honest, open, uncensored, and emotive fashion
> > > without minimizing or discrediting our feelings
> > > > before a loving and understanding Father
> > > > > who listens with great attention, compassion, and concern.[1]

No wound is too insignificant, too old, too stupid, too deep, or too shallow to take before the Lord. All our hurts can be brought prayerfully before our living God, who will capture each and every tear and record them in his book.

Biblical Lament

Have you ever seen waste from the mining process spill out into the environment? It ruins entire ecosystems! It must be dealt with properly or it will poison everything it comes in contact with. Lament is the way God has given us to dispose of the waste that has built up within us. It is our Biblical response to pain, loss, injustice, tragedy, and trauma. Did you know that the Book of Psalms contains more prayers of lament than songs of praise? If the Psalms are man's response to God, and God allows lament to be an important part of our scripture, then they must serve a purpose. If the Bible is God's story of love and his plan of restoration and redemption, then lament must also be a part of that story and plan.

Theologian Walter Brueggemann shares much wisdom on Biblical lament, especially as it appears in the Psalms. He describes lament as cathartic, as "giving expression to what we have felt and known all along."[2] He continues: "In genuine rage, words do not simply follow feelings. They lead them. It is speech that lets us discover the power, depth, and intensity of the hurt."[3]

Take a moment to read Psalm 109. In his study of this psalm, Brueggemann notes the writer's "long recital of rage" through verse 19; how he comes back to "the reality of heart and fear and helplessness" in verses 22-25; and his "final confidence in God" through doxology in verses 30-31. With great insight he states: "The rage is a prelude to the real agenda of attitudes about one's self."[4] Yes, we must process our pent-up negative emotions in order to get to the heart of our true identity. Years of surviving in this world, have left us with "stockpiles" of bitterness, anger, fear, and other negative emotions. These stockpiles build armories of false beliefs designed to hold us captive by the enemy.

Many argue this is not Christian. We've been taught to forgive and forget, to have mercy and compassion, to never speak an unkind word. But how can we have mercy and compassion if we are not willing to walk the way of the cross just as Jesus did? In Gethsemane, Christ pours out his prayers of lament before his Abba Father in such a way that he sweats drops of blood. On the cross he cries out: "My God, my God why have you forsaken me?" All the cruel acts against him combine with the great sin and evil of this world, and yet... for the joy set before him, he endures this great tragedy, giving up his life in complete surrender! Only through the way of the cross can he demonstrate his greatest act of love, mercy, and compassion! How can we expect any less for ourselves? Brueggemann counsels: "We are not permitted a cheaper, easier, more 'enlightened' way."[5] And yet, yielded to the mercy of God, at the end of lament we find ourselves no longer on the cross, but outside an earthly tomb of victory and resurrection. Finally, outside the empty grave, we return to healing and wholeness.

In Psalm 109, Brueggemann reveals that once the writer's "speech of vengeance" is spent, he returns to praise and worship of a sovereign God with the phrase, "But thou..." This "yielding" is a "doxology" that reveals the writer's "final confidence is in God."[6] Notice, in verse 30 the psalmist says, "With my mouth, I will greatly extol the Lord." Yes, with his mouth, the *very mouth* that just spewed curses upon his enemy, he will now speak glory to the God who stands at the right hand of the needy to save his life. Biblical lament always ends in doxology—our lament should end in doxology, as well. Doxology is from two Latin words: *doxa*, which means "glory" and *logos*, which means "speaking" or "word." In literal terms, doxology is "glory-speaking" or "glory-word."

Once our heart is emptied of the stockpiles of pain and loss, we speak out the glory of our God:
>You are sovereign!
>>You are filled with steadfast love!
>>>Your compassion never ceases!
>>>>Great is your faithfulness, Oh God!
>>>>>*Your mercy endures forever!*

Nature's Song of Lament

The National Geographic documentary about the Sawtooth Mountain wolf pack, tells the story of an omega wolf named Motaki. As the lowest ranking member of the pack, she fed last and often felt the brunt of skirmishes for dominance. However, the omega of the pack is not an outcast—they play an important role in pack hierarchy. Motaki's job was to keep peace and initiate play, diminishing tension and rivalry. Yet, Motaki often wandered off to isolated areas of the pack's range, and as a result was attacked and killed by a mountain lion. Her wolf pack set out to find her, and evidence indicates they even chased her attacker up a tree to seek retribution.

After her death, the wolves went into a time of mourning. The documentary reports this phenomenon:

Their howling [took] on a mournful, searching quality as if they are trying to call Motaki back.

Researchers Jim and Jamie Dutcher observed: "Their behavior changed as they appeared depressed; hanging their heads they drifted about their home in a listless manner. As…mentioned earlier, omega wolves instigate play in an effort to diffuse pack tension. Motaki was good at this, and when she died the other wolves lost the desire to play."[7] Read the last statement again: "They lost their desire to play."

Nature is revealing several things about loss and grief. First, our mourning changes the vocalization and tone of our spirit's song. You might go about telling everyone you're fine, but they can hear the anguish in the tone of your voice. The wolf pack doesn't hide its loss: it vocalizes it in the song of its community. Second, notice how the song had a "searching quality" that sought to call Motaki back. Their song is not simply: *"We miss our friend Motaki."* It is:

Motaki, we miss you. Where are you? We need you!
We want you back where you belong. With us. We will never be the same without you!

We must allow our song to take on both a mournful and searching quality, as we grieve our losses. While many questions are left unanswered until we stand before him in heaven, we still search for answers in the midst of our grief. While we know life will never be the same, we still seek restoration of the way things were before.

Thirdly, our mourning also changes our stature and physical being: our heads hang low and we take on a listlessness to our manner. When we are in mourning, there is a slight bent in our physical posture, revealing the true nature of our soul. We cannot hide it. We must give ourselves freedom to walk in this bentness, expressing the emotions we attempt to hide when forcing a smile. Lastly, we lose our desire to play. Activities we used to enjoy are left aside as our reason for play is taken from us. We are left feeling empty and void.

Several years ago I lost my best friend Lynn to a rare, aggressive cancer. As a valuable member of our church and community, her loss was felt by many. Like Motaki, Lynn served a valuable role within our church body and our local community. She was outgoing, loving, hopeful, merciful, kind, and spoke of the mysteries of God as one who had experienced him firsthand. She passed over to the glorious other side in the wee hours of a Sunday morning. While she experienced Sunday morning worship in the wondrous praise of God's throne room, our church body lifted its own song of mournful praise. Some in our body sang out for those who could only weep. Many stood arm in arm, linked together in grief. Like a wolf pack, our howling took on a mournful cry as we sought together for her, for answers, for comfort, for peace, and perhaps even vengeance. As individuals and as a church body, our posture changed as we hunted for answers to questions that will never be answered.

Why, God, did you take her from us?
A piece of our hearts has been ripped out.
What was, will never be.
Why, God, oh why? Why have you forsaken us?

We did not play that morning. We mourned. We cried. We worshiped. We allowed ourselves to question, to feel the loss, to offer a sacrifice of praise in the midst of our great sorrow.

Even now as I write, I weep. I long for what was. I let my writing be my mournful, searching howl, echoing across the plains and valleys of my heart. And as the tears stream down my face, I know God is here collecting…

Every. Single. One.

Lament through Creativity

Like the wolf pack, we must give ourselves permission, freedom, perhaps even encouragement to let our song of grief come out in our creative offerings. As we paint, there's no need to cover our sorrow with watercolor washes of bright yellow and fuchsia. Just like Van Gogh, we must allow ourselves to paint in blue for a long period of time. As we sing and play our instruments, we must allow ourselves to stop singing in major keys and instead express ourselves in minor keys that release the mournful, searching, soulful song within. We must let our song rise up like a howl from deep within to express the grief, the sadness, the robbing of what would've been. As we dance and act we must convey our grief through bent postures—affecting our movement, our expression, our carriage. And that is as it should be.

Given the fact that tragedy lodges itself in the very cells of our physical being, we must take time to explore physical postures of mourning that help us demonstrate our pain to God, our grief finding expression in embodied prayers of mind, body, and spirit. Pounding out clay and hammering metal can become embodied prayers that express our questions, our sorrow, and our anger. Long walks of capturing dying trees, discarded trash, and lonely places rightfully develop into photographs of a soul in deep mourning. Writers need to write longhand with physicality of pen and paper without edit or form, allowing free verse to flow from hands and fingers that hold tightly to all that is lost, broken, and mangled beyond repair. There are many ways to grieve. We must allow ourselves *both* creativity in the process of our mourning *and* the creative process as a way of mourning.

In *God on Mute*, author Pete Greig shares a story of a church's creative expression of grief. Several weeks after devastating mudslides took ten lives in La Conchita, California in 2005, he visited his friend Greg's church one evening. Greg had covered the walls with black paper and planned to use it creatively at the end of the message. He had prepared a sermon that seemed appropriate for the community's struggling spirits, but the tears on their faces led him to set aside *his* plans for the plans of God—a God who heals through creativity. He asked several men to gather dust from the street outside, and it was mixed with red paint. The congregation was then invited to express their "emotions, questions, and prayers" with the "blood-mud paste." While some painted with brushes, others used their hands. Some sat. Some watched. Many wept.

"And all this time, the mud-blood paint just kept splattering off the paper and onto the floor, creating a mess," he wrote of the experience.[8] Indeed, our creative grieving can get messy as we fling our blood-red questions at a wall enveloped in black.

Think back to the Sawtooth wolf pack and how they lost their desire to play as they mourned Motaki's death, and ask yourself:

Where have I lost my desire to play?

What areas of playful creativity have you left behind as a result of ungrieved loss in your life? Creative Christians, we need to play again, but we can't until we've expressed our lament. Let us mourn so we can move into greater levels of freedom and even playfulness in our creativity! It is time to walk alongside Jesus as he comes to redeem, rebuild, restore, and renew the places of our deepest loss and grief.

Mourning Into Dancing

Turn My Mourning Into Dancing is a collection of writings from Henri Nouwen about sorrow and suffering. It was recommended to me by my professor, neighbor, and friend Dr. JoAnn Watson during a particularly difficult time in my journey. She had seen me minister through dance on many occasions and knew the book would speak to my embodied spirit and soul. Let me share from Nouwen's heart:

> We hear an invitation to allow our mourning to become a place of healing, and our sadness a way through pain to dancing. …By greeting life's pains with something other than denial we may find something unexpected. By inviting God into our difficulties we ground life—even its sad moments—in joy and hope. …Ultimately mourning means facing what wounds us in the presence of One who can heal.
>
> This is not easy, of course. This dance will not usually involve steps that require no effort. We may need to practice. …These [steps] will not make the pain go away. They will not mean we can expect to avoid shadowed valleys and long nights. But these steps in the dance of God's healing choreography let us move gracefully amid what would harm us, and find healing as we endure what could make us despair. We can ultimately find a healing that lets our wounded spirits dance again, that lets them dance unafraid of suffering and even death because we learn to live with lasting hope.[9]

He continues: "An early step in the dance sounds very simple, though often will not come easily: We are called to grieve our losses. It seems paradoxical, but healing and dancing begin with looking squarely at what causes us pain."[10]

Just as a dancer must experience the pain he or she is pushing through in order to bring a dance to its true beauty and fulfillment, we must push through the pain and find the root of it all. Do we hurt? Yes! But why? Not simply because life is unfair, but what exactly has happened to you that is unfair? Being able to identify and name your pain is key in the grieving process. Nouwen goes on to say, "Mourning opens us to a future we could not imagine on our own—one that includes a dance."[11] Even amidst my loss and pain, I want the promise of a future that includes dance.

And Dancing Through Our Mourning

Glenn Mercer was a seminary classmate of mine. He was tall, quick to smile, loved athletics, and had a heart for youth. At 24, he was recently engaged to a lovely young woman who attended our church. Life was promising for this wonderful young man of God. But life was also short. He died unexpectedly from a seizure after completing his first year of seminary. It was a deep loss for the community. I had known his parents for many years; his sister Leta was a part of our worship dance ministry; and his mother Susie had been involved in our dance ministry events, as well.

A month before our spring workshop Susie contacted me, saying, "I'm thinking about a black dance." Susie continued:

> Our daughter gave me a blank canvas to paint on my birthday. I painted it all black. My sister also painted when she was healing from cancer, and her art therapist noted that she always filled the canvas. She went on to have my sister consider the benefits of dance, as a means of working outside the canvas to assist with the healing process. Since I had filled the canvas, I decided I too would benefit from dancing with a black flag with which I could "paint" an entire room black.

Susie's grief simply could not be contained within the confines of her 2'x3' canvas. She asked if we could work together with a few others to help her create her black dance. She gathered fabric, props, and poles: I gathered dancers, intercessors, and prayer warriors.

I reminded Susie that it was both the creative process and the journey of letting a dance unfold within a community of like-minded women that would bring its own healing, and I worked to provide her a safe and creative space to mourn. I invited her to consider what song might be used as she prepared to move through her mourning. Of course, a song did come to her, as well as many ideas. Even in the initial stages of her creative process, God met her in powerful ways as she spent time in his presence and revealed to her the idea of creating a light/dark theme. Susie shares:

> Once the song came, it seemed like the ideas came bit by bit each time I listened to the song. Tears came too, and I believe that was a way of letting out some of the pain of death. I think the music helped me realize that it would not be an all black dance, but that there were times God's light would come over the months and years of grieving. Even though I felt run over by a train, God was still in the center of all life, whether I understood what was going on or not. God will not change.
>
> Even the creative process brought clarity of truth and a release of what was taking place inside of me. I was able to name how I felt, so that could be a part of the dance. The experience helped me look at how grief overcame me and was a part of everything I did. I could not escape it. It was a time to look at the pain of death, which was something I had been avoiding. I was able to be honest about how I felt. It was my experience, so it wasn't wrong. It was honest and that was freeing.

The day finally arrived. A small group of women gathered around Susie and her daughter Leta. She described her creative process and assigned us "roles" and "choreography." Each of us was given an item that represented an aspect of mourning or darkness, as well as a role to play. These items were a reminder of how grief is with us all the time—as each dancer was required to have something black with them the entire time. For example, Susie gave me a black shawl and asked me to represent the part of her that moved without emotion through the monotony of sorrowful days. Another was given a black pair of shoes and was asked to simply lie beside them to represent the part of Susie that didn't want to get out of bed in the morning. Another person was given a specific action—the task of running over Susie like a freight train. These items, roles, and actions all became the "choreography" in her dance of lament.

We took our places as Susie took up the large black flag she had created as her "paintbrush" to coat the room with her grief. The music began, and we began to act out our respective roles. Then, as Susie began, the unyielding sound of the black flag whipped through the air—like a violent wind it stormed into our space shattering any sense of shelter or peace. No longer confined by her painting canvas, Susie doused and drenched, smeared and splattered, the walls of the large room with her grief. The forcefulness of it broke into our hearts and minds instantly. What a reminder of the way death sweeps into our lives, shaking us to the core of our very being! Others experienced grief too—in their own unique ways. It was quite touching and beautiful in its own peculiar way.

Susie relates her experience of that day in her own words:

> When it came time for the actual dance, it was a very healing experience. To explain the dance and what role each would play was an opportunity to tell my story. And, of course, just telling your story brings healing.
>
> After the dance, we debriefed, which is always enlightening. Some could hear the anger of my grief come through the flag "painting" the room black. Others physically experienced how stuck I felt. Others sensed the grief like a train running over me. Again, each one had a story to tell of the experience, which also brings healing, love and grace.
>
> Jody invited the others to dance and pray over my daughter and me before ending our time together. I laid down as I felt as though it was my turn to rest in God's care. As women danced over me, blanketing me with worship cloths, it was as if I was covered in God's care—in a way that became a reality: and that brings healing. Our daughter was embraced by her friends in the midst of her grief, and that is healing. I think we do not always know how to care for people we love who are hurting, and this gave opportunity for care and love to be given and received.
>
> Two years after the dance took place I was finally feeling what one dancer prayed over me that day—to be carried by God. To have God and praying sisters be a part of the whole process was a great gift of healing.

For me personally, the memory of Susie's daughter Leta encircled by her friends will be forever etched in my mind as a portrait of sisterly solidarity and God's loving embrace.

Just as a small group of moving women were invited into Susie's embodied prayer of grief, Jesus himself invites us to dance as we allow him into the sorrowful places of our lives. Nouwen writes:

> But it is precisely here, in that pain or poverty or awkwardness, that the Dancer invites us to rise up and take the first steps. For in our suffering, not apart from it, Jesus enters our sadness, takes us by the hand, pulls us gently up to stand, and invites us to dance. We find the way to pray, as the psalmist did, 'You have turned my mourning into dancing' (Ps 30:11), because at the center of our grief we find the grace of God.[12]

Lord, help us take your hand. Help us allow you into our sorrow, our sadness, our grief, our dance.

The following Christmas, Susie and her daughters led their entire family in a simple circle dance at her brother's home. I can picture them: shoulder to shoulder, facing inward—God's children encircling his throne in worship. At last, mourning into dancing. Or rather, perhaps it is…

Mourning through our dancing and dancing through our mourning.

Listen to: "I Am Healed" by River Valley Worship

Digging Deeper Into…

II Samuel 13: And She Lived Her Life a Desolate Woman	Page 112
Psalm 69: Tell It Like It Is	Page 116
Psalm 102: An Offering Poured Out	Page 120
Mark 5: Counting the Cost	Page 124
Lamentations: Creating Your Lament	Page 127

Benediction of Now & Not Yet — Page 131
 Holy Saturday by Heather Escontrías

Next Steps: Resources for Your Healing Journey & Endnotes — Page 132

Coloring Page "Gladness" by Donna Godwin — Page 133

Digging Deeper: And She Lived Her Life a Desolate Woman

Read: II Samuel 13

Like a large pill, this passage is difficult to swallow. If I'm honest, it rips at my heart. But I promised in our last chapter to return to this passage, so let's see what God might be teaching us through his Word.

Allow me to set the stage for this terrible tragedy. Amnon and Tamar were half-siblings. Amnon was the firstborn son of King David by his wife Ahinoam. Tamar was the daughter of King David by his wife Maacah, a princess from the neighboring kingdom Geshur. Therefore, Tamar was not only a princess through her father but also her mother, who would have been one of the highest ranking women among David's wives. Tamar was royal, through-and-through! Moreover, she was both very beautiful and a virgin. As the custom of the day dictated, she was likely promised in marriage to a prince in a neighboring country. As far as women go in that ancient era, she was at the top—the only thing that would've gained her more rank was to be the mother of a son. The future looked bright. Tamar was beautiful, pure, and desired, elevated in a society that did not hold women in very high regard.

And then selfish, evil Amnon destroys her! Filled with lust, he takes what he wants, and then literally throws her out of his room with utter disdain! Notice her actions—she rips her clothing covering herself with ashes—indicating she is grieving a death. Verse 19 says, "And she laid her hand on her head and went away, crying aloud [*zaaq* – a distress signal or cry for help] as she went." The hand to her head indicates that she bears an unbearable burden. And the Hebrew indicates she is sending out a distress signal in her grief. This is not a quiet cry! News of Amnon's actions and Tamar's ruin would've traveled very quickly through the palace.

And then, her father David fails her even more! Amnon should've been punished, but his father lets him get away with what is essentially murder in that culture. David could've forced Amnon to marry Tamar, which may have gone against God's law, but was not out of the question in that culture. By requiring Amnon to marry her, it would've at least secured her place in the king's harem, even if Amnon never had intimate relations with her again. But David fails to act on her behalf.

Should've. Could've. Would've.

So her brother Absalom tries his best to make things right. In vengeance, he takes the life of Amnon and attempts to dethrone David. But as I said, he *tries*—tries, but fails. Eventually this "trying" will cost him his life.

Amidst all the violence, deception, injustice, and death is Tamar. Scripture tells us she lived out her life a desolate woman in the house of her brother Absalom. Once elevated to the highest place in society, she had fallen almost as low as possible for a woman in her culture. Only leprosy would've made her situation worse.

I've often pondered those words—"and she lived her life a desolate woman"—wondering what that meant for her. For us…

The word for "desolate" here is the Hebrew word *samem*. It means stunned, and denotes something so horrible that it leaves a person speechless. Dear Tamar is at a great loss for words, and as we read this horrible passage, so are we.

My heart breaks for her. I long to know what really happened to our beautiful Tamar. I have often looked at the words of her brother Absalom, "Be quiet now, my sister. Don't take this thing to heart," and begin to wonder if this speaks to the real cause of her desolation.

>Her injustice is never recognized.
>
>>Her pain is never given a voice.
>>
>>>No expression: only repression.

Pay close attention to the words and events in verses 14, 16, 19, and 20 below:

Amnon refused to listen to her pleas.
He refused to listen to her even after he violated her.
Her distress signal, her cry for help, went unanswered by her father, King David.
Her burden so heavy, her violation so deep, it left her desolate, stunned, speechless.
Without a voice.

And her brother Absalom, who actually loved and cared for her, tells her to be quiet. The one time when she needed to spill her rage and pain upon the floor, she is told to hold it in. Like poison, it needed expelled. Instead, it killed her. I realize he was trying to say the right thing, but it fell so extremely short of what she needed at that moment.

I can almost hear Tamar's silent cries, echoing in all that *isn't* said in this passage:

"You want me to be quiet?!?!
All that I am and have ever lived for has been stolen from me!
By my own brother! He violated me in the worst possible way!
I will never have a husband who cares for me.
I will never have children to love and be loved by in return.
And don't take this thing to heart?!?!
My heart has been ripped from my very chest with no one to bind my wounds!
There is no hope for me! Ever!
I was a princess!
Now I am nothing!
I am as dead to the world!"

While the men around Tamar paid her voice no heed, her words still echo through this passage that is so hard to swallow. When I question why this story is included in our scriptures, I realize it's because *God wants us to hear* Tamar's voice.

We hear you, Tamar! We hear the depth of your pain calling out from the pages of this ancient story, crying out for justice against the violation you have endured. Keep screaming! Keep weeping aloud! We hear your distressed voice crying out for help, for justice, for the wrong to be made right. We know there is no way *not* to take this to heart—it grows ugly, twisted roots into the very soil of your soul! Even though you are stunned into silence, we hear all the words you cannot say. All the words frozen in your throat, frozen in your heart, frozen in your soul.

I think God not only wants us to hear her voice, but also to learn from Tamar's lack of voice. When you have no voice, it claws at your God-given longings–your need for significance, belonging, and the need to feel heard, safe, and loved. Ultimately only God can fulfill these God-given longings. All the more reason our lament needs poured out before a God who understands us—what we need, our core longings, our true identity, and how the enemy has tried to keep us from walking in our dreams and destinies. He has also placed people around us with gifts of compassion, grace, faith, and discernment to help us process these deep emotions. They are people who, like my friend Pauline Mae likes to say, are "Jesus in skin." People who give Jesus arms that can hold, ears that can hear, faces that can respond with expressions of comfort. This isn't a journey to be traveled alone.

Myra Chave-Jones, author of *Coping with Depression*, describes depression as "frozen rage." David Seamands, author of *Healing for Damaged Emotions*, agrees: "If you have a consistently serious problem with depression, you have not resolved some area of anger in your life. As surely as the night follows day, depression follows unresolved, repressed, or improperly expressed anger."[13] In addition to anger, I would also add grief, pain, fear, and disappointment. Whether or not you suffer from depression, you must be given a voice to express the unresolved or repressed emotions frozen in your own heart.

Remember:
The heart cannot let go of what it has not grieved.

I believe this with all my heart. You must give yourself permission to grieve. Send up your own distress signal to God, expressing the depths of your anger, grief, and pain. If you suffer from depression, don't allow others to quiet you or try to minimize your pain. Find your voice. A caring counselor, a peer group, a caregiver, or a spiritual mentor are just a few of the people who will help you find a voice for pain, anger, disappointment, and for the injustice against you.

I am inspired by these verses from Isaiah 58:

Shout it aloud, do not hold back.
Raise your voice like a trumpet!
…Then your light will break forth like the dawn, and your healing will quickly appear;
then your righteousness will go before you, and the glory of the Lord will be your rear guard.
Then you will call, and the Lord will answer;
you will cry for help, and he will say:
"Here am I."
The Lord will guide you always;
he will satisfy your needs in a sun-scorched land
and will strengthen your frame.
You will be like a well-watered garden,
like a spring whose waters never fail.
Your people will rebuild the ancient ruins and will raise up the age-old foundations;
you will be called Repairer of Broken Walls, Restorer of Streets with Dwellings.
(Isa 58:1a, 8-9a, 11-12)

Take a deep breath. Exhale and let go of all that is building up within you, and read that passage again, this time picturing Jesus declaring it over you.

In this chapter, as you begin to give your heart voice for your pain, anger, fear, disappointment, and grief, may the blessing found in the scripture fall on you and fill the places in your soul left void and empty. May this blessing begin to thaw the frozen rage within so you can walk in freedom, restoration, and healing. Begin to use your creative process as a way to lament. Let your artwork, music, and creativity help you begin to thaw out all that's been frozen in your soul, to shout out the injustices against you, to speak out your pain and grief before a God who loves you and stands ready to comfort you.

Using the quote in italics, the scripture passages, and instructions as your prompts as you begin to explore your lament through creativity, won't you join me in this prayer?

Invite the Holy Spirit into this moment.
Ask the Lord Who Sees (El Roi) to look upon his child as you cry out to him.
Ask the Lord Your Peace (Yahweh Shalom) to purify your imagination and help you picture, sense or create a place of protection and provision around you.
Ask the God of Vengeance (Jehovah Gmolah) to join you in that place and set right all the wrong that has been done to you.

Great I Am, your word says that when I cry to you, you reply, "Here I am." I take you at your word and cry out to you, knowing you are right here with me. I recognize that you satisfy all my needs. So, Lord, in this moment I acknowledge my need to be heard and trust that you acknowledge it, as well. In a sun-scorched land, I believe you and you alone will strengthen me. Like a well-watered garden, may the Holy Spirit's living water fill me and never fail me. Lord, you alone can help me rebuild, repair, raise up, and restore all that has been stolen from me. May I find a voice in him whose voice created the heavens and the earth. As I find that voice, may my spirit be set free! May my voice rise to worship you.

In the Name of the Great I Am, Ehyeh, Amen.

Watch on YouTube: Ad Deum Dance "I Am Silenced" & "Innocence Not Lost" 2.12.2016
And listen to: "Great I Am" by New Life Worship

Digging Deeper: Tell It Like It Is

Read: Psalm 69

    Perhaps by this point you are sensing your need for lament but are still uncertain how to go about it or what exactly it might look like for you? By posing an example, Psalm 69 will help us dig more deeply into Biblical lament. If you've already read it, you might be thinking, "Wow! That's a doozy! That psalmist really tells it like it is," and you are completely right! The examples set by this psalm and many like it, give us permission as God's children to tell it to him like it is, without editing or holding back.

    Psalm 69 is an "imprecatory psalm" which means it contains cursing of an enemy. Now take note this isn't "cussing" as we think of it today (although it can include that). It is the formulation of a curse upon another with intent for God to take vengeance. It might be helpful to think of it as the opposite of blessing. Just as you can bless someone, you can curse someone. It might also be helpful to think of cursing as a dangerous weapon only God can withstand. We can't go shooting these curses off to just anyone. They need to be aimed at God so as not to cause harm to others. Cursing someone to his or her face or to anyone who is within earshot will cause harm to others. Remember: aim this at God.

    Lament isn't about blessing those that curse you. That will, in fact, come later (in chapter 6). But this isn't blessing; this is lament, and lament is about laying it all out there—unfiltered and real—before God. We have complete freedom to say whatever we desire. However, and this is critical: God alone decides judgment and wrath. God alone wages vengeance. As with Absalom in our last study, we see what happens when we take matters into our own hands. Vengeance is God's and God's alone! Lament is complete freedom to shoot your weapon as long as it is aimed at the proper target—God!

    Now notice verse 5. Even as the writer is about to dish out curses upon his enemy, he knows he isn't perfect either. He admits his own guilt before the Lord, asks for mercy, pleads his case, and cries out for help. The writer here recognizes his desperate need of the Lord. Verses 13-18 contain his urgent pleas:

    Answer me!   Rescue me!   Deliver me!
         Come near!   Redeem me!

    Then verses 22-28 are his call for wrath upon his enemies. This is his curse against them—mean and unfiltered. We've been taught this is not Christian, but left unspoken, they become like poison in our soul, and like real poison, you must eliminate it from your body. You can't talk yourself into feeling better and then simply get better. You need to get this out of your system, or it will kill you. If Jesus is the Great Physician, then only he has the antidote for the poison in your spirit. You must expel this from your heart, mind, and soul so he can bring you healing. Jesus alone is the remedy!

Notice the turning in verse 29. These moments of turning in lament are often started with "but" or "yet" or "though." They are the point where the writer has dispelled all their inner toxins, and choose in that moment to proclaim, "But you, oh Lord, are sovereign." Then their hearts turn to worship the God who will handle all they've coughed up. From poison, to promise, to proclamation, to praise: that is doxology.

Bible scholar Craig Broyles explains, "A lament psalm (also called a psalm of complaint or petition or prayer) is a set poetic prayer aimed to present a need to God so that he may resolve it and further his praise."[14] After a lament is poured out, Broyles advises, "There comes a time to seek a way out. …[and] the concluding vows of praise [i.e., doxology] testify that obtaining something from God is not to be viewed as an end in itself. Another aim of lament psalms is to have something to praise God about. Praise should have the last word."[15] The psalms are indeed songs of praise and worship, even these ones of lament and cursing. Bible scholar Samuel Terrien calls them the "Sacrament of Musical Prayer."[16] While churches may not be singing laments today, they were certainly part of the hymnody of Ancient Israel.

Broyles goes on to make several other important points. First, these psalms are not merely a personal lament meant for the psalmist alone:

> [T]hey paint in familiar strokes scenes that evoke the general psychological and spiritual predicaments that worshipers may face. …We should not view a lament psalm as a composition that a psalmist wrote in direct response to his own personal need. Rather, lament psalms are models of prayer composed for the generic needs of God's people. In that respect, [it] is not a mirror reflecting the composer's experience; rather, it provides worshipers a framework to interpret their own experiences and to guide their expression of prayer. …[They are] to lead the worshiper's experience. A lament psalm should be read not autobiographically but rather liturgically.[17]

Secondly, while this part of our ancient Hebrew liturgy has been largely lost in modern churches today, Broyles states:

> Questions and claims of betrayal were not relegated to private counseling sessions with an elder or priest but rather remained a part of authorized prayer services. …Regrettably, lament has been all but censored from most Christian worship services. By always stressing the positive, such worship alienates those suffering pain and depression. And shying away from lament produces unnecessary guilt, and ultimately, a superficial faith.[18]

What's a worshiper to do? These passages of scripture were meant to help God's people process life's tragedy and disappointment, both individually and corporately. However, we are no longer singing and praying these psalms of lament in our Sunday services. It's no wonder we've become so bent, so broken, so bottled up.

Broyles also makes this important point about the Book of Psalms in general, and this is an important point for those psalms we still read on Sunday mornings and those we don't:

> The psalms cannot be regarded as the 'word of God' in the same way as the prophetic word, whereby God speaks *to* his people. But in them, Israel hammered out the most appropriate and effective ways of speaking to God. And they have been regarded by generations of God's people as speech that is appropriate to God and thus a fair reflection of who he is. In this respect, they are the 'word of God' *for* God's people, as they are models of praying to him.[19]

The prayers found in Psalms are to be the models by which we pray. In fact sometimes, when we have no words left of our own to pray, they are to be *the very prayers we pray*.

This "Sacrament of Musical Prayer" is found not only in Psalms, but also in Job, Lamentations, Habbakuk, and many other places throughout scripture. Should you ever question whether the words of lament are permissible, allow these passages to stand as your model of prayer. Open up and let your songs of lament pour forth! Pour forth praise, adoration, and worship, as well as pain, trouble, and cursing.

There is a poignant scene in the 2010 version of Karate Kid with Jackie Chan (Mr. Han) and Jaden Smith (Dre Parker). It is quite possibly the most powerful scene of the movie.[20] The young boy Dre Parker enters his trainer Mr. Han's garage to find the car Han so painstakingly restored now smashed to pieces. Shocked by the destruction, Dre asks:

What are you doing?

Dre discovers that Han relives his guilt over causing the crash that killed his wife and son by rebuilding and then smashing the car, *every year—year after year*. Dre gets into the car and sits there with Han allowing him to mourn. He makes no judgment. He is there, simply there, as Han weeps.

After awhile Dre purposefully gets out, and as Han pours out his grief at the steering wheel, the karate master's training poles, now held by Dre, make their way into the car. With these training tools Dre takes Han by the hands and, in this beautifully and symbolically shot scene of the movie, we see the beginning of a turning point in his lament. In the radiant light of a single intact car light, Dre begins to help Han move through his grief. At one point, he even uses the poles to help Han wipe his tears. Slowly they begin to work through the movements they have done a thousand times in their training. As they embody these movements like a prayer, Han regains his strength and desire to move into healing and wholeness—dancing from the shadows into light.

How often do we sit in the same mess? The same mess we've created over and over in order to assuage our guilt and pain? How often do we relive the sorrowful past? Perhaps if we listened, we'd hear the gentle whisper in our spirit asking:

What are you doing?

And maybe, just maybe, if we are still enough, we sense Jesus beside us as we pour out the tears upon the steering wheels of lives lived in and out of control. Without judgment—he is there, simply there. And perhaps with a little imagination we can picture him taking the master's training tools, pulling us into the light, and using those tools to help us begin to move through our own dance of grief. He will wipe our tears, and together we will move into the beautiful calling of all we were meant to be—from shadows into Light.

As we begin to move into creative process, we call this verse from Isaiah 45:3 to mind:

And I will give you treasures hidden in the darkness—secret riches.
I will do this so you may know that I am the Lord,
the God of Israel, the one who calls you by name. NLT

(continued next page)

Using the questions, the visualization, and scripture passages as your prompts as you begin to explore through creativity, won't you join me in this prayer?

Invite the Holy Spirit into this moment.
Ask the Lord Your Peace (Yahweh Shalom) to quiet your heart before him.
Ask the Lord Who Sanctifies (Yahweh M'Kaddesh) to purify your imagination and help you picture, sense or create a place of protection and provision around you.
Ask the Great I Am (Ehyeh) to join you in that place and reassure you that he is indeed right there with you.

Father, Son, and Holy Spirit, Triune God, the One Who is With Me and Sees Me, I am indeed weeping over my painful past and the broken places within. Please help me sense you gently taking my hands, wiping my tears, and inviting me, pulling me up into your dance of grief. Help me acknowledge my pain. Help me pour out my grief. Help me understand exactly what it is I'm doing and why. Help me mine the secret treasures of dark, hidden places you promised in Isaiah. Help me uncover those dark places within the Light of Your Love to reveal the beauty in the ashes, the oil of joy in the mourning, and a garment of praise for the spirit of heaviness. Like the psalmist I cry, Answer me! Rescue me! Deliver me! Come near! Redeem me!

In the Name of He Who Invites Me to Dance, Jesus, Amen.

Listen to: "Come As You Are" by David Crowder
"Remedy" by Jody Thomae

Digging Deeper: An Offering Poured Out

Read: Psalm 102

This Psalm comes with an opening descriptor in its title:

*A prayer of an afflicted person who has grown weak
and pours out a lament before the Lord.*

This is the only Psalm that comes with a description of this kind. Other Psalms may use the opening explanation to attribute a song to David or Korah or to provide instructions for music or liturgy—this contains none of that.[21] In fact in Hebrew texts, this is actually considered verse 1. So let's examine this descriptor first.

What is translated in English as "pours out" is the Hebrew word *sapak*. It means to spill forth, pour out like a drink offering, or to literally pour out the contents of a vessel. Drink offerings of wine were common in the Ancient Israel. You can find the first occurrence in Genesis 35:14 when Jacob sets up a stone at Bethel following his encounter with God. He pours out a drink offering and oil upon the rock, naming the place Bethel (house of God). In the New Testament, Paul uses this picture as a metaphor for his life being poured out like a sacrifice to the Lord (Phlp 2:17, II Tim 4:6). We often hear of Christ's blood (represented by wine) as being poured out as an offering in his sacrifice upon the cross.

We've already talked about this idea of pouring out, of ridding ourselves of the poison in our soul, of spilling our lament before the Lord. We can equally spill forth praise and worship upon the Lord. Take a moment to picture a large goblet of wine being spilled out as a sacrifice or offering before the Lord. Whether its poison or wine, whining or praise, this act of spilling forth the contents of the vessel of our hearts is a powerful one. It is a sacrifice and offering. Sometimes it's not easy, but every drop needs emptied.

The word for lament is *siyah*, and it refers to a babbling complaint or prayer. This is not a neat and tidy prayer—it pours out without construct or form. To babble is to talk nonsense, gibberish, or rubbish. Lament does not have to make sense to anyone, not even yourself. Like a babbling brook it moves, tossing and splashing along the riverbed to places unknown far down its coursing. The river never asks its source or destination, it simply babbles on. So should our lament before the Lord.

Bible scholar Rolf Jacobson indicates Psalm 102 is "a model prayer for help for any person in need."[22] So let's break this writer's drink offering, his babbling nonsense, down as a model of prayer as we continue our study on lament. Verses 1-2 are the writer's invocation, a cry for help:

*God, listen! Listen to my prayer, listen to the pain in my cries.
Don't turn your back on me just when I need you so desperately.
Pay attention! This is a cry for help! And hurry—this can't wait!* MSG

The writer is desperate to be heard. It is much like other cries of help in the Psalms (see 22:1; 27:9; 31:2; 39:12; 69:17; 71:2; 143:7 for other examples).[23]

In verses 3-11 he pours out his babbling complaint. He is telling God how he feels and what his life is like as a result of his pain. As we read, one gets the sense that the writer knows deep pain or perhaps is suffering from a crippling disease. Jacobson notes how the evening shadow reference in verse 11 paints an image of lengthening shadows that "run away with building speed."[24] Time is short. God must act soon.

In verse 12 we see the psalmist's turning point: "But you, O Lord…" as he begins to reiterate God's promises of compassion, rebuilding, restoration, and responding from scripture. Scholar John Goldingay alludes to the imagery of a seated God rising from his throne to help in verse 12-13:

> [This] does not mean Yahweh is sitting doing nothing; that would be expressed in other ways (e.g., by asking why Yahweh is sleeping). Yahweh's sitting (enthroned) is good news. But when a king decides something needs to happen and/or determines to take action, he stands to make his declaration and/or take the action. It is in this sense that Yahweh must arise from the throne, not stay seated. The king does that when hearing of oppression in the city and rising to fulfill his vocation to show compassion to the weak there. The heavenly King must do that in light of the needs of the city of Zion as a whole.[25]

In verse 14 the psalmist calls God to look upon the stones of the crumbling city walls and the very dust of Mount Zion. Much like the Israelites rebuilding the walls of the city in Nehemiah while enduring the mocking of their enemies (Neh 4:1-9), the psalmist "look[s] upon these fallen stones and this dirt with love, …challenging Yahweh to do the same."[26] The Israelites were taunted with these words in Nehemiah 4:2: "Will they offer sacrifices? Will they finish in a day? Can they bring the stones back to life from those heaps of rubble—burned as they are?" Perhaps they can't on their own, but with God's mighty outstretched hand, their work is sure to prosper! The enemy sees it as impossible, but with God all things are possible!

In verses 18-22 note how the psalmist begins to speak proclamation—speaking into the future even though the present is bleak. These verses stand as an example that we *all* need to develop prayers of proclamation that speak the promises of God into existence over our lives—even (and especially) as our current situations look bleak. Prayers of proclamation speak *as it should be*, not as it currently is. They mock the enemy right back as we declare God will always have the last say. Verses 23-24 indicate another turning point, in essence saying, "It all boils down to this God…" and then and only then, can he enter into doxology in verses 25-28. With his lament poured out upon the feet of his enthroned Yahweh, the writer submits to the will and ways of the Creator of the universe. He who laid the very foundations of the earth can surely rebuild the ancient remains.

Ask yourself:

What lies in ruin in my life?

Imagine the tragedy, trauma, pain, and disappointment as the broken stones, rubble, and dust that lies in ruin in your life. Beloved, it is time to pour out your drink offering upon the rock piles of bitter disillusionment in your life.

Leanne Payne gets to the heart of the matter here, as she encourages us to pour our drink offering before the Cross of Jesus Christ, our own Rock of Salvation:

> As we learn more about the process of healing within the soul, we often find that the power to feel the pain is itself a vital part of the healing. The sufferer has repressed this heretofore and denied it precisely because it is so painful. But now he has to get it up and out. He needs to understand that, if he will stand in the Cross and hurt, there is a place for it to go. An end to the pain. This seemingly endless pain is the way he gets in touch with and names the heretofore repressed grief, fear, anger, and shame underlying his depression. In order to come out of certain types of depression, one must feel the most appalling pain and grief. It often seems that death would be easier. But repressed grief and sorrow and loss remain to afflict us in other ways until we grieve them out. It is a wonderful thing to stand in Christ, identify with his suffering for us, and grieve out our griefs and yield up our angers.[27]

The Incarnational message of Psalm 102 is this: the very God who created the universe empties himself to step into our need. Christ pours out his life like a drink offering so that we may know he enters our pain. He who sculpted the world can surely rebuild the broken-down walls of our lives. The Eternal God rises from his throne and moves in our time-limiting realm, our present moment, to save us: "It is a moment in which the infinite God is asked to enter into the finite world, the everlasting Lord to enter the mortal realm—in order to deliver," says Jacobson.[28]

Scripture reassures us that Christ himself, the one who entered our world, our lives, our pain, and our suffering, died and rose again in power and is seated at the right hand of God the Father. Moreover, Hebrews 7:25 proclaims that Jesus "is able to save completely those who come to God through him, because he always lives to intercede for them." He who is seated at the right hand of the Father lives to intercede for us—for you! Right this very moment Jesus turns to the Father in Heaven and pleads on your behalf. He is praying for you right this very moment! Stop and think about that. Picture Jesus turning to God to pray for you. That should move you to either amazement or tears or both! He is *always interceding for you*. That is astonishing and humbling all at once. Isaiah 53:12 says:

> *He poured out his life unto death, and was numbered with the transgressors.*
> *For he bore the sin of many, and made intercession for the transgressors.*

As he poured out his life as a drink offering for us, he became as one of us (a transgressor), bearing our sin and, even as he was dying, he was interceding on our behalf.

Take a moment to read Acts 7:54-60, noting verse 56 in particular. Here we find Stephen, moments before he would be drug outside the city to be pummeled with rocks until he died from the stoning, looking up into heavenly realms. In that moment of injustice and terror, Jesus has risen to his feet and is *standing* at the right hand of God. Much like our God and King in Psalm 102:13, Christ arises from the throne, determined to take action, standing to make his declaration. Hearing of oppression on the earth, he rises to fulfill his vocation to show compassion to the weak.

If Jesus stood for Stephen, he will certainly stand for you.

Perhaps it's time to ask Jesus to rise to his feet on your behalf.

Today as you enter into your creative process, it might be time to begin writing out your own lament (if you have not already begun to do this). As you quiet yourself before the Lord, ask him if there is an event or a series of events he would like you to begin writing a lament for. Ask him to be specific and guide you to the wound he would most like to address at this moment in your life. Sometimes God will guide you to something that is currently happening, but more often he will lead us back to ungrieved losses from our past. Ask the Holy Spirit to show you *specifically* where to start. As an artist or creative, it is important to both write out your lament, as well as "work it out" through your process of creativity. At some point in your lament process, perhaps it would be meaningful to you to embody the act of pouring out your offering of pain by filling a vessel and pouring it out as an act of remembrance and prayer.

Using the questions, lament instructions, the prayer of proclamation, and scripture passages as your prompts as you begin to explore through creativity, won't you join me in this prayer?

Invite the Holy Spirit into this moment.
Ask the Lord Who Sees (El Roi) to look upon his child as you cry out to him.
Ask the Lord Who Sanctifies (Yahweh M'Kaddesh) to purify your imagination and help you picture, sense or create a place of protection and provision around you.
Ask the Lord Your Healer (Yahweh Rophe) to join you in that place and help you begin to create your lament.

Lord Jesus, like the psalmist, I cry out to you in my deepest places of pain and sorrow. Hear my prayer. Turn your ear to me. Do not hide your face from me. I am in distress. When I call, answer me quickly. I pour out my lament like a drink offering to you. I pour it out upon the rubble of my life. These wrongs done to me are severe. It surely seems like they can never be repaired or restored,
But you, O Jesus, My Lord, sit enthroned
at the right hand of the Father
where you live to intercede for me.
Your fame and renown endure in every generation!
You will arise on my behalf
and take compassion on the ruins of my life!
It is time for you to stand up and show compassion on me,
for my appointed time has come!
In the Name of He Who Rises to Stand in My Defense, Jesus, Amen.

Listen to: "Oh How I Need You" by All Sons & Daughters
"Your Blood" by Matt Redman

Digging Deeper: Counting the Cost

Read: Mark 5:21-43

In this gospel story, we find two healing stories in one. The plea of Jairus and the raising of his daughter are interrupted by the healing of another woman. There are several things to consider as we work through this double healing. Let's dig in.

To begin let's consider how scripture binds these two healings together through words, phrases, and themes. First, the number twelve. At twelve Jairus' daughter would have been close to the age of menarche, as well as betrothal and marriage in that culture. The woman with the issue of blood has suffered for twelve years—the entire lifetime of the dying girl. Twelve symbolizes completeness, and in this double healing, Christ brings both the girl and woman into completeness. Second, the two are connected by the word "daughter." The woman with the issue of blood is called "daughter" by Christ upon her healing, connecting her in a literary fashion to the daughter of Jairus. Third, note the phrases that highlight their faith: the woman with the issue of blood is told by Christ that her faith has made her well, and Jairus is told not to fear but to believe. This parallel ties the faith of the hemorrhaging woman with the faith of Jairus. Lastly, a theme of restoration ties the two stories: the unclean woman is restored to the community after years of separation, and the young girl is restored to life.

Now, let's consider several other aspects of this double healing. The story starts with Jairus. Take a moment to reflect on his potential loss if his daughter dies. Luke's Gospel account tells us this was his *only* daughter. I'm sure she held a special place in his heart. Moreover, close to the age of marriage, she is an asset to her father as this means gifts and the addition of a son-in-law to the family. As you read the passage, you can hear the desperation in his voice. Then imagine his torture as he watches Jesus, on the way to go heal his daughter, stop for the hemorrhaging woman.

Now, let's turn our thoughts to the hemorrhaging woman and the loss she has experienced as a result of her disease. Twelve years is a long time to be sick. She spent *all she had* searching for a cure. According to Old Testament law, as long as the woman had a flow of blood, she was considered unclean and expected to avoid others so as not to render them unclean as well (Lev 15:25-31). Purity rules would have specifically excluded the hemorrhaging woman from contact with her community of faith, because not only are the unclean forbidden from the courtyard of the sanctuary (Lev 12:4; II Chr 23:19; 26:21), but the unclean are banished outside the camp to prevent its defilement (Num 5:1-3).[29] These laws would have affected her relationship with her God, family, friends, and nation. According to Bible scholar Joel Green, she would have "lived in a perpetual state of impurity…in isolation from her community these twelve years."[30] Perhaps she would have been considered 'dead' to her community given the length of her separation from her people and the God whom she worshiped.

Consider the risk she takes to find healing. As she enters the pressing crowd she comes in contact with those who call her unclean. Further, touching Christ "is a premeditated act that will pass her uncleanness on to him."[31] Yet she reaches out and touches just the hem or fringe of his garment thinking no one will see or notice. And of course, Jesus notices! As the story unfolds, she realizes she cannot hide and must reveal herself. She comes trembling, falling down before him. She has broken religious law, 'infecting' and 'stealing power from' this influential teacher, and now she is in dire need of his mercy and forgiveness. Remarkably, instead of rebuking her, Jesus affirms her, calling her "daughter." Through her desperate situation and the action to which her faith called her, she is reinstated into the community that marginalized her. Her faith has healed her physically, emotionally, *and* spiritually. Green indicates that by healing her and calling her "daughter," Jesus is "extending kinship to her and restoring her to the larger community—not on the basis of her ancestry, but as a consequence of her active faith."[32]

Now once again, we turn our focus back to Jairus. As one woman finds healing and restoration, his own worst fears are realized as his servant comes to report his daughter's death. His anxious desperation turns to agonizing grief, but Christ looks Jairus in the eyes and says:

Don't be afraid; just believe.

Dare he hope? Common sense says no, but Jesus says yes. Just as the hemorrhaging woman takes great risk to touch her healer, Jairus takes great risk and trusts in Jesus. He faces embarrassment as the people laugh and ridicule Jesus. But he chooses to trust on behalf of his daughter. By her father's act of faith, the young woman, like the older woman, is reinstated from death into life.

The woman is *figuratively* restored to life: the girl is *literally* restored to life.

And we too are restored to life. Despite our "unclean" nature, he graciously accepts our hesitant yet desperate touch, assures us of our faith, and extends a blessing of peace calling us "daughter" or "son." When all seems lost, he looks us squarely in the face and tells us not to fear, but "just believe." In our spiritual death, he takes us by the hand and brings us back from death into life. He restores us to our own community of faith in right relationship with God.

This Bible study is about counting the cost. The sick woman experienced great loss in the midst of her disease. Jairus and his daughter faced great potential loss as she neared death. With great faith they brought their losses to Jesus, and he brings restoration to all that has been lost and risked in the process. With every wound, with every disease, with every injustice, there is a cost. We must realize everything our wounds have cost us, how they have altered our lives, and the losses we have accumulated as a result. As author Marcia Shoop explains: "Tragedy means that what could have been will never be, what will be is forever shaped by what is lost."[33]

Some might also need to consider what the *process* of healing might cost. The process is not easy and will require you to revisit areas of your life you might rather leave behind. I've already said this, but it bears repeating: soul work is hard work. You will also have to leave behind your identity as a victim as God calls you into your true identity as a beloved child of God with a testimony of healing, restoration, and redemption. Also, people around you might not like it when you begin to walk in your true identity. They can no longer take advantage of you or manipulate you as a victim, and your new identity and freedom might send them into a tailspin as they are faced with their *own* need for a healing journey.

As you consider your loss, listen to the anguish found here in Psalm 42:3-5:

My tears have been my food day and night,
while people say to me all day long, "Where is your God?"
These things I remember as I pour out my soul: how I used to go to the house of God
under the protection of the Mighty One with shouts of joy and praise among the festive throng.
Why, my soul, are you downcast? Why so disturbed within me?
Put your hope in God, for I will yet praise him, my Savior and my God.

This worshiper was once a part of the celebratory procession to the temple in Jerusalem to honor God, the Mighty One. Now his heart is downcast. His tears have become his food. We can hear him counting the cost of his deep sorrow. Perhaps this very psalm crossed the mind of Christ the final week of his life, especially as they mocked him as he hung on the cross? As we consider our own wounds, we must remember that Christ joins us in our suffering.

What have your wounds cost you? What have you lost? What might you risk in the process of finding healing? What lies do you believe about yourself as a result of your wound? Sometimes there is a loss within a loss—sometimes in the midst of one loss, we lose our faith, our identity, our vision. *What is the cost of your wound as you let dysfunction and false beliefs disrupt all God has intended for you? Is it costing you your marriage? Your family? Your friends? Your job? Your passion? Your life?* As you lament, consider the cost.

Using the questions and scripture passages as your prompts as you begin to explore through creativity, won't you join me in this prayer?

Invite the Holy Spirit into this moment.
Ask the Lord Who Sees (El Roi) to look upon his child as you cry out to him.
Ask the Lord Who Sanctifies (Yahweh M'Kaddesh) to purify your imagination and help you picture, sense or create a place of protection and provision around you.
Ask the Lord Your Healer (Yahweh Rophe) to join you in that place and help you to count the cost of the wound. As you begin, create something to represent the cost. Creatively explore and symbolize the lies you believe as a result of your wound.

Lord Jesus, as I open my wound to you, treat it with the most tender of care. Where there is deep infection please pull the contaminated pieces out so you can bring total and complete healing to my innermost being. This wound has cost me deeply, but I recognize that your wounds cost you deeply too. So in your wounds, see my wounds, Lord, and in my wounds, help me see yours. Help me to know it was for my sake that you bore our wounds together on the cross. You alone recognize the depth of my pain and loss, and you alone know all I risk in revealing it to you and others in the process of my healing. Place your healing salve, the balm of Gilead, gently on my wound and bind it up with your compassion and loving kindness. I accept your salvation, redemption, and restoration.

In Your Healing Name, Jesus of Nazareth, I pray, Amen.

Listen to: "Satisfied in You (Psalm 42)" by The Sing Team
"O Sacred Head Now Wounded" by Fernando Ortega

Digging Deeper: Creating Your Lament

Read passages from Lamentations here: (Note: character names in italics added for dramatic effect)

Daughter Jerusalem: Is any suffering like my suffering that was inflicted on me,
that the Lord brought on me in the day of his fierce anger? (1:12)
See, O Lord, how distressed I am!
I am in torment within, and in my heart I am disturbed. (1:20a)

Yahweh: What can I say for you?
With what can I compare you, Daughter Jerusalem?
To what can I liken you, that I may comfort you, Virgin Daughter Zion?
Your wound is as deep as the sea.
Who can heal you? (2:13)

The Weeping Prophet: The hearts of the people cry out to the Lord.
You walls of Daughter Zion, let your tears flow like a river day and night;
give yourself no relief, your eyes no rest.
Arise, cry out in the night, as the watches of the night begin;
pour out your heart like water in the presence of the Lord. (2:18-19a)

The Valiant Man: He has walled me in so I cannot escape;
he has weighed me down with chains.
Even when I call out or cry for help, he shuts out my prayer. (3:7-8)
I remember my affliction and my wandering, the bitterness and the gall.
I well remember them, and my soul is downcast within me.
Yet this I call to mind and therefore I have hope:
Because of the LORD's great love we are not consumed, for his compassions never fail.
They are new every morning; great is your faithfulness.
I say to myself, "The LORD is my portion; therefore I will wait for him."
The LORD is good to those whose hope is in him, to the one who seeks him;
it is good to wait quietly for the salvation of the LORD. (3:19-26)

It is believed the Book of Lamentations was written by the prophet Jeremiah, often referred to as the 'weeping prophet.' In my previous book, *God's Creative Gift*, I wrote two studies on Jeremiah in a chapter on symbolic action: he was the prophet who bought things that often made no sense; he obeyed even when it cost him resources and credibility; and he walked in God's promises when all appeared lost. He was also thrown into a dungeon and a cistern because people didn't like what he had to say. The thing that helped Jeremiah survive his ministry is the fact that he knew how to pour out his grief before the Lord. The Lord had promised to protect him and to rescue him (Jer 1:18-19), so he was obedient to God's voice and will, but he also wasn't afraid to be honest and open before the Lord.

In the verses above we have the makings of a script with several different characters: Daughter Jerusalem, Yahweh, the Weeping Prophet, and the Valiant Man. Daughter Jerusalem, in the midst of her downfall, cries out to Yahweh expressing her grief and confessing her disobedience. Yahweh answers, comparing her grief to the deep, endless sea. And even as he asks, "Who can heal you?" he already knows the answer. He alone can heal her, but his heart is broken, too. His grief mingles with her grief—a God who doesn't simply observe but steps in. The Weeping Prophet then instructs Daughter Jerusalem to cry out day and night, let her tears flow, arise and cry out, rest not, pour out her heart. He himself knows how to grieve, and he calls on Daughter Jerusalem to do the same.

Then enters the Valiant Man.[34] The Valiant Man has also experienced suffering, but he calls on the people to hope. According to Bible scholar Robin Parry: "His transition from despair to hope in 3:19-24 is presented as a model for the community as a whole: a call for them to remember Yahweh's covenant mercies."[35] Verse 21 is his turning point (note it starts with "yet" so it indicates doxology):

Yet this I call to mind and therefore I have hope…

There is no change in his circumstances, only a change in his attitude.[36] Then in verse 22 he begins his prayer of proclamation:

Because of the Lord's great love we are not consumed, for his compassions never fail.

He remembers, and it calls him to hope even in the midst of his suffering. He even turns to Yahweh at one point exclaiming,

Great is your faithfulness!

While the drama before us is still a tragedy, the Valiant Man calls on his fellow characters and the audience watching not to give up hope. This Lamentations drama teaches us how to grieve. It teaches us how to pour out our lament openly and honestly before the Lord; to engage God in a dialogue about our hurt, anger, and pain; to persevere in our lament even when all seems lost; and to put our hope in the character and nature of God.

In her book *Fairy Tale Faith*, author Brenda Waggoner tells the story of a client Serena who worked through the ravages of sexual trauma in her life using painting, poetry, and dance. Although Waggoner had never had a client dance in her office, there was Serena expressing herself through dance and "experiencing a form of healing as she physically released her soul's lament through body movements."[37] Imagine Serena dancing as Waggoner watched: "Serena's movements and facial expressions bypassed the need for words and explanations. They came from her deepest self, demonstrating her acceptance of truths she'd longed to really believe and know about God and his tender care for her."[38]

Sometimes we know things in our head, but we can't really feel it in our bones or express it through our lips. Art helps us transfer head knowledge into heart, soul, and flesh knowledge. Many times in my life, in places of wounding and pain, I have moved through my lament before the Lord. Through dance, movement and symbolic actions, I have released the physical and emotional pain within me. The enemy bit at me, inflicting me with wounds and his poison began to creep into my body, crippling me with fear, hate, and deep sadness. When I moved, this poison was squeezed out of the deep places and released, the anti-venom of God's love saturating and healing my wounded soul, me weeping as I released the deadly toxins. Dancing in the promise of Psalm 56:8, I know that he understands my every sorrow. God collected every tear I cried; he recorded every wound I experienced. He knew, but he needed me to release it to him so he could take care of it. My lament was trapped within my body, and God knew I wouldn't find complete release until I had embodied my prayer in movement. My embodied prayers of grief bypassed all the things I thought I knew, all the things I couldn't say, and I danced what I truly felt. And then God said,

"You are now free."

We think we have to come to God as our best selves, but all he really wants is our *whole* selves, our *real* selves, our *true* selves. How many times have you heard someone say they need to get their act together before they can go to church? I don't know about you, but I'm done putting on my Sunday best and pretending everything is okay when it isn't. Our churches should be safe places to lament. To pour out our hearts before the Great Physician. Why do we have to hide our tears in church when the Lord our Healer awaits to catch every tear we cry? Church is the one place where our tears should be seen as a beautiful offering, a sacrifice of praise.

You see, God wants *every part* of us. Not just the nice, shiny parts but the beat up, broken parts too. He wants the laughter *and* the tears; the righteousness *and* the sin; the whole places *and* the wounded places; the real and fake; the good and bad; the beautiful and ugly.

He's seen us at our best and at our worst,

and he loves us just the same.

Today you will continue to express your lament through your creative process. If you have not done so, it might be helpful to write out your lament, recalling what it has cost you, the lies you believe as a result, and how you felt when it happened. Don't be afraid to say what you really feel because God knows the truth anyway. Let God have it all. Don't worry—he has very broad shoulders. And he's really strong so he can pick you up when it's all over and set you back on your feet again.

And don't forget your doxology. Consider Lamentations 3:21 again:

> *But this I call to mind, and therefore I have hope:*
> *The steadfast love of the Lord never ceases;*
> *his mercies never come to an end;*
> *they are new every morning;*
> *great is your faithfulness. ESV*

> *Yet I still dare to hope when I remember this:*
> *The faithful love of the Lord never ends!*
> *His mercies never cease.*
> *Great is his faithfulness;*
> *his mercies begin afresh each morning. NLT*

Think back to the times and places where God met you in powerful ways, and call those things to mind. Let those memories bring you hope, as you declare:

Great is your faithfulness!

(continued next page)

Using the instructions and scripture passages as your prompts as you begin to explore through creativity, won't you join me in this prayer?

Invite the Holy Spirit into this moment.
Ask the Lord Who Sees (El Roi) to look upon his child as you cry out to him.
Ask the Lord Who Sanctifies (Yahweh M'Kaddesh) to purify your imagination and help you picture, sense or create a place of protection and provision around you.
Ask the Lord Your Healer (Yahweh Rophe) to join you in that place and help you create your lament. While staying in a prayerful state, create something that represents your lament. As you create, tell God how you felt when the wounding event happened and how you feel now. Use your creativity to tell God what lies you believe about yourself, others, and God as a result. Pour out your heart before the Lord.

Lord God, collector of my tears and sorrows, thank you for meeting me in my lament. Thank you for working through my creative process to bring healing, wholeness, and restoration to the wounded, broken, and scattered places within my soul. Thank you for not just listening, but for stepping into my pain with me. I understand that you grieve with me, that you also shed tears and feel my anguish with me. Thank you for being the God Who Sees and Hears and Knows. Now Lord, I ask you, with your righteous right hand, to set me on my feet again, hold me up, and protect me. I look to you now and say, "Great is your faithfulness! You are my portion, and I will wait quietly for you. I put my hope in you and you alone."

In the Name of He Who Brings Salvation, Amen.

Listen to: "I Will Have Hope" by Aaron Wardle
"Great is Thy Faithfulness" by your favorite artist
"Do It Again" by Elevation Worship

ᴥ A Benediction of Now & Not Yet ᴥ

Holy Saturday
by Heather Escontrías

Lodged between two kingdoms,
One is His, and one is not.
Held in tension are the shores
Between which I am caught.

Holy Saturday calls me to wait
In a silence so obscure,
Without the benefit of knowing--
Immobile, breathless, insecure.

This waiting room for those still longing
To yet be made alive,
An interim where pain still reigns
With Peace not yet arrived.

Between the picket fences
And the gleaming pearly gate,
I have no other earthly choice
But patiently to wait.

Now, and not yet--how can it be
That both are fully true?
Do oil and water ever mix
Or darkness change its hue?

In stillness I will wait with You
'Til Easter Sunday's dawn,
The day that You forever will
Make right all that is wrong.

Next Steps: Resources for Your Healing Journey

God on Mute: Engaging the Silence of Unanswered Prayer by Pete Greig

Turn My Mourning Into Dancing by Henri Nouwen

Praying the Psalms: Engaging Scripture and the Life of the Spirit by Walter Brueggemann

The Cure for Sorrow by Jan Richardson

Endnotes

1. Wardle, *Healing Care*, 174.
2. Brueggemann, *Praying the Psalms*, 66.
3. Ibid.
4. Ibid.
5. Ibid., 80-81.
6. Ibid., 68.
7. Accessed April 5, 2016 at https://livingwithwolves.org/sawtooth-pack/our-observations/. For documentary, see https://www.youtube.com/watch?v=-y9uHiJG2k0.
8. Greig, *God on Mute*, 82-83.
9. Nouwen, *Turn My Mourning*, xv-xvi.
10. Ibid., 6-7.
11. Ibid., 37.
12. Ibid., 13.
13. Seamands, *Healing*, 124.
14. Broyles, "The Psalms of Lament," 384.
15. Ibid., 397.
16. Terrien, *The Psalms*, 503.
17. Broyles, 385.
18. Ibid., 395.
19. Ibid., 394.
20. See the scene on You Tube by searching "The Karate Kid—2010."
21. Jacobson, *Book of Psalms*, 748.
22. Ibid.
23. Ibid., 751.
24. Ibid., 753.
25. Goldingay, *Psalms*, 155.
26. Ibid., 156.
27. Payne, 205-206.
28. Jacobson, 758.
29. Westerholm, "Clean and Unclean," 127.
30. Green, *Luke*, 346.
31. Ibid., 347.
32. Ibid., 349.
33. Shoop, *Let the Bones Dance*, 62.
34. Parry, *Lamentations*, 92. The 'Valiant Man' is the term used by Parry in his commentary on Lamentations. I am using it here in this drama, in conjunction with the commentary on the passage.
35. Ibid., 93.
36. Ibid., 100.
37. Waggoner, *Fairy Tale Faith*, 110.
38. Ibid., 111.

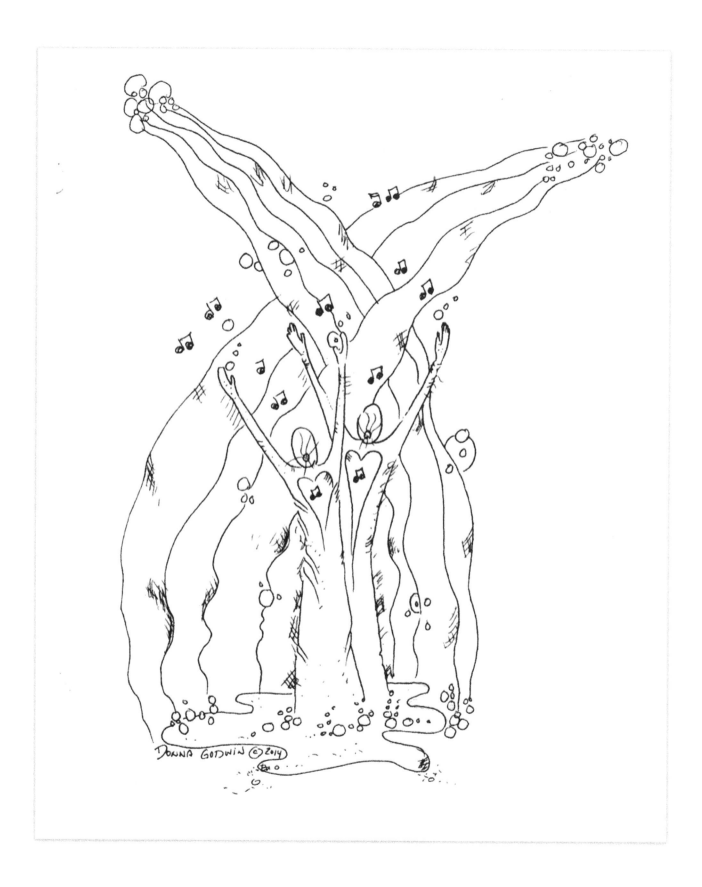

5

Encountering

"And by his wounds, we are healed…"

The healing journey is much like working a jigsaw puzzle. Hopefully you've assembled a puzzle or two in your lifetime so you can follow along on this analogy.

When my family and I work a puzzle, we start with the border—searching through the box collecting all the edge pieces, paying particular attention to find the four corner pieces. Once we've found as many as we can, we begin to assemble the outside border. This creates a framework within which we can begin to fit the rest of the pieces.

As we work the puzzle, some pieces begin to fit together easily. The picture is easy to see, and it comes together with very little effort. There are other times when we struggle to find the pieces that go together. The picture isn't clear, and even though we're examining the box lid, we still can't see where certain pieces fit. Sometimes we set pieces aside because they look similar, and eventually they do make sense, and we can assemble them quickly. I often hold a piece or two aside. When I look at these pieces I think, "These can't possibly fit this puzzle." Yet in the end, beyond my imagination, they do indeed complete the picture.

So it is with our healing journey…

Life is hard—with every painful experience, we become fragmented pieces of our whole self. Broken hearts, shattered dreams, and disintegrated destinies become the puzzle pieces we hold in a box, waiting for the Great Puzzle-Worker to help us put them all back together.

And he does.

I have fervently prayed that God our Healer would use the workbook you hold in your hands as a tool in your healing journey—helping you begin to put together the puzzle pieces of your life. The puzzle won't be complete by the time you finish—it just doesn't work that way. The healing process is a journey that takes our entire life, and we only find complete and utter healing when we stand before his throne in heaven.

But for now, just like my family and I, we start with the border, creating a framework within which to work. It frames the picture but it isn't the whole picture by any means. It is an outline, but not the complete puzzle. I pray God continues to help you sort through the pieces as you read.

You'll find that some pieces go together easily—a "miracle moment" I call them. When heaven reaches down to touch earth and everything just makes sense. Places where, despite the pain, you can see God working it all out for his glory and your good, and the pieces of our shattered hearts begin to form a picture you can recognize without looking at the puzzle box lid for reference.

You'll also find some pieces make no sense and take a long time to sort through and piece back together. You'll finish this book and look at that pile of pieces and wonder if they'll ever fit. Slowly, oh so slowly, they will. God will pick up each piece, one at a time, and help you examine it—to turn it in all directions, to see the places where a piece might fit and come together with other pieces that are already beginning to form a picture.

You will also find a piece or two that need set aside to the very end of your journey. One day, as you stand face-to-face with the God who wipes every tear, and he fulfills his promise, "No more crying here," those last couple of pieces will finally fit. Then you will understand, just as you have been fully understood.

This chapter is about a healing encounter with Christ, through the power and ministry of the Holy Spirit, to bring redemption, restoration, and reclamation to the broken places of our lives. God's word is clear about our healing journey—Christ alone is our Healer and Savior.

As we continue on this road to restoration, let the verses below call our hearts into his presence. These words are faithful and true, even if we don't yet feel them in our bones. When you struggle, return to this list and meditate on these truths. Perhaps you might want to dog-ear the top corner of this page to find it quickly? When you are feeling discouraged, afraid, or too tired to continue, spend time in his presence with these scriptures in mind. Go through each one, and as you inhale deeply, ask God to instill them as truth in the deepest recesses of your being:

- ❖ **God alone is healer:** *"I am the Lord, your healer." Ex 15:26*

- ❖ **He is our Great Physician:** *"He heals the brokenhearted and binds up their wounds." Ps 147:3*

- ❖ **Healing involves the person as a whole—physically, emotionally, spiritually, and psychologically:** *"Have mercy on me, Lord, for I am faint; heal me, Lord, for my bones are in agony. My soul is in deep anguish. How long, Lord, how long? Turn, Lord, and deliver me; save me because of your unfailing love." Ps 6:2-4*

- ❖ **God brings restoration, redemption and reclamation:** *"You intended to harm me, but God intended it for good to accomplish what is now being done, the saving of many lives." Gen 50:20*

- ❖ **Healing brings you righteousness and Him glory:** *"Your light will break forth like the dawn, and your healing will quickly appear; then your righteousness will go before you, and the glory of the LORD will be your rear guard." Isa 58:8*

- ❖ **It doesn't matter what you've done:** *"I have seen their ways, but I will heal them; I will guide them and restore comfort, creating praise on their lips." Isa 57:18-19*

- ❖ **You are not alone:** *"The Lord is close to the brokenhearted and saves those who are crushed in spirit." Ps 34:18*

With these beautiful reminders of truth, let us venture on.

An Unexpected Journey

Some might be asking how we ended up in need of this unexpected healing journey in the first place? Why do people hurt us, and why can't we just get over it? There have been many books written trying to address these difficult questions. I cannot pretend to answer those questions with any thoroughness here. Simply allow me this explanation. Because of the Fall (Gen 3), we are born into a world that is broken and riddled with physical and emotional disease and born into families that are both emotionally and genetically imperfect. Disease and illness threaten our health, and our bodies bear the scars of life in this fallen world, not because God meant for it to be this way, but because there is an enemy who hates us and will do *whatever it takes* to destroy us. Hear me say this again: *the enemy does not want you to walk in the destiny that God has for you!* The enemy's heart is set on destruction, desolation, and deceit, but God's heart is set on redemption, reconciliation, restoration, and renewal!

As we move through life, words and much worse inflict pain on our hearts, and the beautiful inner child becomes wounded and broken. As a result we end up with insecurities, idiosyncrasies, and illnesses that are as much a part of our lives as the destiny, dreams, and design God truly intended. We live unhealthy lives—lives affected by disorders, disease, imbalance, and illness. Our "trust mechanism" goes faulty as we refuse to trust anyone or anything, or quite the opposite, we trust everyone and everything, even what we shouldn't. Psychologically, we cover up emotional wounds with band-aid coping mechanisms—perfectionism, addictions, dysfunctional behaviors, and immature ways of dealing with those around us.

For some people, their emotional wounds are readily apparent because they result in actions and behaviors that alienate people and God. Best-case scenario they end up as grouchy, miserable people with very few genuine friends. Worst-case scenario, they are addicts, murderers, and the mentally insane. For many, the results are much less apparent, and in fact, it may even help them achieve success early on. They are the perfectionists, the do-gooders, the corporate ladder climbers, the people-pleasers. At some point though, unhealed wounds fester until they push to the surface and can no longer be ignored: the perfectionist drives away his family with his OCD tendencies; the do-gooder neglects her own family for the sake of others; the corporate ladder climber finds himself alone at the top with those he's hurt below; and the people-pleaser finds that she's pleased no one except those who take advantage of her for their own personal gain.

But for many of us, we simply awaken one day aware of a discontent deep within our hearts that just doesn't sit well with our spirits. Author Pat Chen describes it this way:

> We've grown so accustomed to the dull ache of life that comes from being unhealed and not cleansed in the deepest parts of ourselves, that we press forward each day with the same lack of abundant life. Some of us have waited so long to be healed deep inside that we've forgotten that we ever believed we could be healed. Others of us have ignored the ache for so long that we don't believe healing is really possible or necessary—at least for us.[1]

Perhaps some of us have lived with the dull ache so long we're not even aware of it? As author Sue Monk Kidd says, "Many of us are shredded inside, split, unable to grow beyond our fragmentation and woundedness."[2] So we live broken lives, stagnating in our present situation with no idea how to move beyond it.

Healings, Cures & Wholeness

Before we proceed, a shared definition of healing is helpful. While physical disease may be more easily grasped and understood in terms of our need for healing, emotional 'dis-ease' may not be. This book delves most deeply into our emotional and spiritual healing. However, we know our emotional well-being is deeply connected to our physical well-being. With this in mind, Mary Farrell Bednarowski, has compiled one of the fullest definitions of healing I've found:

> [Healing is] the bringing of greater wholeness (again) to that which has been fragmented; the restoration of balance to what has been distorted; clear sight to what has been obscured; and resistance to that which is considered destructive.
>
> …A definition of healing points to an overall stance toward life, a straightforward affirmation of the value of life that is also candid about the reality of suffering.
>
> …To be healed is to have sufficient hope to proceed, whatever that might mean in particular circumstances.[3]

Take note of these specific ideas within her definition: wholeness, restoration, balance, vision, healthy boundaries, the value of life, and hope despite surrounding circumstances.

Theologian Paul Tillich further connects healing to salvation: "The word *salvation* is derived from the Latin word *salvos*, which means heal and whole. Salvation is basically and essentially healing, the re-establishment of a whole that was broken, disrupted, or disintegrated."[4] This connection between healing and salvation is important. When you received salvation through Christ Jesus, he comes to your heart to do that which he was specifically called to do. As revealed in Luke 4:14-21, Jesus' identity (what he was created for) is formed by the ancient scripture found in Isaiah 61. It contains another definition of healing—broken hearts bound, freedom for captives, sight for the blind, crowns of beauty, garments of praise, oaks of righteousness, rebuilt ruins, devastation restored, a double portion instead of shame, justice instead of wrong-doing, a bride adorned for her groom, and praise springing up before the nations. In each of these definitions, wholeness, restoration, justice, peace, and hope are evident.

Also note that there's a difference between healing and being cured. A cure relates to the elimination of a disease or illness, often attained through medical intervention. Healing deals with emotional, spiritual, and psychological well-being and is related to a person's belief-system and outlook on life. It implies a sense of hope even when things appear hopeless to others. Thus, a person may not find a cure for his or her terminal illness, but find healing and hope in the midst of the disease. Conversely, a person can be cured of a disease but not be healed of the emotional devastation it has caused in his or her life.

Christ at the Center

As we continue, two truths are of utmost importance: 1) *healing is rooted in an encounter with the Living God, through the person of Jesus Christ* and 2) *this encounter is completely and thoroughly dependent on the ministry of the Holy Spirit.*

First, let's focus on Jesus, our healer.

Healing comes through Jesus. Counseling, therapy, and other methods will most certainly go a long way toward helping us on our journey, but true and complete healing at the depths of our being is found in Jesus, our Lord, Savior, and Friend. Please hear me: I am not saying those methods do not help. They do! Tremendously! I am *not* saying quit therapy. But complete healing in the deepest places comes when Christ works *through* those methods. Terry Wardle encourages us in this vein:

> Only Jesus Christ has the power to set the captives free! In and of themselves, prescriptions, programs, and processes offer at best short-term relief. But when Christ Jesus is recognized as the source of healing and all else the means of grace, there is great hope for permanent wholeness. Why? Because of Calvary! On the cross, Jesus paid the debt, defeated the foe, and insured an inheritance for all who believe.[5]

Do you hear that? Debt paid! Foe defeated! Inheritance insured!

Apart from Jesus, there is no true restoration, redemption, and renewal at the deepest level of our being. Counseling, therapy, and other methods are the "means of grace" that aid us in our journey, but we must journey alongside Jesus. He is the Suffering Servant who bears our grief and pain:

> *Surely he took up our pain and bore our suffering,*
> *yet we considered him punished by God, stricken by him, and afflicted.*
> *But he was pierced for our transgressions, he was crushed for our iniquities;*
> *the punishment that brought us peace was on him,*
> *and by his wounds we are healed.* Isa 53:4-5

Henri Nouwen once wrote: "I let Christ live near my hurts and distractions."[6] As the part of the Godhead who suffered earthly pain, Jesus understands what we experience in this world. He joins us in our suffering even as we join him in his (Rom 8:17). In him we find salvation, wholeness, and healing. The burden of the punishment we deserved was laid upon his shoulders, and he carried it all the way to Golgotha. There the yoke of our burdens became the crossbar of his crucifixion cross, and the full extent of his love was demonstrated as he died to bring us life. Yes, *by his wounds, we are healed!*

Before he was betrayed, in the Garden of Gethsemane, Jesus cried out in deep anguish of soul, and God the Father met him in powerful, life-sustaining ways. As Jesus hung naked and exposed on the cross, he offered forgiveness to those who nailed him there, to those who mocked him, and to those who offered bitter vinegar for his thirst.

Jesus understands suffering.

Should you ever find yourself questioning or doubting whether Jesus understands your pain, return to the powerful passages that describe what he endured in the Garden of Gethsemane on the Mount of Olives and at Golgotha, the Mount of Calvary.

And yet there, in his place of greatest suffering and shame, was his greatest victory! Let me state that again:

> *Jesus Christ's place of greatest suffering is his place of greatest victory!*

The only defeat that day came to the enemy of our souls, *not Jesus.* "This victory is one of the most important truths that the broken can embrace," states Wardle.[7] As sons and daughters of God, we too can claim that victory. Doesn't matter where you've been, what you've done, or what's been done to you! Jesus will take your places of greatest suffering and turn them into places of great victory!

Leanne Payne writes of taking people before the "Cross of Christ" as she works with them to receive deep healing. Up to this point, these people have tried to trust and believe, but this has all been a matter of the mind. They have tried to think themselves healed, but now the "difficulties erupting from the deep mind and heart" have brought them to their knees at the foot of the cross:

> Then we kneel down before God and with my arm around the sufferer, I ask him or her to look up and see Christ on the Cross, dying to take into himself whatever is amiss in his [or her] heart. Invariably, within a matter of minutes, the 'diseased matter' within starts surfacing. It comes right up and is given to [Jesus]. I ask them to see with their hearts this being done, and it is amazing what they see. All that they have never been able to receive through painful thinking and striving now comes with 'interest' as God does over and above what they were able to think or imagine. The connection is now made between the heart and God. As this healing takes place, peace and healing comes to the conscious mind and mental processes as well.⁸

What a powerful encounter! And this encounter is available to all who will receive.

The Holy Spirit Working in a Holy Exchange

Now, let's attend to our second truth: this encounter cannot be done apart from the ministry and power of the Holy Spirit. It cannot be done in human strength or effort, apart from the Holy Spirit working a miracle of heavenly exchange, a "holy exchange," in an encounter with our Savior and friend Jesus in the deepest places of our spirit.

Won't you take a moment to stop and read Psalm 42, taking special note of verse seven?

We now recognize Psalm 42 as a lament, as the psalmist takes his grief and feelings of abandonment before the Lord. In anguish, with his deepest longings exposed, he comes before the Lord and pours out his heart, recognizing his great thirst and hunger. He speaks words of hope to remind himself to praise God despite his feelings (vs 5). He calls his mind to remembrance of God's faithfulness in his life (vs 6). Let's read verse seven in two translations:

> *Deep calls to deep in the roar of your waterfalls;*
> *all your waves and breakers have swept over me.* NIV

> *Deep calls to deep at the thunder of thy cataracts [or waterfall cascade];*
> *all thy waves and thy billows have gone over me.* RSV

Here we see the Holy Spirit (Deep) as it speaks to the writer's spirit (deep) in a tidal wave of grace, love, and mercy. We recognize this as the Living Water offered to the woman at the well (Jn 4) but instead of being ladled out in small portions, it is poured out lavishly, almost recklessly, upon this writer so deep in anguish and pain.

Through the ministry and power of the Holy Spirit, our grief is poured out like a drink offering at the feet of Christ. In a heavenly, holy exchange, the One who offers Living Water in great abundance; the One whose own drink offering was poured out even until death; the One who cried, "My God! Why have you forsaken me?" at his death enters into our sorrow and drinks fully of the offering we pour out. He stands beside us, takes the guilt, shame, ridicule, and pain for us. We, who once stood guilty, wounded, and afraid, are now cleansed in the rushing torrent of his cleansing flood. As our deep cries out to his Deep—as our spirit cries out to his Spirit—the thunderous sound of his Living Water erupts like a gusher and fills the dry, parched places of our spirits. We exchange our drink offering for the communion cup of his blood. We exchange our grief and pain for his healing love. We exchange our ashes for his beauty. We exchange our captivity for his great freedom! Hallelujah! Christ is Lord!

Under the Holy Spirit's lead and counsel, we bring our wound before Jesus and lament. We tell him how it has affected our life and how we view the world and others as a result. After we have expelled our grief, pain, and sorrow, we ask Jesus to step into that wounding moment. We ask him where he was, and ask him to give us a picture, word, or sense of his actions in that moment of wounding.

In the very place of our wounding, we ask Jesus to step in and meet us.

As we find him in that moment we ask him to speak truth into the lies. Through our dependence on the Holy Spirit, Jesus replaces the lies and distortions of the enemy with truth and acceptance. As we allow that truth to soak over us, our emotional turmoil is quieted through the power of his comfort and peace. From this place of holy encounter, we seal the work of the Holy Spirit as we begin to move out in empowered living that begins to shape, mold, and change our life into one that moves in wholeness and freedom.[9]

Please read Psalm 42 again—this time, as if *you* are the writer. Allow yourself to feel the thirst of your soul. Call your spirit to praise him amidst the pain, to hope against the anguish you feel. Picture yourself at the edge of a mighty ocean representing his great love for you. Imagine a mighty wave sweeps ashore, taking you under. You fight to hold your breath as the torrents of his love hold you under. At last, you cannot hold your breath any longer, and while you fear you might be overtaken in the power of his overwhelming love, you take in his Living Water and miraculously, like a baby in the womb, you find the water in your lungs does not drown you, but nourishes and protects you. Over and over, his waves of love crash into you, pulling you in and under. You are tossed about in reckless abandon, yet you are completely safe, secure, and unsinkable.

We fear we might drown in our darkest wounds. We fear experiencing the great emotional upheaval that occurred at the moment of our greatest woundings. This fear is undeniably real. Wardle writes:

> Wounds are ugly, dark, and destructive. They often bring with them feelings of shame and fear, and no one wants to re-experience such negative emotions. As a result people develop elaborate mechanisms to distance themselves from any remnant of what occurred. Memories are locked away, denied, minimized, or marginalized. All the while these untouched wounds continue to bring harm to peoples' lives. Though hidden far below conscious awareness, they remain powerful and destructive. They must be remembered and addressed by the Lord if the broken are to experience freedom and wholeness.[10]

When we take those wounds before a loving and gentle, yet awesome and powerful Savior, he meets us there. A "holy exchange" happens when through the help and guidance of the Holy Spirit, we encounter Jesus in those wounds. We do this sheltered and protected by a Heavenly Father, guided by a comforting, counseling Holy Spirit, and through the power of our Savior and friend, Jesus Christ. This beautiful exchange happens in the communal presence of the Holy Trinity. There is no other way to true freedom.

This "holy exchange" truly is our "kintsugi of the soul"
...and it is where Jesus Christ does his most powerful work!

Are you ready for Jesus to do that work in you?

The Story of Ruth

I met Ruth[11] through my association with Healing Care Ministries. She has experienced trauma at many levels throughout her life. Prone to illnesses as a young child, she nearly lost her life to an infection. As a pre-teen, she suffered repeated sexual abuse. Early in her marriage, she lost three children to miscarriages, including the twin of her eldest daughter. She has also experienced the pain and betrayal of spiritual abuse. She currently struggles with chronic illness for which there is no known cure. Despite all that the enemy intended for evil (Gen 50:20), she walks an unexpected journey of healing, not only for herself, but for others to whom she ministers. Ruth has used the creative process since she was a small child as a way to deal with the pain and trauma in her life, writing songs, stories, and poetry to help navigate and process wounding in her life. She courageously shares her testimony with us here so we might explore her story as an avenue towards creative insight on the healing journey.

Ruth's creative exploration started as a small child. Even though she was unable to fully articulate what was happening within, she began writing. She shares: "It seemed to spring up organically. As a child, I would not have been able to understand writing was helping me to integrate the left and right sides of my brain. Through study, I have come to understand that what is true does not always feel real, and we require this bilateral integration of the mind to make sense of our life experiences." In the creative process of writing, she was able to integrate the thinking left-brain with the feeling right-brain and understand more fully the trauma she had experienced.

Note how this was an innate, organic process for Ruth. No one instructed her to use creativity to help her: "I don't recall having been told that these activities would help me," and yet she knew. I love how God uses the creative mind and instinct to bring restoration to his children! Ruth continues: "Particularly during times when I have not had someone to walk with me on my journey, God has used these creative outlets to provide a space in which I could explore my thoughts and feelings." I am amazed how her creativity has given her a sense of God's presence with her in the loneliest parts of her journey—a miracle of great beauty and wonder! God also uses creativity to reveal truth to her:

> God may reveal some truth to me when I am driving, cooking dinner, talking with a spiritual friend, or creating. One of my songs was written on a series of post-it notes, stained with blueberry juice as it came to me when I was making Christmas pies. I cannot control when creativity strikes. All I can do is to be quiet and receptive to hear the truth God is trying to communicate to me. Many times, this truth is highly personal, but I believe that what is most personal is often most universal. So, I often share the songs, poems, and stories that God gives me in the hope that they will encourage someone else.

I love how the creative process of baking opens her spirit to God's presence! Ruth also shares that silence and solitude is crucial on her journey. In silence and solitude Ruth can practice the presence of God and Safe Place—where God can meet with her and instill his truth deep within. Also notice how her healing brings others into wholeness and restoration.

While admittedly difficult to articulate, Ruth shares with us a testimony of healing in an encounter with Jesus:

> During prayer, I was in Safe Place, and I asked Jesus to show me what he wanted me to look at on that particular day. I was led to a room in which I had been sexually abused. I saw myself in the corner, shrinking from Jesus' touch. I had my knees pulled to my chest in a defensive stance.
> With a tearstained face, I told Jesus, "Don't come close! I'm a bad girl!"
> He smiled as he reached out and touched my face and said, "Not bad—just a girl."
> Then he walked to the middle of the room where there was a chalkboard. That room was a bedroom and didn't actually have a chalkboard in reality, but I had noticed it when I first saw the image of that room in my mind. At the time, I had wondered why a chalkboard was there. He took the chalk and drew a line down the middle and put my name on one side and the name of my abuser on the other side. Jesus slowly took the chalk and made a mark under the name of the other person. He said, "I'm not chalking this up to you." Of course, I had heard ad nauseam that it wasn't my fault, but on some level, the younger me didn't get that.

Notice the lies Ruth believed as a result of her sexual abuse: it was her fault because she was bad. However, Jesus revealed the truth in their encounter: she was neither bad nor to blame. Of course, she had been told that, and even though she knew that in her head, she couldn't feel it in her bones. In the depths, she still *felt* as if she was guilty. She carried the shame of that terrible tragedy against her—until Jesus came and told her she didn't need to carry it any more. While the story above seems rather short and simple, understand Ruth probably spent 30 minutes or more in Safe Place prayer, visualization, and lament as she processed this event, not to mention the years of processing prior to this!

Ruth also graciously shares portions of her writings as a creative testimony of her healing. In this story, Preciosa represents the "teenage part" of Ruth. First, notice the physical effects of trauma and abuse:

> Breathing was often problematic for Preciosa. She often found herself gasping for air after several seconds of having held her breath. She never held her breath on purpose; she just found that it happened. She had a fear of exhaling and losing something in the process. She held everything so tightly inside of herself that exhaling seemed like a dangerous prospect. It seemed as if she didn't even know how to breathe, like she needed to relearn that skill. She would often find herself having to remind herself to breathe. There was a strong voice inside of her that would command her to breathe in and out. Like a tiny drill sergeant, the voice would take control when her most basic functions seemed to be failing. Preciosa wondered if she would even be alive without that voice shouting orders and keeping her focused on survival.

Now, notice how God meets Preciosa through the warm, inviting character of Mrs. López-García, who pulls Preciosa into her embrace of love and acceptance:

> Mrs. López-García didn't let go. Preciosa had never been hugged for this long before, but she reveled in the sound of the stout woman's heart that could still be heard through all of the mounds of flesh surrounding it. That steady rhythm began to invade Preciosa's body, and she felt her own heart taking on the slow, consistent pace of the older woman's heart.
>
> It was then that she felt something she had never felt before. It was a warm feeling that began to creep over her whole body. She felt peaceful, yet fully awake and alive to all that was around her. She could hear the gentle ticking of the clock on the wall, and she could feel her chest as it would rise and fall with each breath. She was fully in the present moment, and it was a wonderful feeling. She wondered if this is what it felt like to be able to feel Jesus. She would ask Wonder later, but for now, she would just breathe and allow herself to do nothing but exist and feel how amazing it was to have this woman so happy that Preciosa was alive.

Wonder (mentioned above) represents the "inner child" part of Ruth. Wonder loves to dance for Mrs. López-García, who delights in her creativity and joy. Listen as Wonder explains why she dances:

> Wonder lifted her head to look at the beaming woman.
> "You know why I like to dance so much?" she questioned. Mrs. López-García said she didn't know.
> "Well, I like to dance because Jesus likes it. Sometimes when I'm dancing, I can feel him smiling and then I feel him just come all up inside of me."
> The brown-skinned woman laughed and said, "Yes, I know the feeling, that one."

I love how this story captures the awe, freedom, and playfulness of the little girl in Ruth, aptly named Wonder. Likewise, I am struck by the hesitancy, trepidation, and honest vulnerability of the teenage girl in Ruth. Despite the guilt and shame she carries from the abuse and trauma she has endured, she is still fittingly named Preciosa—for she is indeed precious! This story reveals much about coming to terms with the wounding moments of our lives.

Like many other healing stories I've heard, it reminds me of a quote:

> *Life isn't about waiting for the storm to pass;*
> *It's about learning to dance in the rain.*

I pray that Wonder encourages all of us to dance... even in the rain.

By His Wounds

As we move through the Bible studies in this chapter, we will follow the leading of the Holy Spirit as we encounter Jesus through our creative process. Throughout this book we've read testimonies of hurt, wounded people who found healing through creativity. I truly believe that when we add our Savior Jesus Christ to the creative experience, there is even more powerful healing available to us. We must remember to keep Christ at the Center.

Jesus came and walked among his people, touching, blessing, and healing them. It was vital to his identity as Messiah and Savior. He took on the vilest of wounds so we could find healing from ours. His wounds were not just physical, but emotional, spiritual, and psychological too. We will study Jesus in the Garden of Gethsemane, revealing the depth of pain and anguish Jesus Christ suffered—not just for God, but on our behalf. We often think as Christians we should be exempt from suffering, but even a superficial read of Acts or the letters of Peter or Paul demonstrates that is not true. In fact, the opposite is true—as Christians we join Jesus in suffering. How can we share in Christ's glory without also sharing in his suffering? We can't if we are to be conformed to his beautiful image.

I believe the late author Madeleine L'Engle summarizes it best: "Wounds. By his wounds we are healed. But they are our wounds too, and until we have been healed we do not know what wholeness is. The discipline of creation, be it to paint, compose, write, is an effort towards wholeness."[12] Let her wisdom lead us on in our journey, as we pray together:

Lord, may our own creative "efforts toward wholeness" be for your glory. May our artistic endeavors bring us healing in the deepest places of our being. And may we, being on a healing journey, be transparent enough to bring others into freedom, peace, and wholeness through our own healing, creative process. We pray that the Holy Spirit will meet us in mighty ways with great reminders of Jesus Christ's great love and saving power. Lord, help us keep our eyes open—we never know what symbol might appear in our lives to reveal the truth of God to us. We want to be aware—in this very present moment. We breathe deeply, and as we exhale, we let go.

In the name of Jesus, whose wounds bring us healing, we pray, Amen.

Listen to: "Miracles" by Jesus Culture

Digging Deeper Into...

Luke 13: Encountering Christ	Page 147
Luke 6: Wondering Which Wound	Page 151
Mark 14 & Luke 22: Lamenting Our Loss	Page 154
Revelation 21 & 22: Hearing Jesus Speak	Page 157
Romans 8: Embracing the Victory of the Cross	Page 160

Benediction of Completion — Page 164—165
The Antique Rocking Chair by Sarah M. Wells

Next Steps: Resources for Your Healing Journey & Endnotes — Page 166

Coloring Page "Lion of Judah" by Donna Godwin — Page 167

Digging Deeper: Encountering Christ

Read: Luke 13:10-17

There are many beautiful aspects of this healing story to discover as we dig into this passage. As we begin it's important to note this healing occurs right before several teachings on the Kingdom of God. So it serves as a kind of preamble pointing to Jesus as Lord: Lord of the Sabbath and Lord over God's kingdom. It is a symbolic action that illustrates the teachings that follow—a prophetic movement that looks to the future. Now onto this healing story and the beauty it reveals.

First, it's immediately stated this healing occurred on the Sabbath, serving as revelation that Christ is Lord over the Sabbath. The fact that the religious leaders don't recognize this doesn't stop him. On God's sacred day, the day of Sabbath rest, Jesus acts with great authority and power. Next, scripture tells us there is a woman there who has been crippled by a spirit. It also states that because of this crippling spirit she was *both* "bent over" *and* "could not straighten up at all." These two descriptors are for emphasis. The length of her deformity is also indicated—eighteen years. Given shorter lifespans in Ancient Israel, this is a long time. These explanations stress the gravity of her crippling deformity.[13] The word for crippled in Greek is *astheneia*, and it signifies she's not only without strength and powerless, but also points to an "infirmity of the soul." Both physical and spiritual weaknesses are implied here.

Bible scholar David Garland relates that although this woman was an outsider within ancient culture, she came to the local place of worship—not to be held back despite her deformity and low rank in society.[14] In complete recognition of her need for God, her infirmity does not hold her back from hearing, learning, worshiping, and gathering with other believers, even those who might possibly reject her. She comes to the synagogue because she desires freedom from that which holds her captive and bound. Since she was an outsider, we might assume she was most likely in the back of the crowd. And yet somehow, she caught Jesus' eye, and he called her to come to him. Bible scholar James Edwards reveals that in this culture, a woman would never approach a rabbi nor would a rabbi speak to a woman, so "personal encounters between rabbis and women were consequently rare occurrences."[15] And yet Jesus breaks the rules again to establish his authority and power.

Notice Christ does three things: he *sees* her; he *summons* her, and he *speaks* to her.[16] Further, he does not speak to the spirit of infirmity that holds her captive. This moment is all about her, and he speaks to her directly:

Woman, you are set free from your infirmity.

And with the power of one single touch from the hand of the Lord of the Sabbath, she *immediately* straightens. She is *immediately* set free from that which has held her bound. Hallelujah!

Then when confronted by the synagogue ruler, Jesus uses a word picture, a metaphor—one of a bound animal that needs untied in order to lead it to water. Jesus questions his accuser: "Who wouldn't untie an animal and lead it to water, regardless of it being the Sabbath?" The answer is obvious! Of course, one would untie the animal and lead it to water!

Take that in for a moment: the animal is tied up—kept from life-sustaining and life-giving water! In the same way, like a donkey, this woman has been bent over, tied up, and bound by her infirmity. Garland paints the picture of this metaphor most vividly: "She was bent over, face to the ground like a bound draft animal."[17] As an outsider she was unable to reach life-giving water! If we would take a donkey to water, why wouldn't we do the same for a daughter of God?

When Jesus addresses her as a "daughter of Abraham," it's an expression of honor, and he's using it purposely to reinstate and welcome her back into her community.[18] Jesus is proclaiming that as a "daughter of Abraham," she has every right to freedom from captivity as her Israelite ancestors set free from the bondage of Egyptian slavery many years ago. "Let my people go" echoes through this passage as Jesus powerfully proclaims:

You are set free!

Earlier in Luke (4:18), Christ announced that part of his mission is release or freedom for the prisoners or the oppressed. The Greek for 'set free' in 13:12 is *apolyo*, which means to set loose as from bondage or imprisonment. In essence, Christ is using this specific word to indicate he is doing exactly what God the Father had destined him to do. Edwards goes on to say:

> It was not coincidental but "necessary" that Jesus should free a woman bound by Satan, and to do so *on the Sabbath*, for Jesus, who is Lord of the Sabbath, must complete his mission of redemption on Sabbath, just as God completed his mission of creation on Sabbath. …The mission of Jesus and the Father are one, and thus inseparable.[19]

Furthermore, this healing must occur on the Sabbath to reclaim this woman bound by satan to establish that Christ *and Christ alone* is Lord! It is time for Jesus to set the captives free and for satan to let God's people go! While the religious rulers grumble, the people who've seen this crippled woman healed join her in worship to celebrate her newfound freedom.

In this story we find a person full of hope despite the circumstances of her life. My suspicion is that several things are at the root of her hope: faithfulness, gratitude, worship, and prayer. Despite her condition, she comes to the synagogue to hear the reading of the Torah, learn from the rabbis' teachings, and worship with her fellow Israelites. Her deformity could've easily held her back, yet she comes to receive. She could've stayed home in misery and isolation, yet she chooses to faithfully come. Unlike the hemorrhaging woman who risks everything to touch the hem of this garment, the crippled woman seems resigned to her condition as she takes her place in the back of the crowd. Yet still she comes, as she so faithfully came many times before. And in her faithfulness, she finds Jesus—the God Who Saves! Consider your own circumstances for a moment, and ask yourself these questions:

> *What holds me in bondage and keeps me from life-giving water?*
> *Have I been faithful?*
> *Have I continued in gratitude to worship?*
> *Have I continued to seek the Lord in prayer?*

I am afraid it is all too easy to get discouraged and give up. To stop being grateful for God's faithfulness in our lives. To stop gathering in community to worship, to learn, and to hear the good news of Jesus. To stop showing up to see what the Holy Spirit will do, because for so long we have been bent over, crippled, and bound by the enemy.

We must persevere and come before the Lord—again and again. We have experienced many losses in our lives. We must come to him over and over so he can heal us—wound by wound. We must continue on with hope, faithfulness, and gratitude despite our circumstances. Consider these thoughts from Henri Nouwen:

> If mourning and dancing are part of the same movement of grace, we can be grateful for every moment we have lived. We can claim our unique journey as God's way to mold our hearts to greater conformity to Christ. The cross, the primary symbol of our faith, invites us to see grace where there is pain; to see resurrection where there is death. The call to be grateful is a call to trust that every moment can be claimed as the way of the cross that leads to new life.
>
> …Gratitude helps us in this dance only if we cultivate it. For gratitude is not a simple emotion or an obvious attitude. Living gratefully requires practice. It takes sustained effort to reclaim my whole past as the concrete way God has led me to this moment. For in doing so I must face not only today's hurts, but the past's experiences of rejection or abandonment or failure or fear.[20]

Yes, we must cultivate an attitude of grace with daily tending and uproot the weeds of the enemy's lies in our lives.

Like the crippled woman we come to the place of learning, prayer, worship, and community—over and over. In our crippled and bound state we come—again and again. There we discover healing, restoration, and freedom as we encounter Jesus Christ, our Lord and Savior.

We must also persevere in prayer. Wardle warns: "Emotional healing cannot happen apart from prayer."[21] I know many give up conversation with God when they perceive nothing's happening or think they cannot hear or see God's answers. I fear our wounds often blind and deafen us to the answers he offers. Jesus is right there in our midst, and we fail to see. God's still small voice whispers, and we fail to hear. The Holy Spirit moves and acts on our behalf, and we fail to take notice. We must encounter Jesus time and time again—giving him space and time to bind our wounds, to apply his healing salve, to work his miracles in our lives. This is a continual process requiring a consistent practice. Wardle candidly shares: "I link my ongoing well-being to various types of prayer, more than any other aspect of my inner healing."[22] *Any other aspect!* Prayer is the root. The beginning, middle, and end. It must be *in* all things and *through* all things. We want to walk in the kingdom power of Jesus Christ, yet apart from regular and intimate times in his presence, we cannot.

This study is about encountering Christ. That encounter happens within the practice of our Safe Place exercise (remember: if the word "safe" causes difficulty, replace it with peaceful, restful, or calm). In the protection and provision of his presence we come, just like the crippled woman, before the Lord Jesus Christ, for only he can save us from our bent and bound lives. Won't you accept Jesus' invitation found in Matthew 11:28-30?

> *Come to me, all you who are weary and burdened, and I will give you rest.*
> *Take my yoke upon you and learn from me, for I am gentle and humble in heart,*
> *and you will find rest for your souls. For my yoke is easy and my burden is light.*

(continued next page)

Using the questions and scripture passage as your prompts as you begin to explore through creativity, won't you join me in this prayer?

Invite the Holy Spirit into this moment.
Ask the Lord Your Shepherd (Yahweh Rohi) to guide you as you pray.
Ask the Lord Who Sanctifies (Yahweh M'Kaddesh) to purify your imagination and help you picture, sense or create a place of protection and provision around you.
Ask the Lord Your Healer (Yahweh Rophe) to join you in that place and help you come before him with honesty, transparency, trust, gratitude, and deep faith in his healing power.

Jesus, like a beast of burden I am crippled, bent over, unable to straighten under the weight of the load I carry. Though I see your living water, I am still bound and unable to slake my thirst at your life-giving well. Lord of the Sabbath, untie me! Where I have been ungrateful, help me cultivate gratitude. Where I have failed to continue on in prayer, instill me with new strength to persevere. Where I have been stubborn, gently prod me on to your water where I will drink freely and deeply. Today I come before you. I come before you because I need you; because I can't do this without you; because I know you are Lord over all. In myself I am full of weakness, but in you I have strength. Take my burden! I declare I will no longer be a beast of burden! Instead I take on your yoke—where you pull the full weight of the load, and I walk steadily by your side. Bandage my wounds, Lord. One by one.

In the Name of He Who Carries Our Burdens, Amen.

Listen to: "Come All Ye Who Are Weary/Deep Calls to Deep" by Rita Springer
"Satisfied" by Jordan Feliz

Digging Deeper: Wondering Which Wound

Read: Luke 6:6-11

Imagine for a moment…

He stood in front of everyone—the man with the shriveled hand. Exposed. Revealed. Ashamed. All eyes on him and his deformity: the deformity that would keep him from the temple courts; make it difficult for him to work or farm; keep him from grasping anything. And Jesus makes him stand before everyone. The one who would rather stay invisible becomes the prop, the object lesson, the teachable moment.

The writer Luke is a physician, and in his thoroughness he points out that this is the *right* hand—the other gospel accounts of this story don't. Assuming the man is right-handed then it has great effect on his life. We don't know if it's been this way from birth or if an accident or disease has rendered it useless, but it is useless all the same. According to Biblical scholar Francois Bovon, the hand has great significance, not just physically in this man's life, but in all areas of his life and in the culture he lived:

> The hand can hold, sense, love, and be creative; in it the analogy between the Creator and Redeemer is most evident. The symbolism of the hand thus has deep roots in the Hebrew Bible and refers anthropologically to every aspect of the human existence. The hand is important for this reason, because it can become, in its universality, a sign of the delivering Christ. With his hand Jesus heals (8:54), and with the finger of God he drives out demons (11:20).[23]

This is more than just a hand—it's a symbol of life, and Christ has come to give life, abundant life. The man with the shriveled hand is so much more than an object lesson. He and his hand represent all that Christ came to do: restoration, redemption, and salvation!

I am often curious what went through the man's head when Jesus asked him to stand…

    Did he hesitate, looking at those around him?

        Or does he stand immediately in awe of this great teacher and healer?

           Did he hide his withered hand in the folds of his robe?

                Or did he hold it out bravely hoping Christ would heal it?

                    Could he even hold it out at all?

    Or did the weakness render it completely useless?

        We don't know. All we know is that Jesus asks him to stand. And he does.

Of course, it isn't long before all eyes are on Christ instead. Will he break Sabbath law to heal? Although not written in the law, it was well established and clearly understood that you could only heal on the Sabbath if a life was in danger.[24] Clearly this man's life was not, but Jesus challenges the religious authorities. And by challenging their authority, he establishes his own, and they don't like it. Essentially Christ is asking: "Is it right to do good as I intend to do? Or is it right to do evil as you intend to do?" He's challenging their motives, and it shines a negative light on the religious leaders.

All the while, the man with the shriveled hand is wondering if Christ made him stand only to let him down. Or would Jesus actually heal him? Imagine. The one thing he'd rather hide or ignore, and Jesus is asking him to stretch it out.

"Stretch out your hand," Jesus commands him.

Stretch out the one thing that deforms you, defiles you, defines you. And yet, in spite of his fear of exposure, the man refuses to hide any longer, and he takes a risk, wondering if today's the day. Just as he gathered the courage to stand, he now gathers the courage to stretch out his hand—all the while wondering if Jesus has the courage to defy the authorities and heal him.

But Christ doesn't even touch the man—he simply stretches out his hand, and it is whole. Since Jesus didn't physically touch the man, no one can accuse him of healing on the Sabbath. Christ catches the religious authorities on a technicality, but he's proven his point. The shriveled hand is completely restored—not just usable, but *completely restored* as God intended.

Today, think about the wounding events in your life. Big and little. Traumatic and incidental. Think of all the things, like the withered hand, that deform, defile, and define you. Picture yourself in the passage above. As Jesus scans the faces of those gathered around him, his eyes fix on you. *How does that make you feel?* As you consider that, imagine him asking you to stand. I imagine the man slips his hands into the folds of his robe hoping Jesus won't notice. *How would you hide your own deformity from Christ?*

And yet… what if then he asked you to stretch out that very thing for all to see?

Would you dare? Would you dare hope for healing? Think of all the things you'd rather keep hidden away and the things you'd boldly hold out for Christ to heal if he stood in front of you at this very moment.

As you consider your own woundings, be careful not to dwell on present circumstances, instead allow them to help you look back at the wounding events that may be contributing to them. Try to take note of anything that comes to mind. It doesn't matter if it seems trivial or insignificant. "What is forgotten is unavailable, and what is unavailable cannot be healed," Nouwen tells us.[25]

Yet at the same time, be careful not to rack your brain to drudge up everything from your past. Brenda Waggoner rightfully states:

> None of us could face all the ugliness and weakness in ourselves all at once, so God in his mercy reveals it to us a little at a time. We needn't go probing into the darkness of our unconscious, pressure ourselves to "figure out" things we don't yet understand or rush the healing process. It's enough to face the truth as God brings it into light.[26]

Give yourself time. God has plenty of it, and so do you. Simply take note of the things he brings to your mind today and jot them down. Don't worry about creating an exhaustive list. Allow God to reveal what you need in this moment.

Once you've spent some time doing this, ask the Holy Spirit to lead you to the *one wound* that the Lord wants to work on with you. Ask him earnestly:

What one wound is most standing in the way of my on-going relationship with you, God?

And allow him to guide. I am often surprised at the wound God singles out. Many times, it seems so insignificant. Yet in the end I am shocked at the lasting effect it has had on me and how it's stalling my current relationship with God. Trust God to lead you down the right path:

The Lord leads me beside waters of rest.
He restores my soul.
He leads me in right paths for his name's sake. (Ps 23:2-3)

Using the questions and scripture passage as your prompts as you begin to explore through creativity, won't you join me in this prayer?

Invite the Holy Spirit into this moment.
Ask the Lord Your Shepherd (Yahweh Rohi) to guide you as you pray.
Ask the Lord Your Peace (Yahweh Shalom) to quiet your heart before him.
Ask the Lord Who Sanctifies (Yahweh M'Kaddesh) to purify your imagination and help you picture, sense or create a place of protection and provision around you.
Ask the Lord Your Healer (Yahweh Rophe) to join you in that place and help you remember several wounding events in your life. Ask the Holy Spirit to help you identify a wound that has held you captive to the enemy's lies. Don't go to the wound you think you should work on, but to the one the Holy Spirit leads. Listen to his prompting, for that is where he wants you to start. This is the wound you will continue to explore through the rest of this chapter as you join Jesus on this healing journey. So it is vital that you listen to his leading and explore only the wound he would have you explore. Once you've identified the wound, begin to tell the story of the event, without discounting, minimizing, or rationalizing it away. Try to recapture and reconstruct the event, remembering as many details as possible: images, sensations, feelings, behaviors, meanings. Create something that represents the wound while continuing to stay in a prayerful state. Use your creativity to explore and symbolize the wound. If you feel unsafe at any point, return to Safe Place.

Let the words of Fernando Ortega's song "Father of My Heart" be our prayer today:
"Be still my child, for you must know I am the Father of your heart.
It is I who goes before you on this journey."
Through the dark, still it's hard for me to see and harder still to believe
Help me now to give you every part.[27]

Father of my heart, wrap me safely in your arms and protect me from any attack of the father of lies. Lord, as I recount my wounds I am overwhelmed by how the enemy has tried to pull me down and ruin me. Lord, help me remember there is redemption, restoration, and salvation in each and every wound—just as in the man's withered hand. Help me to hear your voice say, "Stretch out your hand," and help me to have the courage to do so. I trust in you alone, for you alone are the Father of my heart.

In the Name of the Trustworthy One, Amen.

Listen to: "Father of My Heart" by Fernando Ortega
"King of My Heart" by Sarah McMillan

Digging Deeper: Lamenting Our Loss

Read: Mark 14:32-42 & Luke 22:39-46

If there is ever a portrait of Jesus that reveals his humanity, it is this one found in the Garden of Gethsemane. Both passages speak of his great anguish as he prayerfully comes before God the Father to prepare for the trial ahead. Jesus is:

Deeply distressed
Troubled
Overwhelmed with sorrow to the point of death
Let down by his closest friends
Falling on his knees before God
In anguish
Praying earnestly
Sweating profusely, like drops of blood falling to the ground

Luke 22:44 uses the Greek word *agonia* for anguish. This is indeed pure agony—a deep inner tension in his soul. The Greek here is indicative of someone dreadfully anticipating an intense conflict. Like a soldier preparing for combat, he is steeling himself for battle. Bible scholar James Edwards interestingly notes:

> Jesus' inner torment manifests itself in physical trauma. Dripping blood would be expected to describe the crucifixion, but no blood attends that narrative. The most intense description of Jesus' suffering in the Gospels occurs not at Golgotha but at Gethsemane, in his decision to submit to the Father's redemptive will. On the Mount of Olives, Jesus' soul is crucified; on the Mount of Calvary, his body is surrendered.[28]

Do you understand the implications? The Gospel accounts of the crucifixion do not mention blood. While we know and understand Jesus bled while being whipped and dying on the cross, it is here in the garden that the direct reference is made to his blood. It is here *in the garden* where Jesus' heart was laid bare before the Mighty One, the Everlasting God, who could take this cup of suffering away from him. And yet did not.

If there was one Biblical story of Christ that illustrates how he identifies with your pain, it is this one: Jesus is at the very edge of himself. Faced with a redemptive plan that included the most humiliating of all punishments by death, he has never been more human than now. It is here that his suffering joins with ours.

And what is Jesus doing to prepare for the battle ahead? He's brought friends along to pray with him, but they fail him. He's alone in this world. So he relies on someone from another world. He comes before the Father, *his* father, his Abba Father. In his darkest hour he pours out his anguish, his grief, his lament before Abba. In his wrestling, he asks the cup be taken from him, yet at the same time submits to God's will. As Jesus pours out his turmoil before his father, God sends an angel to strengthen him. This is no worldly friend who cannot keep his eyes open long enough to intercede for Jesus. This is a heavenly friend of angelic proportions!

Wardle writes about the experience of both Jesus and his disciples in contrast to one another:

> Jesus grieved before the Father in Gethsemane and received strength for the upcoming suffering. The disciples did not deal with feelings that night, but instead slept through the dark hour. As a result, when the pressure became great, they denied Christ, ran in fear, or lashed out in anger.[29]

Jesus comes before God with his experience of pain. The disciples do not. Jesus finds strength and power to face his darkest moment. The disciples do not seek and therefore find nothing to sustain them in the days ahead.

The Garden of Gethsemane is Jesus' Safe Place. This is where he's gone time and time again to meet with God his Father. This is where he's listened and heard the voice of Abba Daddy. This is where he's aligned his will with the Father's in all matters related to the revelation and glory of God's kingdom on earth. Communing with his Father is a regular part of Jesus' every day life. It is here he's refreshed, guided, and loved. It is here in this place of protection and provision where Jesus can be brutally honest, before a Father who loves him in every way. This is no superficial prayer session—he is praying with his whole being. From the depths of his anguish and agony, he is pouring his heart out before the Lord.

We don't know what Father God or this angelic messenger said to Jesus, but we know he was strengthened to the point of resolve. Dr. Curt Thompson paints a beautiful picture of empathy and attunement between God the Father and Jesus his Son:

> It is not too much to imagine the Son hearing echoes of the Voice at his baptism telling him who he is even as he pleads, 'Father…take this cup from me!' As he speaks, he surely senses the Father hearing and responding to every word, every crimson drop of sweat. He feels God feeling him. He sees himself in the Father's eyes. The mentalization is as attuned and alive as it has ever been. The Son senses the Father's presence, and the Father's persistent invitation to the Son to trust him. Then Jesus responds, 'not my will, but yours.' The Son senses the Father's presence, his love, and his acceptance.[30]

There is a touching painting by artist Lucy Dickens called *Gethsemane – His Will*.[31] In this painting Jesus sits alone amid the trees in Gethsemane, shoulders slumped in a posture of hopeless despair. As I ponder the painting, I'm first captured by the olive trees with thick trunks and strong roots. They speak an ancient tale of strength and wisdom—trees rooted down deep into the soil, prepared for wind and storm. The artist shared that she witnessed these trees firsthand in a visit to the Holy Land, and her experience is revealed in the way she depicts these primeval trees. Jesus is cradled within the strength and wisdom of a tree while a ray of bright light filters through the treetops towards him—God speaking in the darkness of Christ's despair. It was there in the Garden that Jesus said yes, despite all that he would endure on our behalf:

> *During the days of Jesus' life on earth, he offered up prayers and petitions*
> *with fervent cries and tears to the one who could save him from death,*
> *and he was heard because of his reverent submission.*
> *Son though he was, he learned obedience from what he suffered and, once made perfect, he became*
> *the source of eternal salvation for all who obey him.* (Heb 5:7-9)

Because of his obedience, we have life. Thank you Jesus for being with us, even in our own suffering. May you be glorified! Even in our weakness, may you be glorified.

Staying with the same wounding event identified in the previous study, and using the scripture passage and instructions below as your prompts as you begin to explore through creativity, won't you join me in this prayer?

Invite the Holy Spirit into this moment.
Ask the Lord Your Shepherd (Yahweh Rohi) to guide you as you pray.
Ask the Lord Who Sees (El Roi) to look upon his child as you cry out to him.
Ask the Lord Who Sanctifies (Yahweh M'Kaddesh) to purify your imagination and help you picture, sense or create a place of protection and provision around you.
Ask the Lord Your Healer (Yahweh Rophe) to join you in that place and help you create your lament. While staying in a prayerful state, create something that represents your lament. As you create, tell God how you felt when the wounding event happened and how you feel now. Use your creativity to tell God what it has cost you and the lies you believe about yourself, others, and God as a result. Pour out your heart before the Lord. Let your tears flow as God collects and records each one. Release your grief and pain to the Only One who can heal your soul completely. If you feel unsafe at any point, return to Safe Place (remember: if the word "safe" causes difficulty, replace it with peaceful, restful, or calm).

Lord Jesus, I know you understand my suffering. In your short life you endured great anguish, and you endured it on my behalf. It is hard to comprehend that the Perfect One would take on the imperfect nature of all humankind so that we could be made whole. Did the Father really turn his face away or are those just lyrics to a song? Perhaps it was you, Lord Jesus, who had to turn his own face away instead—the Once Perfect, Now Imperfect One no longer able to look his Father in the face because of the sin, our sin, you bore on Calvary? Help me understand more and more how you bear my suffering with yours. How you pray for me when I cannot. How you turn my tears of lament into a prayer for the deepest places of my spirit. Be with me in my own Garden of Gethsemane, when the night is dark and evil lurks nearby to destroy me. In my own anguish, let me feel your comforting presence, just as you felt the Father's presence in your own agony. I pour out my lament at your feet. Heal me as I do.

In the Name of Jesus, My Fellow Sufferer, Amen.

Listen to: "How Deep the Father's Love for Us" by your favorite artist
And watch: "Heal" Contemporary Dance Piece - Tom Odell
(posted on YouTube by Mary Strause)
Listen to: "Garden" by NEEDTOBREATHE

Digging Deeper: Hearing Jesus Speak

Read: Revelation 21:1-22:6

In the passages above, God and the Spotless Lamb are restoring creation to its original condition. The writer is describing a New Jerusalem, restored to all its glory and splendor. He is also describing a restored Garden of Eden. Just as the garden contained many trees and a flowing river (Gen 2:9-10), this restored Eden does too. In ancient Jerusalem the water was dirty and polluted, but here the water is crystal clear. On earth, trees only bore fruit in season, but here there aren't just twelve crops a year, but twelve crops month! There is plenty, and no one goes without.

Let us read these verses from Revelation 21:3-7 again allowing me to add emphasis (in italics) as we do:

> And I heard a loud voice from the throne saying, "Look! God's dwelling place is now among the people, and he will dwell with them. *They will be his people*, and *God himself will be with them and be their God. He will wipe every tear from their eyes. There will be no more death or mourning or crying or pain*, for the old order of things has passed away."
>
> He who was seated on the throne said, "*I am making everything new!*" Then he said, "Write this down, for these words are trustworthy and true."
>
> He said to me: "*It is done.* I am the Alpha and the Omega, the Beginning and the End. To the thirsty I will give *water without cost from the spring of the water of life*. Those who are victorious will inherit all this, and *I will be their God and they will be my children.*

God makes his dwelling among his people, repeating covenantal language that declares we are people meant to be in his presence. In his presence there is no more pain or grief! No more bottles to hold our tears or scrolls to record our lament, because here he wipes each tear away. All is saved, redeemed, and restored. All that has gone before is done. Do you remember our definition of healing from earlier? This passage describes kingdom healing!

Now many of you might be thinking, "Yes, this sounds great, but this is for some day far away, not now." While I agree to a point, I also believe God has healing and restoration right here, right now!

In John 11 we find the story of the raising of Lazarus from the dead. In this story, Jesus and Martha discuss resurrection and life. Martha thinks Christ is talking about the resurrection of the last day, but Christ proclaims, "I AM the resurrection and the life!" Present tense—right here, right now! Mary comes out to meet him, falling at his feet. Notice both sisters tell Jesus that if he'd been there, Lazarus would still be alive. They're not afraid to express their disappointment, grief, and lament directly to his face. And they don't mince words! As Jesus looks at Mary, Martha, and all the others mourning Lazarus' death, he is moved deep inside and what does he do?

He enters in.
He steps into their grief, and *he weeps*!

Jesus weeps with us!

But he isn't just moved to compassion, he's moved to action. Moments later, Lazarus, still wrapped in his grave clothes, appears from the tomb. Lazarus rises from the dead—not one day far away, but right there, right then!

Do we dare hope that these verses of Revelation are not just for some day but also for right here, right now? Madeleine L'Engle speaks to the possibility:

> We are hurt; we are lonely; and we turn to music or words, and as a compensation beyond all price we are given glimpses of the world on the other side of time and space. We all have glimpses of glory as children, and as we grow up we forget them or are taught to think we made them up; they couldn't possibly have been real because to most of us who are grown up, reality is like radium and can be borne only in very small quantities. But we are meant to be real and to see and recognize the real. We are all more than we know, and the wondrous reality, that wholeness, holiness, is there for all of us, not the qualified only.[32]

God has so much more for us than the tattered, broken lives we lead. He longs for us to walk in our true identity and rightful inheritance—here on earth! The enemy and his awful lies are the only thing that stands in the way of us walking in our true identity. *Do you remember the glimpses of glory from your childhood? Can you think of just one?* When I was a little girl, there was a lion head fountain hidden in the shrubs of an overgrown garden at the local seminary. Finding that fountain was, for me, like Lucy meeting Aslan face to face, and every time I returned, it was a glimpse into glory—a thin place between heaven and earth. Think back to those glimpses and thin places in your life, then turn towards your Savior and see him face to face.

Today you will ask Jesus to enter into your wounding memory with you and speak truth into your heart and mind. Revelation 22:4 tells us we will see his face, and his name will be written on our foreheads. Today we will ask to see his face—right here, right now—and ask him to mark our foreheads with his words of truth. Still don't think it's possible? Hear God's voice whisper to your inner child:

> *"Forget the former things; do not dwell on the past.*
> *See, I am doing a new thing! Now it springs up; do you not perceive it?*
> *I am making a way in the wilderness and streams in the wasteland."* (Isa 43:18-19)

Asking Jesus into our memories is asking to look into the face of Christ, to see him face to face. The promises of a new life and healing found in Revelation are the promises he will partially fulfill right here on earth and fully reveal later in eternity. Each restored memory and healed wound helps us know and understand Jesus more—each is a restoration of the way things should be and as God had originally intended. Each time we ask Christ in, a piece of us is restored, and we begin to reflect more and more how things should really be. New Jerusalem is being created in our hearts and minds each time we invite him in. Asking Jesus into our wounding event is not erasing the memory and replacing it with something that didn't really happen. It's asking Jesus into the moment of your wounding to bring healing and restoration. It's asking him to speak truth into all the places deep within where the enemy spoke his devastating lies. It's asking him to shed light on the dark places of your soul. It is asking Christ to bring freedom to all the places in our lives that have brought bondage and oppression.

As you work through your creative process today, you will be asked to picture your wounding event and ask Jesus into that place. As he does, you will want to notice what you are sensing, seeing, and hearing. Even if you haven't had someone with you as you've worked your way through this book, today might be the day that you ask a friend, counselor, elder, or pastor to be with you to offer support, safety, comfort, and intercessory prayer as you work through the process.

Staying with the same wounding event you've been processing in the previous studies, and using the scripture passages and these instructions as your prompts as you begin to explore through creativity, won't you join me in this prayer?

Invite the Holy Spirit into this moment.
Ask the Lord Your Shepherd (Yahweh Rohi) to guide you as you pray.
Ask the Lord of Hosts (Jehovah Sabaoth) to protect you from the enemy.
Ask the Lord Who Sanctifies (Yahweh M'Kaddesh) to purify your imagination and help you picture, sense or create a place of protection and provision around you.
Ask the Great I Am (Ehyeh) to join you in that place and reassure you he is right there with you.
Ask the Lord Your Healer (Yahweh Rophe) to meet you face to face in your place of your wounding. Invite him in, and with a purified imagination, picture him there. What are you sensing? Seeing? Hearing? As he meets you there, open the eyes and ears of your heart and allow him to speak the truth related to your wound and the lies that surround it. Allow those words of truth to be written across your forehead—deep in your mind and spirit. Listen for words from scripture, too. Do not rush this step. Wait until you have heard from the Lord for the truth revealed to you through what you are sensing, seeing, hearing, and feeling. If you feel unsafe at any point, return to Safe Place, remembering that if the word "safe" causes difficulty, to replace it with peaceful, restful, or calm.

Once you have spent some time with Jesus listening to his voice of truth, create something that represents those truths. Again you can create something new or continue to build on what you've already created. Continue to stay in a prayerful state while you create a symbol of his truth. Ask Jesus to give you a scripture verse that relates to the truth he's speaking into your heart. You can incorporate the verse into your work as well.

Dear Jesus, my Lord and Savior, thank you for being here with me now. Please fill me with your comfort and peace. Lord, erase the lies of the evil one and rewrite your words of truth on my heart and mind. Hold the hand of my inner child and comfort him/her as only you can. You have known me since before my creation, and you knit me together in my mother's womb. You have been with me since I was conceived so you alone know my true destiny and calling. Speak into those places. Let your Deep call to my deep.

Where this wound has led to sickness, illness, and disease in my life, I pray that you bring my body into restoration and wholeness, along with my heart and mind. Help me to see glimpses of eternity from ages past. Help me to see glimpses of glory for my future as I walk in the truth of your great love and care for me. I pray scriptural promises over my life, and I stand in the truth of your word. I pray these truths will be sealed deep within my spirit so that the enemy will not be able to cover them again with his lies. Continue to bring healing, restoration, and wholeness to my spirit. Continue to speak truth into my heart and mind.
    In the Name of Jesus, my Redeemer, my Restorer, my Healer, I pray, Amen.

Listen to: "Right Now" by Centric Worship
"Voice of Truth" by Casting Crowns

Digging Deeper: Embracing the Victory of the Cross

Read: Romans 8:28-39

Romans 8 is a powerful passage of scripture! I've turned to it during many times of trial when I sought reassurance of God's sovereignty in all situations, as well as his love for me in the midst of my doubt and fear. While it is impossible to uncover all the scholarship and commentaries on this important passage to the Christian faith, let's allow God to reveal the verses that are most critical for our healing journey.

In hindsight it might be possible to see God working all things together for good, but surely, if we are honest with ourselves, in the midst of our most difficult circumstances, we question if this is true. I first discovered the truth of this passage when I was 16. On a beautiful day in August my brothers, my friend, and I were enjoying a day of fun and sun at the lake. A perfect day until my friend dove into shallow water, breaking his neck. The whole event was quite frightening—watching someone you truly care about losing feeling in his feet and legs as you worked to get him the medical attention he needed in a remote wooded area at the base of an inaccessible ravine. As they finally shut the ambulance doors and drove away, I feared he would never walk again. By the time I was permitted to see him many hours later, he was lying flat and helpless, traction pins in his temples, uncertainty in his eyes.

I'm not sure how, but God soon led me to Romans 8, and there I found verse 28:

> *And we know that in all things*
> *God works for the good of those who love him,*
> *who have been called according to his purpose.*

To say I clung to that verse like a life preserver in a stormy sea is truly a vast understatement! I did *not* know how God could work this tragedy out for his good, but I was willing to wrestle God night after night until the truth of that blessing had been revealed in my friend's life. Months later, when he walked, yes *walked*, out onto the football field to a cheering crowd celebrating his full recovery, I understood God's truth. So many people in our community were praying for him, and many of our fellow high school students watched amazed as God had completely healed him. God's glory revealed!

Bible scholar William Greathouse helps us enter the mind of Paul (author of Romans) as he states:

> It would never have entered Paul's mind that all things just work out on their own in some mechanistic or magical way; he is discussing divine providence. Although God may act anonymously and invisibly in the only apparently coincidental events that transform life's tragedies into triumphs, it is God who acts. The death of Jesus did not just work out for the best after all; God intervened, disrupting the normal course of events to vindicate his faithful and obedient Son by raising him from the dead.[33]

It isn't just a coincidence that led me to that verse in the midst of my heartache. I also believe it isn't just a coincidence when a special sign appears at the exact moment I need encouragement from God. And it isn't just a coincidence that God has led you to this book at this moment in your life.

In *all things* we must seek the Lord. If you are still struggling to see what good can come from your past or current situation, surrender to his sovereignty and love. If you are still clinging to the hurt and pain, relinquish your heartache to the Lord. God can't turn a situation around while you're still clutching to it for dear life! Let go, and let God!

At verse 31 we begin to see the language of a courtroom drama. Who will bring charges against us? Our offenders? Our accuser? Most certainly they will try, but if God is on our side no charge brought against us can stand! They are powerless in the face of God's unsparing gift of his Son given at the cross and the One who rose victorious over sin and death and hell! The Crucified One is now the Resurrected One![34] Hallelujah! We are justified in the resurrection of Jesus Christ!

Recalling our study of Joshua the High Priest in chapter three, in Romans 8:34 we again find the best lawyer money *can't* buy at our side as our vindicator and counsel:

> *Christ Jesus, who died—more than that, who was raised to life—*
> *is at the right hand of God and is also interceding for us.*

Once again we see Christ who lives to intercede for us! Also, note in I John 2:1, it indicates that Jesus Christ, the Righteous One, is the one who speaks to the Father in our defense. In that passage the Greek *paraclete* is used—the imagery is one of a legal counsel or advocate that comes forward on behalf of another. He is the atoning sacrifice (2:2) satisfying God's demand for sinless righteousness in our lives and assuages the judicial wrath required for justice against the evil we commit. As our atoning sacrifice he doesn't simply cover our sins--he removes them once and for all!

In the final verses of Romans 8, we hear the judge proclaim, "Not guilty!" as our offenses are erased from the Book of Law, and our name is entered into the Book of Life! As the verdict is read, we hear that we are *more than conquerors* through him who loves us. This phrase in Greek is *hypernikao* and it means we are hyper-conquerors—thoroughly victorious well beyond the current conquest. This victory is not a temporary one but for all time and far into eternity! Doesn't matter what awful situation you've come through, what you've done, what you're currently enduring, or what the enemy has dished out at you—*nothing separates* you from the love of God through the death and resurrection of Jesus Christ our Lord. We stand as victors ourselves through his resurrection power and love.

This love is vast and deep and wide. We must understand and cleave to this truth! Jesuit priest and scholar Joseph Fitzmyer refers to these verses as a "jubilant hymn of praise" as Paul expounds on the great love of God through Jesus Christ, and insists we claim it as our own:

> The love of God poured out in the Christ event is the basis of the Christian life and hope. No created being or force can unsettle that foundation. In all of the uncertainty of human, earthly life there is something fixed and certain, Christ's love and God's election. These are unshakeable; and Christians must learn to trust in them and take them for granted.[35]

How can we take this great gift for granted? I am awed and overwhelmed at the thought of his great love and sacrifice on my behalf! At the same time I must live as if this is "a given"—for as a child of God, it is! This is faith in action. I pour out my praise and thanksgiving to you, Lord! Thank you! Thank you! Thank you!

This is the victory of the cross we are to embrace as we move forward in healing and wholeness. One of my greatest fears is that to reject this love of God through Jesus Christ is to say his death and resurrection meant nothing. I refuse! Every time we find healing, every time we hear his truth, every time we experience his love we must embrace it as if our life depends on it—for surely it does! He longs to meet you in your places of pain so he can bring restoration to all the enemy has attempted to steal from you. I implore you, do not reject his love, grace, and mercy.

As you continue your creative process, you will be asked to extend forgiveness and celebrate the victory of the cross. I suspect that you, like me, will be more willing to celebrate the victory of the cross than forgive those who have hurt you, let alone shape a blessing for them. Yet scripture is clear: as we have been forgiven, we must also forgive. Extending forgiveness is not a face-to-face event with your offender(s)—that is not required of you. This act takes place in prayer with Jesus at your side. Forgiveness is letting go of this person(s) control over you.

Forgiveness is both an act and a process. We've all heard that unforgiveness is a prison that holds us (not our offender) captive. In the act of forgiveness we choose to let go and to *free ourselves* from this prison. Note that you may have to forgive a person, God, or yourself. We will speak more of this at greater length in the next chapter, but for now, remember forgiveness is a vital part of the healing process.

Without forgiveness, your offender will continue to hold you captive. Forgiveness is not done in your own power, but through the power of Christ in you. As we forgive, we ask the Holy Spirit to help us form a simple blessing over them. This is based on Jesus' mandate in Luke 6:28: "Bless those who curse you, pray for those who mistreat you." This blessing can be as simple as, "Bless them with your grace (or love or mercy)." The blessing never has to be spoken to the person who has harmed you. This happens within the safety of the presence of a loving God. Again, we will discuss this further as we go on.

Forgiveness is like a cage you let yourself out of. You hold the key, but it is up to you with Jesus' help to insert it, turn it, open the door, and let yourself go free. It's time, brothers and sisters, to walk in freedom!

(continued next page)

Staying with the same wounding event you've been processing in the previous studies, and using the instructions and scripture passages as your prompts as you begin to explore through creativity, won't you join me in this prayer?

Invite the Holy Spirit into this moment.
Ask the Lord Your Shepherd (Yahweh Rohi) to guide you as you pray.
Ask the Lord Your Peace (Yahweh Shalom) to quiet your heart before him.
Ask the Lord Who Sanctifies (Yahweh M'Kaddesh) to purify your imagination and help you picture, sense or create a place of protection and provision around you.
Ask the Lord Your Healer (Yahweh Rophe) to join you in that place and help you extend forgiveness and shape a blessing for the person(s) who wronged you.
While staying in a prayerful state, allow your spirit to forgive and let go of the person(s) who wounded you. Allow God to take care of their issues. Ask God to help you create boundaries that will protect you from further wounding. Ask God to help you form a simple blessing for them. Now use your creativity to celebrate your newfound freedom and victory. Create something that says, "Hallelujah! He is alive! I am alive!"

Crucified One, Righteous One, Risen One, Victorious One, today I choose to forgive and celebrate. I forgive _____ for their sins against me, and I pray a blessing of _____ over them. As I forgive and bless, I let go. I release their hold over my life, now and forever, through the strong name of Jesus Christ of Nazareth. Today, Lord Jesus, I walk out of the cage of unforgiveness that has held me captive. I choose in this moment to let go of the control they have over me by forgiving them in the power and strength of your great love for me. I bless them as I throw away the keys that have kept me locked in the hurt of my past. Like the filthy rags of prison garb, I feel the weight of this unforgiveness fall away from me, and I run into the freedom you have for me, celebrating the victory of the cross over the trauma of my past. I rejoice in your great love for me. I am more than a conqueror through God's love, and I proclaim:

Neither death nor life, neither angels nor demons, neither the present or the future,
not any powers, neither height nor depth, nor anything else in all creation,
will be able to separate me from the love of God that is in Christ Jesus out Lord! Amen!

Listen to: "The Conquering Lion" by Grace Falkner
"Nothing Ever (Could Separate Us)" by Citizen Way

❧ A Benediction of Completion ❧

The Antique Rocking Chair
by Sarah M. Wells

The carpenter is not disappointed
by the ruined finish or the broken arm,
loose spindles, failed glue joints.

He checks the chair for its rhythm,
rests carefully in its solid seat and tests
the sway, hums an ancient hymn,

feels the wind that wore away the finish,
drove the rain between the grains
and diminished the lacquered polish.

A chip along the armrest where a son
discovered mischief with a chisel
can be remedied, the crimson

scribble across the headrest should be
buffered out easily. He takes a pin punch
and hammer, twists the spindles free.

The worn seat board is planed to true
the surface; he's careful to avoid removing
too much wood. And when he's through

clamping cauls, filling end-grain breaks
and feathering maple wedge ends, he
carefully spreads the stripper paste

in heavy coats, waits for the softening
and scrapes away the residue. A putty knife
lifts bubbled layers of tired stain.

Away goes the ache of discoloration,
oil dissolved, original grains exposed.
Every crevice is cleansed, each abrasion

doctored with twine between the grooves,
brass-bristled brushes in each recess.
He sands away the raised grain, removes

the marks in the concave seat. With glue
that's slow to set, the seat and arms are raised
and then the spindles and splat. It's almost new,

the way the old has been removed. The carpenter
knows the chair won't last without stain
and picks a distinguishing shade to bear the wear

of another century. It is set apart, protected
with three coats of clear wood finish. The rocker
holds the woodworker: *it is finished.*

Next Steps: Resources for Your Healing Journey

Thin Places: a Memoir by Mary E. DeMuth

His Healing Hands: Finding God in Broken Places by Margaret Feinberg

The Shack by Wm. Paul Young

"Come Away With Me" extensive care retreat. Based on the model used in this book, this 7-day retreat in the beautiful hills of Southeast Ohio takes participants through times of teaching, worship, one-on-one sessions, and deep healing ministry in God's presence. Find out more: www.hcminternational.org

Endnotes
1. Chen, *The Depths*, 143.
2. Kidd, *When the Heart*, 160.
3. Bednarowski, *Religious Imagination*, 152.
4. Tillich, quoted by Shapiro, *Your Body*, 88.
5. Wardle, *Wounded*, 172.
6. Nouwen, *Turn My Mourning*, 11.
7. Wardle, *Healing Care*, 196.
8. Payne, *Healing Presence*, 174.
9. This encounter or "holy exchange" with Jesus, through the power of the Holy Spirit, is rooted in the Formational Prayer Model developed by Terry Wardle. Please see *Healing Care, Healing Prayer*, particularly pp. 140-142 and 189-210 for a more in depth discussion of this model.
10. Wardle, *Healing Care*, 189.
11. Name is changed to protect her privacy.
12. L'Engle, *Walking on Water*, 74.
13. Garland, *Luke*, 547.
14. Ibid., 553.
15. Edwards, *Luke*, 395.
16. Ibid.
17. Garland, *Luke*, 553.
18. Ibid.
19. Edwards, 397.
20. Nouwen, *Turn My Mourning*, 18-19.
21. Wardle, *Wounded*, 146.
22. Ibid., 147.
23. Bovon, *Luke 1*, 204.
24. Henderiksen, *Luke*, 321.
25. Nouwen, *Dance of Life*, 121.
26. Waggoner, *Fairy Tale Faith*, 79.
27. Ortega, "Father of My Heart," Urgent Records, 2009.
28. Edwards, 645.
29. Wardle, *Healing Care*, 203.
30. Thompson, *Anatomy of the Soul*, 139.
31. Lucy Dickens painting and remarkable story behind the painting can be viewed at: www.lucydickensfineart.com/portfolios/journey-through-the-holy-lands/gethsemane-his-will
32. L'Engle, 69.
33. Greathouse, *Romans*, 272-273.
34. Ibid., 284.
35. Fitzmyer, *Romans*, 536

6

"Be merciful, even as your Father is merciful."

    During my first ministry position, our church experienced major upheaval. Anyone who's been through church conflict knows the pain is quite intense. The one place you expect to be safe isn't. It is unsettling. Words cannot describe the pain I experienced through this period: it robbed me of all joy. In the midst of my grief and despair, God went silent on me. I could not feel or sense his presence or peace. All that I thought I knew about God changed, and this new revelation of God's hidden nature was more than I could bear. Every night for months, curled in a fetal position, I lay in bed crying out to God to answer, my tears soaking the pillow. I cried until I had no tears left to cry. Then, I was simply silent. My silence crying out to God's silence—deep calls to Deep.

    In the midst of this, I attended a two-week course on embodied prayer at Boston College taught by Father Robert VerEecke, a Jesuit priest. One assignment was to tell our God-story through movement. I thought through the last several years and created my painful testimony. What I presented to the class was a story of hopes dashed, dreams unfulfilled, crying out and seemingly not being heard, pain and disappointment, reaching out and pulling back. At one point, I pounded my fists upon the ground. When I was done telling my story of pain, there was complete silence. My constant friend, Silence. Finally an older, wiser woman spoke and simply said, "I saw blame." I realized in that moment I had blamed God—for all of it. I had not recognized or admitted this until that very moment.

    Given permission, I had processed my pain through cathartic creativity, expressing what no words could give voice to. I could talk of my pain, but words failed to translate the language of my despair. Through the creation of my story with movement and through the presentation to a small community of like-minded artists, I was able to dig deep into the hurt places of my soul. I had painstakingly gathered all the broken, fragmented pieces of my shattered heart and laid them before God to put back together. And somewhere in the process, he did just that.

Kintsugi of the Soul.

I came back from Boston a different person. The despair had lifted. No more numbness or debilitating pain. God was still silent, but my joy was back. I was healed and being healed. I can't say that everything went back to the way it had been before but I was markedly different inside. It's been many years since that experience, and in many ways I am still coming to grips with a sometimes silent God, but I am assured of his presence, and my faith is strong and unwavering as a result.

Life can be hard. Separated from our heavenly home, we journey between now and not yet. Moments of joy and blessing are interspersed with great sorrow and tragedy. The climb to the mountaintop is arduous and rugged, requiring strength and perseverance. Once we finally arrive at the peak, it seems but a moment before inevitably we're called to travel back down to the valley below. The passage is long. Moreover, we are called to walk this path in community, but often we lose step with our fellow travelers, and people we thought would be with us for the long haul suddenly disappear with little or no explanation. Left seemingly alone, we struggle to find our way. We look around for clues left behind by others who've journeyed before us. Caught up in the difficulty of the voyage, we become fatigued and must stop to rest. Yet... if we look upward, and search for the Son through the clouds that attempt to obscure our vision, we find a Light that guides us—onward and upward.

In this chapter we will talk about journeying through life in an imperfect world, with imperfect people around us, and imperfect hearts within us. This chapter is particularly important for us right-brained souls. We are truly sensitive to the world around us. God designed us this way for a reason—he needs us to see, hear, feel, and sense things around us to interpret them for others who cannot. That is our priestly calling. But this sensitivity also leaves us vulnerable if we are not secure in our identity in Christ and spending valuable time in his sweet presence.

Christ's Community

In his ministry here on earth, Jesus gathered a tribe around him. There was a large group that followed Jesus, caring for him and the disciples. There were others who welcomed him in their homes. There were the twelve, and there was a more intimate group of three (Peter, James, John) included in more private settings. He lived and modeled community.

During his final days, however, that group scattered. Scripture records that only John, Mary Magdalene, his mother Mary, and her friends stayed with Jesus to the end. And it was Joseph of Arimathea who went to Pilate on his behalf to give Jesus a proper burial. All the others had deserted him in his most critical hours of need. They couldn't even be counted on to collect his lifeless body.

And yet... at some point they regrouped, and there in that place of community Christ appears to them, *in their midst* (Jn 20:19). For some reason Thomas isn't present when Jesus first appeared to everyone, and of course, he doubts their word. That is, until he is *gathered with them* (Jn 20:26) and sees the resurrected Christ with his own eyes. Shortly following these encounters is the miracle of Pentecost—a miracle beginning with them *all together in one place* (Acts 2:1). In the midst of their gathering, the Holy Spirit comes in tongues of fire and *all are filled* with the Spirit's great power.

This is how it is in community. Fact is, the people around us let us down, especially in the places of our greatest need and pain. But still, within the context of community—the very one that has let him down—Jesus comes and makes due on all his promises, fulfills the prophetic words he's spoken, reassures them in their doubt, and fills them with the very same power that resurrected him from the dead.

Is community faulty? Why, yes! Community is made up of faulty people. No one acts or loves as they should all the time. People will let us down, won't fulfill our expectations, and won't be there when we need them. Still we are called to love, forgive, and work towards unity together as the body of Christ. Is it easy? No. *Only through Jesus,* can we journey together as a tribe. As God's chosen people, we are called and commanded to live and love in community:

> *Therefore, as God's chosen people, holy and dearly loved,*
> *clothe yourselves with compassion, kindness, humility, gentleness and patience.*
> *Bear with each other*
> *and forgive whatever grievances you may have against one another.*
> *Forgive as the Lord forgave you.*
> *And over all these virtues put on love which binds them all together in perfect unity.*
> *Let the peace of Christ rule in your hearts,*
> *since as members of one body you were called to peace.*
> *And be thankful.*
> *Let the word of Christ dwell in you richly*
> *as you teach and admonish one another with all wisdom,*
> *and as you sing psalms, hymns and spiritual songs with gratitude in your hearts to God.*
> *And whatever you do, whether in word or deed, do it all in the name of the Lord Jesus,*
> *giving thanks to God the Father through him. (Col 3:12-17)*

Community in Christ

As defective as it is, God created us to be in community: "It is not good for man to be alone," says Triune God in the midst of creative process (Gen 2:18). And while God created us to be in relationship, sin interrupts the perfection of our God-ordained need for relationship. Where God designed us for perfect peace, we are often sidetracked and distracted by life's struggles in an imperfect world where there seems little peace. So how do we do it? How do we live in communion with God and others? How do we journey with people who let us down? Only through the power of Christ in us—our hope of glory!

We all long for safety, security, nurture, significance, purpose, understanding, acceptance, belonging, and love. These core longings[1] were placed within us to draw us towards God. However, in a world ruled by the enemy, these longings push us to place expectations on others, as well as drive others to place expectations on us. In our need for significance, we strive for popularity and recognition. In our need for belonging and love, we grasp at others who instinctively pull away from our grappling. In our need for security, we accumulate wealth and hoard the blessings God has bestowed on us. In our need for safety, we build walls to keep others out and find ourselves alone.

Now these longings are not sinful—*except when they are misplaced* (as in the examples above). Instilled in us to draw us to God, they only find true fulfillment in his loving presence. At the same time, safe and healthy people around us can be used by God to help fulfill these God-given core longings. As previously mentioned, my friend Pauline Mae calls those people "Jesus in skin"—they act as the hands and feet of Christ. God uses them to love and speak life to others around them. But scripture tells us that the enemy appears as light, so there are times when we place our trust in someone the enemy is using in his dark pursuit of our soul. Moreover, our woundedness can sometimes obscure our understanding of the intentions of those around us, and we misinterpret their actions and words. Even "Jesus in skin" people have issues and circumstances that leave them seemingly unavailable. Oh how the enemy loves when these things happen.

As followers of Christ we are called to be "one" (independently relying solely on Jesus) and also "another" (journeying in community with others). The New Testament is filled with "one another" commandments. The first was uttered by Jesus himself: "A new command I give you: Love one another. As I have loved you, so you must love one another" (Jn 13:34). All others are part of the New Testament letters written to churches to encourage and offer instruction (see Rom 13:8; I Pet 1:22; 3:8; I Jn 3:11, 23; 4:7, 11-12; II Jn 1:5). If the apostles are addressing these problems, then surely they were struggling with them. The early churches were filled with real people—just like our churches—and real people aren't perfect. They make mistakes. They act selfishly. They fail one another. It happened thousands of years ago, and its still happening today. Yet we are called to fulfill these instructions as we live in community, and we can only do that if we are rooted in Christ and filled with his empowering Spirit.

We must rely on God to fulfill our core longings at the deepest level. And there's more required of us: we must also use our own gifts to help God fulfill other's core longings in a healthy and encouraging way. As we give our gifts of artistry, beauty, creativity, and worship to the world, in line with the clear direction and leading of the Holy Spirit, we are doing just that! God calls us to specific tasks as we serve others—he has uniquely designed each of us to fulfill his kingdom here on earth. Listening to the Father's voice, we give our gift unselfishly.[2] "But they aren't helping me with *my* core longings!" we whine. This is such an unfair dichotomy—a dichotomy that the enemy preys on and uses against us. And yet scripture is filled with dichotomy (the poor are rich, the last will be first, etc). We must live fully dependent on God but also be willing to be vessels as the hands and feet of Jesus.

As artists and creatives it is important to find community with other like-minded creative Christians. If your church or community does not have a group of gathering artists, perhaps you could start one? Don't be discouraged if it takes awhile to take root—creatives are difficult to gather. There are also places to connect online through social media. I am the member of several groups on Facebook and am deeply encouraged by the posts there.[3] Creative community can be elusive, but it's important to seek it out.

Wounded Healer

In his book *The Wounded Healer*, Henri Nouwen writes of our role as people who have experienced pain and suffering (wounded) called to minister to the hurt and broken of this world (healer). The "wounded healer" is best described by an old legend Nouwen found in the Talmud:

> The Messiah, the story tells us, is sitting among the poor, binding his wounds one at a time, waiting for the moment when he will be needed. So it is too with the [creative] minister. Since it is his task to make visible the first vestiges of liberation for others, he must bind his own wounds carefully in anticipation of the moment when he will be needed. He is called to be the wounded healer, the one who must look after his own wounds but at the same time be prepared to heal the wounds of others.[4]

The injustice in your life brings justice and freedom to others—that is the life-giving purpose of the wounded healer. Is this not the life that Christ modeled for us? Just as Jesus gave his life in sacrifice on our behalf, we give our lives as a sacrifice so others can find him through our stories of healing, our testimonies of restoration, our words of hope formed in the crucible of our souls.

Zechariah 8:23 says:

> *This is what the Lord Almighty says:*
> *"In those days ten people from all languages and nations*
> *will take firm hold of one Jew by the hem of his robe and say,*
> *'Let us go with you, because we have heard that God is with you.'"*

People from every tribe, tongue, and nation are called to firmly take hold of the hem of Jesus Christ in order to be renewed, redeemed, and restored. God is indeed with him! The power of God flows out of Christ as we reach for him, and in the midst of our grasping we are healed. He turns to us in that moment, and as we admit our need of him, he looks us straight in the eye and says:

> *Daughter! Son! Your faith has healed you. Go in peace.*

As we go in peace we find we can freely give our creative gift without hoarding or giving away too much of ourselves in the process. The amazing thing about being creative is that deeper fulfillment is often found in the offering and giving of your gift of artistry and beauty. God has instilled you with a treasure—a treasure that not only brings *you* great joy, but can also bring *others* great joy. You are given the awesome privilege of being a wounded healer through art, beauty, creativity, and worship. Grab hold of his hem, beloved! It is time to journey forth as wounded healers!

A Place and a Purpose

Do you remember our story of Motaki and the Sawtooth wolf pack from Chapter 4? Through nature's revelation, we discover more truth in this story: we all have a place and a purpose in whatever community you find yourself. As the Omega wolf, Motaki's role was one of peace-keeper and play-maker. Even though she was the lowest ranking wolf in the pack, she had an important purpose. Sadly, it seems it was difficult for her to see that purpose. As a loner she put herself in a dangerous position, and the mountain lion attacked and killed her. When we separate ourselves from our own pack, it leaves us vulnerable to the enemy's attack, as well. One powerful tactic of the enemy is to isolate us from community. When we are alone it's very difficult to fend off his assault.

Moreover, because we have a place and a purpose, others will feel loss in our absence. Even though it would seem she was an outcast in her pack, the wolf pack's actions all reveal her importance. When she went missing they went looking for her. They sought to avenge her against her attacker, wanting justice for her death. They returned in mourning as they grieved her loss. All signs of her significance to their community.

If you have left (or are considering leaving) your pack or fellowship abruptly without explanation, they will notice your absence, come looking, and grieve your "passing." You may think to yourself, "No one came looking so I must not be missed." Truth is, your pack did come looking for you: you just weren't aware of it. In this day and age, out of "courtesy" and not wanting to make you feel guilty for your decision, your pack knows you left and went searching for answers. No matter what answers they found, they are mourning the loss.

Don't ever think you can run away from a situation or difficulty and not be missed by your pack or fellowship. If you are considering running, do your pack the courtesy of telling them why, and allow them to address the situation if possible. If no resolution can be found, take a break. If it still cannot be resolved, do everything on your part to separate amicably and with peace. On the other hand, if someone has left your pack, go looking for answers and seek resolution. As much as you are able and it is within your power, seek justice on their behalf. Let them know they were important to your community.

Father Forgive Them

We learned in our previous chapter that an important aspect of celebrating Christ's victory in our healing process is forgiveness. Forgiveness is mandated by scripture; necessary to survive this journey; and connected to our freedom in Christ. Matthew 18 tells the story of the unmerciful servant who receives forgiveness but does not offer it. In these verses we are told to forgive as we've been forgiven, but it's not always that simple. It's hard to forgive those who've hurt us. However, if we don't, they hold power over us. When we forgive, their hold over our lives disappears, and we find freedom.

In the midst of his greatest pain and rejection, Jesus modeled forgiveness:

"Father, forgive them, for they do not know what they are doing." (Lk 23:34)

If he can do it from the cross, certainly we can too, from whatever cross we bear (Mt 16:24). Forgiveness is not forgetting what happened. Forgiveness is not necessarily allowing that person back into your life as if nothing happened or excusing the sin as if it doesn't matter to God. Forgiveness doesn't require you to speak to the person(s) or make them apologize. Forgiveness is never fair. It transcends justice and requires sacrifice. Forgiveness is giving up our right for revenge and blame. Forgiveness is giving up control to God so you can also give up the offender's hold over your life, and he can seek justice on your behalf. Forgiveness allows you to separate yourself from the person who's hurt you. It's not about changing the other person; *it's about changing you!*

Forgiveness is giving up the hope of another "better" past. We cannot change our past, nor can we put our hope there. The hope must be for the present and into the future—that any given day, any given moment, is a chance for God to reveal himself in not what could've been, but in *what could be!* God's word is filled with promises, and those promises are yours to claim. God is not a liar, and he will not go back on his word. This is the hope that anchors our souls. We are firm and secure in the redeeming, renewing, resurrecting power of Jesus Christ. He alone is our hope and salvation! He alone gives us strength for the journey and the power to forgive.

Setting the Stage for Jesus

As we move into this chapter's Bible Studies it is important to set the stage for our main character, Jesus. At this point in his life and ministry, after spending an entire night in prayer, Jesus chooses twelve disciples to journey with him. He then sets out with his new tribe, and here in Luke 6 he's come to a "level place" (plateau or plain) where a large crowd of people has gathered around him. Often referred to as the Sermon on the Plain, in Luke 6:18-19 we read what has attracted them:

[The people] had come to hear him and to be healed of their diseases.
Those troubled by evil spirits were cured, and the people all tried to touch him,
because power was coming from him and healing them all.

Truly a drama with a miraculous plot! People were simply reaching out to touch him, and they were healed!

    And isn't this exactly what we've been doing all along?

           Reaching out to Jesus?

    The Word Made Flesh is not only making his dwelling among us,

        but healing us,

           redeeming us,

                and restoring us.

Here in this passage, he takes authority over demons and disease. The Greek for power in the passage is *dynamis*. It has a divine and miraculous connotation. It also has a sense of this power residing within Jesus making him fully capable—he is able to heal because the power of God rests upon him as the Son of God. Power truly does come from him, and he heals us as we reach out to grasp his hem.

What strikes me even more is that out of this place of healing power, Christ looks out over his disciples and begins to teach. Seeing them, he recognizes their need, not just to be healed, but to live a life of health, wholeness, and well-being. He recognizes their need to have not just "right bodies" but "right minds and hearts." Verse 20a indicates that Jesus has turned to his disciples (not the crowd) to instruct them. Others may have overheard, but he's directing his counsel to those with whom he has a rabbinic (teaching and mentoring) relationship.

I believe that through these passages Jesus will teach *all of us* how to live a life of healing, especially within the context of community. These teachings are directly from the mouth of Jesus. If you are reading this in a red-letter edition Bible, everything we read in the following studies ahead is lit up in red. As his disciples, we should pay attention. We will do well to listen and heed his voice—it is wisdom for the journey.

Listen to: "Fill Me Up/Overflow" by Tasha Cobbs

Digging Deeper Into…

Luke 6:17-26: Blessings and Woes — Page 177
Luke 6:27-36: Love Your Enemies — Page 181
Luke 6:37-42: Judging Others — Page 184
Luke 6:43-45: Tree and its Fruit — Page 187
Luke 6:46-49: Wise and Foolish Builders — Page 191

Benediction of Wholeness — Page 194—195
Blessing for a Whole Heart by Jan Richardson

Next Steps: Resources for Your Healing Journey & Endnotes — Page 196

Coloring Page "Creator God" by Pauline Mae Blankenship — Page 197

Digging Deeper: Blessings and Woes

Read: Luke 6:17-26

My friend Chris returned from his first medical mission trip from Africa with amazing stories—stories that remind me of the "blessings" spelled out in the beginning of this passage. The people he witnessed experienced extreme poverty, hunger, disease, and pain, yet they worshiped with wholehearted jubilation. They raised their voices in praise, joined by simple instruments unifying them with an uplifting beat. They danced and celebrated the goodness of God together as one body. They truly were blessed despite their circumstances. Upon returning home, he noticed the stark contrast of our Western life and the way in which we worship. When we should be celebrating the blessings God has bestowed on us, we hold back, hold still, hold silence. It was deeply troubling to him.

"They have no hope but God, so they worship him with all they are," Chris noted. "We have everything, and yet we fail to worship him fully. It is so backwards."

I fear we are so self-absorbed in our "first-world problems" and ungrateful for the many blessings in our lives that truly the woes will come to us if we do not take notice of the poor and hungry, those who weep, and those who are hated and ridiculed for their faith in God.

In this passage, the blessings in verses 20-23 (also referred to as beatitudes) stand in stark contrast to the woes in verses 24-26, which mark a complete reversal in condition and position. They point out two extremes—two ways of living in this world: one leads to blessings and one to woes.

First, let's take a moment to re-read the blessings. Notice the heavenly blessings for those who experience injustice, inequality, and prejudice in this world:

Poor	Kingdom of God
Hungry	Satisfied
Weeping	Laughter
Hated	Leaping for Joy
Persecuted	Great Reward

For every situation of need, Jesus speaks out prophetically in a call for justice.

Notice in verse 22 how Jesus refers to himself as the Son of Man, identifying himself with humanity. While the power with which he healed revealed his divinity, now he refers to himself with a title of humility, identifying him with the people. Those who followed Jesus sacrificed a life of ease and comfort to follow him, and many would have been ostracized for their choice.[5] So too, as we stand for Christ in this world, we will face persecution. We will be told that our views are narrow-minded, judgmental, and wrong. In some cases, some of our brothers and sisters in Jesus face great persecution and death for our beliefs. We are called not only to pray, but to speak out against the injustice and brutality they endure. We stand together with them, Jesus at our side.

Now let's examine the woes. Woes act in several different ways in scripture—sometimes as a kind of curse and at others times a kind of sorrowful pity. They always act as an admonition to those who will forsake their warning. Notice the affliction that comes to the greedy, prideful, and popular of this world:

Rich	No more comfort coming
Well-fed	Hunger
Laughing	Mourning and weeping
Spoken well-of	Fate of false prophets

In this case they have already received any reward of comfort here on earth and will receive no further reward in heaven. God will act justly, and they will reap the harvest they've sown as they followed the ruler of this world. While they have enjoyed a sense of well-being on this earth, their pride will be their fall. No amount of self-assurance or wealth will help them when they face judgment before God. God sends rain on the just and unjust of this world, but in heaven all will be set straight before him.

My initial gut reaction as I read the beginning of this passage is great joy and bright hope, yet as I get to the end, I feel like I need to get it together. However, this isn't a passage about works or one to make us feel guilty about not having done enough. It is a call to two things as we journey in community and in this world. First, it is a call to understand that great blessings come to those who suffer; that God will right all wrongs; that God is a God of justice; and that he will reward those who seek after him even in direst circumstances. Second, it is a call to respond to the needs of others; to stand up for injustice in this world; to give out of excess; to fight complacency in the our great abundance; and to not be lured in by worldly standards that reward the greedy and prideful.

God's intended kingdom on earth is turned upside-down as the ruler of this world (satan) brings his evil injustice to bear in this age. But the kingdom of Christ is right-sided when we walk his path in this world, aware of the broken and in need. Don't rely on your government to do this—this is what *we must do* as the body of Christ, this is what *we must do* as individuals called to serve those that face injustice, scarcity, prejudice, and mistreatment of any kind. A time is indeed coming when satan will be bound and all will be set straight. In the meantime, it is up to us to act justly, love mercy, and walk humbly with God (Mic 6:8).

Bible scholar Darrell Bock reveals how the blessing and woes serve an important function in this sermon to his disciples. The teachings of Jesus following the blessings and woes are hard to swallow if we have no faith God will set all things right in his time. He states: "The premise of the sacrificial spiritual life is the promise of God's faithful justice."[6] We must be assured God will care for those in need in order to live a life where things often seem upside-down. Matters are not fair in this world. Yet we cannot act, live, or walk as others do. We are set apart as subjects of a heavenly kingdom who follow a ruler who sets things right-side-up when we function in line with his will and ways. How can we as artists, creatives, worshipers, and revealers of beauty turn this upside-down world around through the things we do? Let me offer two examples.

I recently saw a video of a girl missing the lower part of her leg. Her mother and sister sit back as they bestow on her a very special gift—an American Girl Doll™ fitted with a prosthetic leg just like this young girl. She clings to this doll and weeps aloud as she realizes the beautiful meaning of this precious gift.

"It's got a leg like me!" she cries.

The company that did this was A Step Ahead Prosthetics, and they do this *free-of-charge*! Their company website states: "We feel that it is absolutely crucial to boost the self-confidence, self-esteem, and feelings of inclusion for little girls with limb loss, and that something as small as a doll that resembles them can have a profound effect on their mental and physical well-being."[7] I am so grateful for the person(s) who developed this creative solution. Through their ingenuity, they have righted a small piece of injustice in this world. Does it change the world? No, but it changes a little girl's world, and that's all that matters. The same is true of us: we may not be able to change the world, but we can change one person's world.

My artist friend, Elva Robinson[8], was recently in the process of generously giving away numerous pieces of artwork. She was creating new artwork, and her studio had become crowded. So, she began to give away her art through Facebook. I was blessed to receive a piece called "Overwhelmed." I was indeed overwhelmed by God's generosity to me demonstrated through this artist. Every day I see her artwork on my wall, I am reminded of his overwhelming generosity in my life. All because an artist listened to the voice of the Holy Spirit and began to give away her artwork. Now, she could've ignored that quiet voice, decided to give in to uncertainty and greed, and hoarded her artwork. Instead, as an act of worship and obedience, she gave it away. I know God will bless her for surrendering these treasures from her heart.

Through our artistry, beauty, creativity, and worship we can make a difference, even if it is in a small way. That is the role of the wounded healer. As we share our creative gift with others, we give hope, we uncover potential, we act against injustice, we speak to righteousness and goodness, and we reveal God's love. We bring blessing to those in need.

And if not us, then who?

Take a moment to consider:
How can you be a blessing to the people around you?
How can you bring blessings to a world already overflowing with woes?
What does it look like to act justly, love mercy, and walk humbly with God?

(continued next page)

Using the questions and scripture passage as your prompts as you begin to explore through creativity, won't you join me in this prayer?

Invite the Holy Spirit into this moment.
Ask the Lord Your Shepherd (Yahweh Rohi) to guide you as you pray.
Ask the Lord Who Sanctifies (Yahweh M'Kaddesh) to purify your imagination and help you picture, sense, or create a place of protection and provision around you.
Ask the Great I Am (Ehyeh) to remind you that he is indeed right there with you.
Ask the Lord Your Healer (Yahweh Rophe) to lead you as his wounded healer.
Ask the Lord Your Victory Banner (Jehovah Nissi) to help you reveal his glory and love to a world in need of his blessing!

Lord of the helpless, poor, hungry, needy, mistreated, and persecuted, I call out to you for blessing for those in need of your love, grace, and mercy. I cry out for justice Lord—for others and for me. Help me to embrace the blessings of this passage where I am left feeling poor, hungry, grieved, and persecuted, and then out of that blessing help me act justly, love mercy, and walk humbly with you, God. In my journey, I want to be a vessel of your love, a tower of your protection, a giver of your goodness, a revealer of your beauty. Help me to give out of the abundant blessings in my life to those in need. Help me to speak up on behalf of those who voices have been silenced. Help me, Lord, to direct money, time, energy, and resources to the avenues of your grace where you would have me help. Direct my paths so that I might give my creative gift to the exact person or audience you have in mind. If there is a specific way you would have me help, Lord, reveal it, and convict my heart to action.

In the Name of God the Just I pray, Amen.

Listen to: "Micah 6:8" by Northland Church
"You Said" by Shane & Shane

Digging Deeper: Love Your Enemies

Read: Luke 6:27-36 & Matthew 5:38-48

This passage calls us to actions that are so counter to our own feelings, our need for self-protection, and society's rules for survival.

Love your enemy.
Do good to those who hate you.
Bless those who curse you.
Pray for those who mistreat you.
Turn the other cheek.
Give to those who steal from you.
Do not seek restitution.
Do to others as you would have them do to you.
Be merciful, just as your Father is merciful.

This is certainly a difficult teaching to live out in this dog-eat-dog world! I dare say it scarcely makes sense. Yet again Jesus is calling us to journey with him in this upside-down world with his right-side-up kingdom ways.

Marietta is a play by Stephen O'Toole performed by Forgiveness 360, a project of Spirit in the House, a non-profit organization exploring spiritual diversity through the arts.[9] Based on the true story of Marietta Jaeger, it explores both the difficulty and possibility of forgiving the unforgivable. Marietta, who forgave her daughter's kidnapper and murderer before she even knew if her daughter was dead or alive, claims, "Forgiveness is not for wimps."[10] Marietta understood that unforgiveness would hold her captive. She readily admits at first she wanted to kill him in revenge, but she soon realized that she was becoming the very man who abducted her child. Not wanting to be another "victim" of his crime, it took daily commitment to prayer and reaching out to the One who forgave her first. She knew she needed to travel this road with Jesus by her side.

When her daughter's kidnapper called on the anniversary of the abduction, Marietta had already done the hard soul-work of forgiveness and was able to ask how he was doing. He was stunned. He called back several times to try and shake her. She was unshakeable. Praise God! She told him she was praying for him. He was eventually moved to confess, and Marietta was finally able to lay her daughter to rest.

This is a remarkable story! A story of forgiveness in the deepest sense and a story of God's inevitable justice and reconciliation only available through the healing power of Jesus Christ. In today's passage, Jesus is not saying to let people walk all over you: he is instructing us to extend grace and mercy. Marietta is doing just that, and in doing so God begins to right the wrong.

Bible scholar Robert Tannehill proposes a view of this passage that requires creativity on our part:

> Jesus' teaching uses forceful and imaginative language, which is to be clearly distinguished from legal language. Legal language must try to provide clear definitions in order to regulate external behaviors. Forceful and imaginative language is not concerned with clear definitions…[but] serves to stimulate moral insight by challenging the ruts in which people move. Such language succeeds when it stimulates the moral imagination to imagine the possibility that breaks out of these

ruts. It can change action by working through the imagination, challenging old assumptions, and suggesting a new possibility while trusting the hearer to work out the details. Luke 6:27-36 is a carefully crafted attempt to awaken the imagination so that radically new ways of relating to enemies will result.[11]

Jesus stimulating our imaginations! As a creative, that should cause us pause! Think on this a moment:

*How can we use our creative minds
to imagine new ways to walk in forgiveness
and to let go of those who seek to harm us?*

Read Jesus' expectations of us again. This list of ideals is hard enough with the people in our own faith communities, but he calls us to do this for our enemies! However, when we act in obedience and do this, we break the chains of injustice by stopping satan in his tracks. Forgiveness is not about lying down and allowing our enemies to walk all over us. It is about taking control back from the enemy. When Marietta chose to ask her daughter's killer how he was doing, she stopped him in his tracks. He tried again and again to rattle her, but she refused to walk into his trap. She stood immovable in the power of the presence of Jesus. Only Christ could help her do what she did.

And if he can help Marietta, he can help you too.

Today you will continue to forgive as you create. As you forgive, see yourself letting go of the person who offended you (also realize sometimes we need to forgive God, as illustrated in the opening testimony of this chapter). As you forgive, form a simple prayer of blessing for them. It is an important step to form a simple blessing for the person who's wronged you. Luke 6:28 instructs us to bless those that curse us and to pray for those who mistreat us. I realize it's hard enough to forgive them, let alone bless them, but scripture mandates this. This blessing helps you release their power over you. It is a vital step to heal your spirit. Romans 12:14 reminds us:

Bless those who persecute you; bless and do not curse.

Only by your power, dear Lord!

(continued next page)

Using the instructions and scriptures as your prompts as you begin to explore through creativity, won't you join me in this prayer?

Invite the Holy Spirit into this moment.
Ask the Lord Your Shepherd (Yahweh Rohi) to guide you as you pray.
Ask the Lord Who Sanctifies (Yahweh M'Kaddesh) to purify your imagination and help you picture, sense, or create a place of protection and provision around you.
Ask the God of Vengeance (Jehovah Gmolah) to set right all the wrong done against you.
Ask the Lord Your Healer (Yahweh Rophe) to lead you into deeper and greater healing.
Ask the Lord Your Victory Banner (Jehovah Nissi) to give you victory over hate as you choose to love others with the love of God.

Lord Jesus, you alone can help me in this difficult step in my healing journey. I know I cannot do this without your help, without your great love for me. Those who have harmed me do not deserve this gift of forgiveness, yet you call me to forgive them as I have been forgiven. So I obey simply because I long for nothing to stand in my way of complete healing. In the midst of forgiving, I realize that it's indeed truly a gift to my own self. I pray to forgive those who have hurt me. I forgive _____ for their sins against me, and I pray a blessing of _____ over them. Lord, where I am unwilling to forgive and bless, make me willing. As I forgive and bless, I let go. I release their hold over my life, now and forever. Thank you for your strength in this. I cannot do it apart from you.

In the strong name of Jesus of Nazareth, Amen.

Listen to: "Losing" by Tenth Avenue North
Watch on YouTube: "Forbearance" from Ad Deum Dance, Project Dance Houston
(Choreographed by Caleb Mitchell)

Digging Deeper: Judging Others

Read: Luke 6:37-42

Author and poet Kathleen Norris tells a wonderful story of a troupe of dancers who came to her town to give their creative gift in a wide variety of ways, breaking down barriers and changing misunderstandings of stereotypes, race, and the artistic spirit. As their visit neared its end, they fellowshipped together over several meals. After their final meal, feet became the subject of discussion, and in a show of unlikely camaraderie and transparency, those gathered together began to bare their feet—propping them up right there on the tabletop upon which they had just feasted.

Now to have a full appreciation of this story, you must understand dancers' feet—they are an absolute and utter mess! Corns, calluses, deformities, and blisters all tell the story of what they've been through, how hard they strive, and what they're willing to endure for the sake of giving their gift of beauty to the world. And yet here they are, bringing their feet out "above board" for all to see. In baring their feet—their broken and battered feet—they are symbolically baring their souls. Kathleen states, "As we talked I realized that we had, by this odd gesture, stumbled into community."[12]

Isn't that the way it is? We stumble into community as we bare our souls—the broken and battered parts of our souls we'd rather keep under the table, hidden away from everyone's view. But these are the very places that reveal where we've been on our journeys, how hard we've struggled, and the perseverance and determination it took to give the gift we bring to the world. In the baring of these delicate places, we find community.

Now, truth be told, I have more than once bared my soul only to have been judged, criticized, or ignored. That is always the risk we take when we expose ourselves to others. And despite the nicks to my soul, I give again—perhaps more wisely measured or, in opposition, with greater abandon. Over the years, I have learned to give from a place where my identity is rooted squarely in Christ, and my mission comes from a place of surrender and obedience. As we look to Jesus, and Jesus alone, we find the world's chastisement means very little to us. We must listen to the one who calls us to give our dance of beauty, no matter the outcome. My feet might get bruised in the dancing, but I refuse to stop.

We live in a time when judgment is freely exercised and given without merit or sound judgment. A quick look on social media illustrates my point. Share an opinion that is different than typical pervasive thought, and you will be judged. New York Times columnist David Brooks writes about a new culture of shame in America, where the moral relativism of the late 20th century has been replaced with moral judgment. Citing an article based on studies of anthropologist Ruth Benedict where the previous "guilt culture" has been replaced with a new "shame culture," Brook states:

> In a guilt culture you know you are good or bad by what your conscience feels. In a shame culture you know you are good or bad by what your community says about you, by whether it honors or excludes you. In a guilt culture people sometimes feel they do bad things; in a shame culture social exclusion makes people feel they are bad.[13]

Whereas in cultures and eras where shame was based on whether you were an honorable citizen, this new shame culture seeks "to be attention-grabbing and aggressively unique on some media platform."[14] Seek to stand against the current flow popularized on social and news media, and you will be ostracized. As a prophetic voice, I have often faced this public outcry from the "in-crowd" that attempts to shame me back into line.

Given this premise, this passage in Luke 6 might be even harder to live by than we anticipate. In a culture built on judgment, we must be willing to stand against the social engineering of modern media and seek God's mind on matters. We must also be those that lead the way in *not* judging others—criticizing their beliefs or opinions. We must follow the teachings of our Rabbi Jesus before we form our opinions (6:39-40) and examine our own thoughts—find our own plank—before we examine the speck in the eye of another (41-42). This is a difficult task given the world in which we live, but it is indeed the task to which we are called in our journey on earth.

And yet, if we dare take this journey, there is great reward:

Give, and you will receive.
Your gift will return to you in full—pressed down,
shaken together to make room for more, running over, and poured into your lap.
The amount you give will determine the amount you get back. Lk 6:38

If our culture is indeed attention-grabbing and aggressively striving to be unique as Brooks proposes, then we must strive in the opposite direction. Not necessarily of the current opinion, for it may have truth to it, but against the attention-seeking aggressiveness that characterizes this culture of shame. We must seek to flow in the opposite direction of judgment and condemnation as this passage commands. We must forgive, even when others seem to be getting it wrong, and seek unity among our fellow brothers and sisters in Christ, offering grace in matters of societal norms and issues.

We must be willing, within the context of community, to prop our feet upon the table of fellowship. To be brave enough to show our blisters and calluses to one another. To be merciful and kind as we figure out how to journey through this thing called life on planet Earth. To examine our ways and remove our own planks, and then to work gently and patiently with others as we help them with their tiny specks. Can you imagine the creative "dance" that would pour forth? A dance that returns in fullness, pressed down and shaken together to make room for more! As we hand out peace, grace, mercy, and loving-kindness, we dance upon the bonds of injustice! In the dancing, we will get all these things and more in abundant return. Those are the promises of God's word!

In the words of the prophet Isaiah (52:7):

How beautiful are the feet of those who bring Good News!

How BEaUtiful, trUly BEaUtiful, indeed!

(continued next page)

Using the challenge presented and scripture passages as your prompts as you begin to explore through creativity, won't you join me in this prayer?

Invite the Holy Spirit into this moment.
Ask the Lord Your Shepherd (Yahweh Rohi) to guide you as you pray.
Ask the Lord Who Sanctifies (Yahweh M'Kaddesh) to purify your imagination and help you picture, sense, or create a place of protection and provision around you.
Ask the God of Vengeance (Jehovah Gmolah) to set right all the wrong done against you.
Ask the Lord Your Healer (Yahweh Rophe) to lead you into deeper and greater healing.
Ask the Lord Your Victory Banner (Jehovah Nissi) to help you shout the good news of Jesus to all who will listen!

Lord, Rabbi, Teacher, and Friend, I long to bring the Good News of the Gospel of Jesus Christ to a world so desperately in need of you. In a world of judgment and shame, give me strength, wisdom, insight, and courage so that I may not give verdict on a case I do not have authority to decide. Help me to speak up on behalf of justice in a way that brings acceptance of others opinions and not condemnation of them. Help me dance upon injustice. This is a difficult task, Lord. I need your help. Holy Spirit, convict my spirit when I am going for the speck in my brother or sister's eye. Help me look in the mirror at my own plank. Examine my ways. Let there be found no iniquity in me. You are the Friend to Sinners—let me follow in the steps of your beautiful feet. I want to dance with you.

In the Name of He Who Brings Good News, Amen.

Listen to: "Jesus, Friend of Sinners" by Casting Crowns
"With Every Act of Love" by Jason Gray

Digging Deeper: Tree and Its Fruit

Read: Luke 6:43-45

This passage reveals guidelines for two areas of our lives: how we act with others and how we act with others. Yes, you read that right. And no, it's not a typo. One is about *others* and one is about *you.*

Let's start with others, and as we do let's read the first part of verse 45 in the New Living Translation:

A good person produces good things from the treasury of a good heart,
and an evil person produces evil things from the treasury of an evil heart.

As we apply this to our interactions with others, it lends discernment and wisdom to how we respond to them and journey with them. Now we realize from our interactions that some people are trustworthy and kind and others are not. This is fruit. A "tree" that bears the "fruit" of love, joy, peace, forbearance, kindness, goodness, faithfulness, gentleness, and self-control (Gal 5:22-23) symbolizes one who walks with the Holy Spirit. They are trustworthy, and from a heart of God's love, grace, and mercy they speak love, grace, and mercy to all they meet. Their words disclose what's in their heart. However, a "tree" that bears the "fruit" of envy, strife, condemnation, lust, pride, wrath, anger, and offense demonstrates one who has allowed their roots to grow down into enemy soil.

Dr. Henry Cloud and Dr. John Townsend have written several books on boundaries. Boundaries tell us where one thing ends and another begins. Physical, mental, emotional, and spiritual boundaries are necessary to live healthy lives in an otherwise unhealthy world. These boundaries help us know when to say yes (who/how/when to trust others), as well as how to say no to those who would overstep healthy limitations in order to harm us or demand something from us to which they have no right. I consider this a must-read, especially if you come from a family of high dysfunction.

This concept of boundaries informs how we interact with others whose fruit reveals a tree that is wrongly rooted. When someone displays negativity, anger, and offense, they are what we might call "toxic"—being around them brings us down. We walk away feeling worse. They make us feel bad about ourselves or others. These are people with whom we should set physical, emotional, mental, and spiritual boundaries. As we interact with them, we must be Light to their darkness, but we cannot allow their darkness to overwhelm and devour us. In dealing with people of bad fruit, we must exercise caution, wisdom, and discernment. We must also practice grace, mercy, and forgiveness. When you leave an interaction with them you may need to "shake the dust off your feet" as you walk away (Mt 10:14, Mk 6:11).

Now I realize this is much easier said than done. I don't know about you, but I have a tendency to replay disappointing encounters in my head over and over trying to think of what I should've said or how I should've acted. This is a bad habit that leaves me feeling bad about myself and gives room for the enemy to add his "fertilizer" of strife, anger, and offense. If I tend to this too long, my roots can start to grow down into bitterness and hatred, and the fruit of my life will not be edible. When the Bible says to take every thought captive, these are the very thoughts I must confine. Over and over I have to instead replay the words of truth Jesus has spoken over my life. I must get in the presence of his safety, under the shelter of his wings, in order to keep myself from dwelling on the negative. I speak from experience when I say this is difficult, but doable with Jesus!

Consider for a moment—you have to *take* or *pick up* an offense. People around us can range from being simply dense, dim-witted, and unaware of the havoc they wreak upon our lives, to very offensive, aggressive, and downright abusive. However, no matter what they say or how they act, we *choose to take or pick up the offense.* It might be handed to us or dropped at our feet, but we don't have to take it or pick it up. *It is always a choice.* We live in an age and society where taking offense is just what we do—like a nasty habit it's become our *modus operandi* of functioning in this world. The media enforces this in many destructive ways. Children of the Living God, it is time to stop this nasty habit! Believe me: I am just as susceptible as the next person to this ploy of the enemy. Yet God in his infinite patience is working on my heart, helping me catch my automatic response of taking offense. We must stop this behavior, brethren—it's not Biblical. Turn off the social media and the news if you need to for a time of fasting from this behavior. Allow yourself to return with eyes wide open, heart keenly aware, and mind in line with God's ways.

It boils down to this: would you eat rotten fruit? No! Then why do we eat the rotten fruit handed to us by the enemy through the mouths of unhealthy people around us? We need to stop taking rotten fruit from people and encourage those around us to do the same. We must be strong in the Lord and in the strength of his mighty power (Eph 6:10). This is a devious tactic of the enemy, we cannot fall prey to it. By Jesus' strength alone are we able to spot and counter this attack!

Secondly, this guideline is also for us. So let's read the second part of verse 45 in the New Living Translation:

What you say flows from what is in your heart.

My friend Matt Durbin[15] painted during our worship services at church while he was a college student at our local university. The painting from one particular service hangs in my friend's home. The sermon that morning was from John 15 about the vine and the branches. This passage tells us to remain in Christ because apart from him you can bear no fruit. The tangled roots in this painting work their way down into Jesus and the branches of the vine reach heavenward, sprouting green leaves and the words of the fruit of the Spirit from Galatians 5. The painting beautifully illustrates a life deeply rooted in Christ, one that abides in him and allows him to prune away the dead branches. It also exemplifies the fruit on display in the lives of those who abide in Jesus.

We too must abide in Christ so that the fruit in our life attracts others to come see the tree of life that is our source. We must display the fruit of the Spirit in our lives! Just as other's words reveal what is in their hearts, *your words disclose what's in your heart.* Pay attention to the words coming out of your mouth. *Are they filled with love, grace, mercy, and forgiveness? Or fruit of envy, bitterness, greed, and condemnation?* The Bible gives much instruction related to the tongue—indeed it has the power of life or death (Pr 18:21)!

Consider how these words from Colossians 1:9-12 inform the lives of those rooted in God's wisdom and will:

We continually ask God to fill you with the knowledge of his will through all the wisdom and understanding that the Spirit gives, so that you may live a life worthy of the Lord and please him in every way: bearing fruit in every good work, growing in the knowledge of God, being strengthened with all power according to his glorious might so that you may have great endurance and patience, and giving joyful thanks to the Father, who has qualified you to share in the inheritance of his holy people in the kingdom of light.

Paul and Timothy were praying this powerful prayer over fellow believers in Colossae. They longed for their brethren to seek wisdom and understanding through the Holy Spirit so they could bear fruit, grow in knowledge, be strengthened to persevere, and to give joyful thanks. This is what we are to aspire to as God's holy people! Perhaps you can find an intercessor to pray this over you and your life?

Where in your life have you let the enemy get the better of you? In what areas of your life do you feel the Spirit convicting you to change your attitude or behavior? Of what might you need to repent to come not just into alignment, but also into abiding with the Holy Spirit's healing presence in your life? Go back to the 6 R's of Repentance in Chapter 3 and repent where you have failed. Ask the Lord to prune away the branches that are bearing bad fruit and fill you with his empowering Spirit in order to bear the fruit that ushers others into the kingdom of God. Isaiah 37:31 says:

*Once more a remnant of the kingdom of Judah
will take root below and bear fruit above.*

Won't you join me as his remnant? A remnant of artists, creatives, and worshipers that take root into Jesus Christ so that we can bear fruit for all to see and taste? Oh, that the world would taste and see that the Lord is indeed good (Ps 34:8), and may we be the trees that display your splendor (Isa 61:3), oh Lord!

(continued next page)

Using the questions and scripture passages as your prompts as you begin to explore through creativity, won't you join me in this prayer?

Invite the Holy Spirit into this moment.
Ask the Lord Your Shepherd (Yahweh Rohi) to guide you as you pray.
Ask the Lord Who Sanctifies (Yahweh M'Kaddesh) to purify your imagination and help you picture, sense or create a place of protection and provision around you.
Ask the Lord Your Healer (Yahweh Rophe) to join you in that place and lead you into deeper and greater healing.

Gentle Gardener, prune away all that is dead and destructive in my life. Clear away the old to make way for the new. Call forth your remnant of the Root of Jesse! I root myself down deeply into you, and I unearth you through the fruit of love, joy, peace, patience, kindness, goodness, faithfulness, gentleness, and self-control. Let the words of my mouth reveal your grace, love, mercy, and truth. I want to be a part of the army of artists, creatives, worshipers, and revealers of beauty that you are calling forth to bring and display your glorious kingdom here on earth as it is in heaven. May the words of my mouth and the meditation of my heart be pleasing in your sight, LORD, my Rock and my Redeemer.
In the Name of God the Father, Christ His Son, and the Holy Spirit, Amen.

Listen to: "I Love Your Presence" (Extended Version) By Bethel Live
"Keep Your Eyes Open" by NeedToBreathe

Digging Deeper: Wise and Foolish Builders

Read: Luke 6:46-49

Wrapping up his sermon on the plain, Jesus ends with a parable. If you recall, Jesus was addressing his disciples, but many others had gathered around him and were listening in to these counter-culture teachings. And after this right-sided kingdom instruction, we have arrived at the crux of the issue at hand. In the words of Bible Scholar Robert Tannehill, "Now the crucial question is whether they will not only come and hear but also act."[16] And this is what Jesus asks:

> *"Why do you call me, 'Lord, Lord,' and do not do what I say?"*

A question that cuts to the heart.

Imagine *you* were there on that plain, a plateau on a mountain somewhere in Ancient Israel. You have heard of this teacher, a teacher with the power of God flowing out of him in such a way that the sick and demon-possessed are being healed in his very presence. Many have gathered. You strain your neck to hear the teachings that go against all you have experienced in this world. And yet, the kingdom life he describes is one you desire. This abundant life is calling out to you through his words. In the silence of your heart you call out to him, "Lord."

Then he looks around and asks this question. It is a critical question. Perhaps he even looks *you* in the eye as he asks:

> *"You! The one who just whispered 'Lord'—are you really ready for me to be Lord? If I am your Lord, then you will obey. As hard as all of this is, will you do it? Because deep down your heart knows it will never be satisfied apart from me. You call me teacher and Lord for that is who I am. I do not promise an easy life, but I promise you an abundant life in my presence. Won't you do as I say? I know your heart teeters at the edge.*
> *Beloved, can I tell you a story?"*

Stories are remarkable ways to touch another person's heart. Have you ever heard one that drew you in completely or was so good you couldn't put it down? That's the power of story—and Jesus uses it often.

In his story Jesus tells of two men—builders, in fact. One man hears and obeys. He does the hard work, the heart-work, of putting all this into practice. He builds his life—the way he interacts with others, responds to others, and journeys in faith—on the Solid Rock of God's instruction. He lets the Master Architect direct him to a sure foundation before he builds, and he drills down deep into the bedrock below. But there's another man who hears the good instruction from the Master Architect but chooses to do it his own way. With no foundation he constructs a life on shifting sands. When the rivers rise, as they most surely do, only one house can withstand the torrents of life. The man who built on the Solid Rock stands firm. The man who built with no foundation is washed away.

As a listener of this story I'm sure you would agree that the first builder got it right, and the second got it wrong. But listening and agreeing with the story is not the same as taking action based on that story. It is easy to read these passages and agree with them, but it is much harder to put them into practice.

Chip and Joanna Gaines are the popular stars of HGTV's *Fixer Upper*. Their faith is evident in all they do: so is their creativity. According to their website, "[Joanna's] specialty is making old things new and seeing the potential in every project—no matter how hopeless it may seem in the beginning."[17] A fitting description for a woman of faith using creativity to rebuild, restore, and renew. Sounds like Jesus to me! And in both flipping houses and redeeming lives, we know it's not simply about making things pretty on the outside, but about stripping things back to the barebones so you can get things right on the inside. It's only when we strip everything away that we see the foundation and are able to secure the weak places in need of repair.

Take a moment to read Philippians 2:1-18. The words in verses 6-11 are believed to be an ancient hymn of the Risen Christ. This song is encased in teachings that echo the precepts taught in Luke 6. Are these high ideals we journey by? Yes indeed! But here, encased in these teachings, Jesus himself sets the most beautiful and poignant example. Christ was God incarnate. And yet he let go of that. He became like us, and then he emptied himself for us. And in the emptying, he was filled.

So how will you respond to his question?

"Why do you call me, 'Lord, Lord,' and do not do what I say?"

When he looks you in the eye and asks, how will you answer? After hearing his story of the two builders, how will you respond then? Is his story convincing enough? Or do you look at the *whole* story? The story that also includes a sinless man beaten within an inch of his life. The story that includes that same man dying on a cross for the sins of all humankind? The story that includes that man rising again from the dead and rolling away a stone that took several strong soldiers to move.

Will that story be enough to convince you?

In the emptying of himself, he was filled. And the same is true of each of us. As we empty ourselves and walk in the steps of Jesus we come to look more and more like him. We are filled in his presence. Do we still have things to work on? Of course, but we are *working out* what God is *working in* (Phlp 2:12-13). We trust him to work all things together for good for those who love him and are called according to his purposes in our lives (Rom 8:28). We trust the Master Architect as we build our house upon the Rock of Ages, our sure foundation.

(continued next page)

Using the questions and scripture passages as your prompts as you begin to explore through creativity, won't you join me in this prayer?

Invite the Holy Spirit into this moment.
Ask the Lord Your Shepherd (Yahweh Rohi) to guide you as you pray.
Ask the Lord Who Sanctifies (Yahweh M'Kaddesh) to purify your imagination and help you picture, sense or create a place of protection and provision around you.
Ask the Lord Your Healer (Yahweh Rophe) to join you in that place and lead you into deeper and greater healing.

Master Architect, I want to follow your plan for my life. I hear your stories, and I am drawn into the Greatest Plan that I could ever know or imagine. Sometimes I don't understand why things happen as they do. I struggle to live in this upside-down world with right-side-up kingdom thinking. But I desire to live abundantly despite my struggle. I long to know you in the deepest places of my being. I want to build my house upon the Rock of Your Salvation. I want my foundation to go deep into the bedrock of your love for me. I trust your plan for my life—even when I don't understand. Empty me so I can be filled again to overflowing.
In the Name of Jesus Christ, My Firm Foundation I pray, Amen.

Watch: "It's Gotta Stop Somewhere" by Jon Jorgenson Spoken Word
Listen to: "My Hope is Built on Nothing Less (On Christ the
Solid Rock I Stand)" by your favorite artist
"You Are" by Colton Dixon

🙦 A Benediction of Wholeness 🙤

Blessing for a Whole Heart
By Jan Richardson

You think
if you could just
imagine it,
that would be a beginning;
that if you could envision
what it would look like,
that would be a step
toward a heart
made whole.

This blessing
is for when
you cannot imagine.
This is for when
it is difficult to dream
of what could lie beyond
the fracture, the rupture,
the cleaving through which
has come a life
you do not recognize
as your own.

When all that inhabits you
feels foreign,
your heart made strange
and beating a broken
and unfamiliar cadence,
let there come
a word of solace,
a voice that speaks
into the shattering,

reminding you
that who you are
is here,
every shard
somehow holding
the whole of you
that you cannot see
but is taking shape
even now,
piece joining to piece
in an ancient,
remembered rhythm

that bears you
not toward restoration,
not toward return—
as if you could somehow
become unchanged—
but steadily deeper
into the heart of the one
who has already dreamed you
complete.

See the beautiful artwork accompanying this blessing from Jan Richardson at: www.paintedprayerbook.com/2015/01/25/epiphany-4-blessing-for-a-whole-heart.

Jan carries a small playing-card-sized piece of artwork in her purse from her friend Priscilla. It is a collage with the word "Wholehearted" printed across it. This gift from a friend has served as a poignant reminder to Jan along her healing journey. It also serves as a reminder to us as we use our artwork in such a way that we are the hands and feet of Christ in a world where the fractured and shattered all around us desperately need a blessing of wholeheartedness.

Next Steps: Resources for Your Healing Journey

The Wounded Healer by Henri Nouwen

Boundaries: When to Say Yes, How to Say No by Dr. Henry Cloud & Dr. John Townsend

Crossroads by Wm. Paul Young

I Do Hard Things by Havilah Cunnington. Four-part video/audio series with accompanying workbook. At www.havilahcunnington.com.

Endnotes

1. Terry Wardle writes extensively on core longings in *Wounded*. See pp. 63-72.
2. I write extensively on giving our creative gift in my first book *God's Creative Gift—Unleashing the Artist in You*. Visit www.jodythomae.com to learn more.
3. Visit www.jodythomae.com and search "Facebook Friday" for ideas of groups related to your individual area of creativity.
4. Nouwen, *Wounded Healer*, 82.
5. Bock, *Luke*, 121.
6. Ibid.
7. www.weareastepahead.com. Look for "Doll Prosthetics" under the "Community" tab.
8. You can find Elva Robinson's artwork at www.robinsongart.com
9. Seal, "Forgiveness 360," 31-38. You can read more about Marietta's story at www.journeyofhope.org.
10. Ibid., 33.
11. Tannehill, *Luke*, 117.
12. Norris, *Dakota*, 111-112.
13. Brooks, "The Shame Culture," paragraph 6. Accessed September 15, 2016 at: www.nytimes.com/2016/03/15/opinion/the-shame-culture.html
14. Ibid., paragraph 13.
15. Matt Durbin's art can be found at www.mattdurbinart.com.
16. Tannehill, 122.
17. From www.magnoliamarket.com/about. Accessed October 17, 2016.

7

Adventuring

*"The One who breaks open the way will go up before them;
they will break through the gate and go out."*

CinDay Academy in Southwest Ohio is one of the most creative school environments I've encountered. Based on principles that emphasize creativity, complexity, curiosity, and collaboration, faculty and administration believe that every child can succeed given the right environment and teachers. Serving children from preschool through high school, CinDay Academy's mission is to give every child his or her deserved chance to learn, in whatever way he or she needs to learn, because every child is unique and every child matters. Any given topic is studied across multiple disciplines and mediums, including art, drama, music, and physical activity. Children learning about the Gettysburg Address will not only study it in history class, but also in English, drama, and art. Classrooms are innovative and a vast improvement on the row upon row of desks in the typical, crowded American classroom. Butterfly bushes and vegetable gardens adorn the campus where minds and imaginations are given flight and room to grow.

Interestingly, this remarkable learning experience is the result of the negative childhood experiences of founder and principal Gina Pangalangan. Hiding from the noticing glances of her teachers and developing complex coping mechanisms that helped her fly under the radar, Gina struggled through most of her education.

"I always felt like I was hiding or in prison. I felt like a lost child—neglected, invisible. I was dumb. Never good enough. I knew the answers but only got credit for writing them down. There was no credit for knowing and saying," shares Gina. "I often heard, 'If only you could only learn to read, you'd be smart.' So for me, reading equaled intelligence, and since I struggled to read, I was unintelligent."

"And shame. I felt shame."

It wasn't until much later that she realized she had dyslexia, a learning disability that made it difficult for her to succeed in traditional American classrooms. Despite being mocked by her guidance counselor (yes, her *guidance counselor*) for wanting to go to college, she succeeded in being accepted and sought a degree in education. It was at that time, and through the love and patience of some amazing tutors throughout her life, that a dream was planted within her of an educational experience that fosters a love of learning and acceptance of strengths *and* weaknesses.

Upon graduation she taught in a typical school environment where she quickly realized that if she adapted her teaching to the individual needs of each student, they experienced greater success. At one point when her children were young, she decided to stay home with them for a time. Of course, her love of education never went away, so she went about teaching them, working with them in their own unique interests and strengths. When they were school-aged, Gina sought creative and nurturing school environments for them but quickly became frustrated. As a result, she set out on an adventure to start a preschool. Soon she added first grade, then more elementary grades, then secondary, and finally in 2016, she added high school classrooms to her seven-acre campus in Springboro, Ohio.

In touring the facility with Gina, it is evident that her educational struggles became the impetus for founding this school and is her continuing motivation as the school grows and impacts children on many levels. She works with a deep sense of justice for *each* child who attends and gathers a community of other like-minded educators around her to help her fulfill her vision.

"A learning environment that is safe, creative, and helpful will ultimately lead to fulfilling and meaningful lives for these children," says Gina. "It is my desire that each one learns who they were truly meant to be —and they learn to walk in their unique giftings and passions."

I believe they will, and they do!

I have known Gina for more than 30 years. Her passion for a creative, individual learning experience inspires me. I know she is changing generations to come through the loving experience she brings in serving each child individually. But this did not come easily to her. She had to fight to silence the negative words that were spoken over her time and time again. Yet as she walks in her true identity, she brings an amazing gift to this world. She brings hope, beauty, intelligence, and a strong determination to see every child succeed.

She could've easily given up a long time ago—allowing negative voices to hold her back. But something deep in her spirit (the Holy Spirit) pushed her to keep going. Kind, patient tutors offered encouragement and spoke life and light into the shame and fear that attempted to overwhelm her. Like an anchor deep within, her faith in God held her firm. Now, as she adventures forward in the dreams, design, and destiny God had planned for her, she is alive in his presence.

Our final chapter is about living abundantly; walking in our unique giftings, passions, and callings; and being the hands and feet of the Lord as we adventure through life, Jesus by our side. For it is only in the giving away of our gifts that we walk in resurrection power and make his praise glorious. In this chapter, you will hear four separate testimonies of fellow creative Christians. They all have something to teach us, so may you be inspired by their adventures. Jesus said:

I came that they may have life, and have it abundantly. Jn 10:10

It is time to live adventurous lives, abundantly alive in his presence!

Jesus the Breaker

Before we read these testimonies of adventure, we must know that it is Jesus our King who goes before us. Let's read Micah 2:13 in several translations:

The One who breaks open the way will go up before them;
they will break through the gate and go out.
Their King will pass through before them, the Lord at their head. NIV

Then I, God, will burst all confinements and lead them out into the open.
They'll follow their King. I will be out in front leading them. MSG

He who opens the breach will go up before them;
they will break through and pass the gate, going out by it.
Their king will pass on before them, the Lord at their head. RSV

Your leader will break out and lead you out of exile,
out through the gates of the enemy cities, back to your own land.
Your king will lead you; the Lord himself will guide you. NLT

Like a great and valiant king, he mounts his warhorse and breaks out before his people. The Lord here is referred to as "the Breaker" (*happores* in Hebrew). Notice each translation words it differently: the one who breaks open; the God who burst all confinements; he who opens the breach; or the leader who breaks out. While the language differs, the image does not. The King breaks open the barrier that entraps us, creating a breach in the wall, bursting through all that confines us. As he breaks down the gates of the enemy armies, he leads us out of exile and guides us back to our true place and calling.

This is a powerful passage—one that encouraged me in the deepest places of my being during the darkest places in my journey, even while I was still trapped behind enemy lines in exile. I memorized this verse and began to speak it over my life, trusting that God would be true to his word. I would visualize a mighty king who was fighting the battle on my behalf in order to form a breach in the wall. It reminded me that all I had to do was wait in expectant assurance of his victory and be prepared to rush out behind him when he broke through ahead of me.

Take a moment to stop and read Matthew 10, the sending out of the twelve disciples. Jesus the Breaker has already gone ahead of them, healing diseases and casting out demons. Now he places a calling on the disciples and gives them authority in his name. The passage starts out inspiring enough, but then we get to verse 16 and the tone changes to one of grim warning:

I am sending you out like sheep among wolves.
Therefore be as shrewd as snakes and as innocent as doves.
Be on your guard…

This adventure is not easy! But he also promises great provision—they will be given the precise words to speak, the Holy Spirit will whisper in their ears, and all darkness will be brought into the Light.

Just as Christ went ahead in life, he would also go ahead in death. Many disciples would give their lives on behalf of the gospel of Jesus Christ. And as it goes with Christ and his followers, so it will go with us. How can we expect a life of ease when Jesus warns his followers that it will not be so? In the age of the early Christians (and many places still today), it meant physical death. In our lives it's easy to think this passage doesn't apply to us, but it does. We undergo a death of the soul each time the enemy attacks. We must stand strong and be the light just as Jesus was the Light before us. We must adventure forward on the path of sacrifice and obedience.

An abundant life alive in his presence may not mean what you think it means. It is not defined by worldly standards. Abundance does not mean wealth, health, and blithe happiness. Abundance means giving our lives as an act of service to the Lord. It means giving our resources away for the sake of Jesus. It means leading others by being transparent in our testimonies. It means shaking the dust off our feet when others do not receive us as we expect. It means interceding on behalf of a fallen world. It means taking the broken, shattered pieces of our lives to Christ so he can perform *kintsugi* of our souls. It means that he will shine brightly through the cracked places of our history. Read the first six paragraphs of the preface again. This is our calling, our story, our mission. Look at the life of Christ our Breaker. The life he demonstrated should be the life we expect.

And yet, amidst all the struggle and pain, we know he is with us, he goes before us, and he will never leave us nor forsake us. That is the abundant life of adventure. It's your destiny, beloved.

Now, are you ready to hear some very powerful testimonies from fellow artisans? Let's adventure on!

Dancing in the Darkness

Matthew Palfenier is a professional dancer, who has performed with Las Vegas Contemporary Dance Theater. I have had the joy of crossing paths with this young man in my own adventure. I want to share a portion of his testimony in his own voice:

> The Lord rescued me years ago from demonic opposition that came as a result from sharing His Gospel. I was not expecting to share this story but there are some ears that need to hear it. Maybe, even my own? Honestly, I feel so removed from that period in my life that it seems strange to revisit those memories. But how could I forget? Those events occurred over 10 years ago…
>
> I remember how I was so scared and felt so powerless. Every day felt like death was standing at my door. How do you fight with an enemy that cannot be seen, but only felt? By the name of Jesus, and by the blood of the Lamb! It was by God's grace and mercy that I was not overtaken by them. The enemy did not win; they couldn't take my life. They may have made me gravely ill, struck me with severe depression, gave me endless nightmares, and trapped me in this endless cycle of sin, but Jesus was my way out. He continues to be my protection even today. I praise you Abba for how you are still in the business of delivering people from Lucifer's hand. May this year be a year of deliverance for those who find themselves ensnared by the demonic forces of our enemy, in Jesus name. For satan is the enemy of ALL who bear Your image and the witness of Your Gospel.

I met Matthew six months after losing my nephew by the same name. And while he looked nothing like my Matthew, when I heard his name and saw the incredible light in his eyes, I had an immediate affection for this young man. I did not know his testimony. I did not know the depth of demonic attack upon his life. All I saw was the Light of Christ within.

The name "Matthew" means "gift of Yahweh," and truly he is a gift in the lives of so many he touches through his testimony, creativity, and dance. Jesus broke through the walls of the enemy for Matthew, so he could follow Christ out of exile. Now his testimony and life leads others out, as well. That is abundant life, adventuring forth with Jesus the Breaker!

Performing the same evening of the Paris bombing in 2015, Matthew recounts a powerful experience of dancing amidst the heartache of a broken and fallen world. As they readied themselves in their dressing rooms, they heard the news of those held hostage within the Bataclan Theater for the first time. Matthew shared: "I remember thinking how crazy it was that while we were stepping onstage to *entertain* here, on another stage in another theater at that very moment people were *fighting for their lives.*" It was this thought, filled with heartrending irony, that became a powerful driving force as he danced that evening, while across the world great tragedy was at that very moment taking place. Listen as he relates his experience:

> I danced because I believe. I believe God (at His Word) that I am worthy of the calling that He has given me. I danced because I believe in the mission of this company, and because I know that art can heal broken souls. I realized that I'm dancing among those to whom the Kingdom is promised: humans. Humans who know that they are fully human. Exceptionally flawed...
>
> By an act of the Spirit, somehow, when I went out and danced, I entered the Kingdom in a way I have never experienced before. I've never smiled so much and for so long in my life. For a night, even among the terrible news of the global terror occurring throughout the world, I found Hope hiding within my dance. And there, in that place, I encountered a deep penetrating joy that covered the vast open wounds, which the very same dance has inflicted upon me.[1]

This is the power of art, beauty, creativity, and worship! The power to heal and bring life, hope, and joy—to ourselves and to others!

Matthew's testimony illustrates that being on your own intentional journey of self-discovery, exploration, and healing helps you be the kind of artist that helps others on their journeys. As a wounded healer, you open doors and windows for others to find restoration themselves, no matter if you are in sacred or secular ministry. The artist should be driven to reflect the Light of Jesus our Breaker in this dark world, no matter what setting they find themselves in or medium they find themselves working with. It also beautifully illustrates the redeeming power of the blood of the Lamb! May Christ be praised!

His Love (and Patience) Endures Forever

Donna Godwin is a prophetic artist from Virginia. Her artwork dons the cover of this book. Speaking of her creative process as she paints, she shares with the heart of a true artist:

> The piece I am currently working on is taking me to the depths of the human heart. As I have been sitting and painting I have felt like a heart surgeon. This morning I have felt as if I were peering into the window of the heart of our Father. As I painted heaven's light like roots, I have been reminded of a time in Texas with a friend and stopping along a dirt path to take a picture of some tree roots and rocks that looked the wall of Jerusalem. Father is always speaking to our hearts, are we listening?
>
> As I grow (and groan) I realize that I AM creation groaning. I have trees and plants and stars and planets and galaxies living within my heart because my Father placed them there when he created the world. I AM creation, and I AM filled with the Light and Love of our Father in Heaven through His Son Jesus, our Lord and Savior, Redeemer and Friend... oh what a friend he *is*... the best kind... there is no other.

> As I have come before the Lord in the way he's instructed, I have experienced a True Friendship, one that I will never have to question and one that I can always trust. So, as I continue to lean in and listen to our Father's Heart, I want to encourage you to do the same. Turn off whatever is distracting you, close the door, and get real before the Lord, and let him take you on a journey through his heart. I guarantee you will never be the same again, and you will know what it means to have a Friend and be a friend to the Lord.
>
> We are human beings filled with light, love, laughter, and joy. We are also living in a fallen world, which means there are temptations surrounding us. Sometimes we stumble and fall in sin and the only one who can lift us up is Jesus, our Brother, our Friend, our Savior, our Lover. While we are here to walk with each other along this path, we cannot carry each other in the same way that Jesus does. That's his job. As a person who's extremely sensitive and loving, I am having to relearn what Love truly *is*. It is not enabling, agreeing, fearful, judging, nor condemning. It is reverence to the Lord, awe of the Lord, wonder of the Lord. It is being discipled in the Word, discipline, order, boundaries, compassion, mercy, grace, peace, hope, faith, and love. The greatest of these is *love*... of our Lord. When we love him, we love others. Sometimes in our lives, the love we've learned has been twisted up into something it was never meant to be. It takes time to untangle lies and hear Truth.
>
> So this brings me to my real message—and that is patience. I am thankful for the enduring patience of our Father in Heaven. He has seen it all, and he knows exactly what we need and when. If the unraveling happens too fast we cannot handle it, so we wait upon the Lord, and we let *him* untangle us and make us into something new and bright and loving and pure. God is Light and his Light lives in me, and it is this Light that shines in my darkness and brings all things into the Light of his love. Hallelujah!
>
> So as my painting grows, I see our Father's Heart expanding forevermore into all of eternity, and I am blessed to be called his and his alone. Blessed indeed is she who loves the Lord![2]

Blessed indeed are those who love the Lord. There is so much wisdom in what she has shared. As God works deeply in us to bring healing, we can easily become discouraged. Donna's testimony illustrates how an open and grateful heart helps us endure the healing journey. May we all be blessed with this beautiful attitude of gratitude.

Incarnational Ministry

Randall Flinn is the Founder and Artistic Director of Ad Deum Dance Company in Houston, Texas. He has inspired many, not only with his dance, but also with his writing. Let me share his testimony of why he dances:

> In talking to a friend about my desires and my actions in life, I came to this very clear conclusion about what I do "artistically and vocationally." I'm not involved in dance simply because of dance. I think the art of dance is a beautiful gift and expression, but that is not why after 40 years of dance experience and journeys that I'm still pressing on in this movement. The purpose and passion of my remaining in dance is way beyond a love for the art form, skill, performance, and aesthetics. I have discovered and feel very assured that I've been called to embrace and preserve with an even deeper core value in this gift—a redemptive core value—one which has a spiritual and sacramental virtue. I'm no longer all that concerned with who likes or

doesn't like my work. It's not so much about me anymore—my choreography, my company, my career. Perhaps at one time it was the profession I chose to pursue for various personal reasons, but now it has become much more intertwined with a sense of holy and grace-given calling and mission.

You see, I really dislike darkness, injustice, suffering, evil, corruption, and destruction of life.

In my own small (or perhaps not so small) way, I know I have been called to contribute to the healing and to offer a greater hope from the massive amount of chaos and brokenness in this world. It's so clear to me now—this is why I'm involved and can't get away from this thing called dance. It's my offering for the sorrow—it's my medicine for the illnesses I see of spirit, soul, and body—yes, even my own.

A very broken and brave shepherd-king once said, "The Lord has turned for me my mourning into dancing." Another very wise and broken king said, "There is a time to mourn and a time to dance." And my favorite King of All said, "In the Father's house there was music and dancing." So maybe, just maybe, this whole gift of dance has its original intent in the role of restorative and renewing redemption for the heart and soul of humanity.

Well, this sounds like a great purpose and pursuit for me, and I'm pretty convinced that this is indeed my calling in this art form. So if by grace (and ongoing conditioning) I get to hang out with this dancing stuff for another 10-40 years, this is where and why my heart will be fixed, and I will continue to have faith and hope in this pursuit—believing with all my heart in its present and eternal value. For this, I will give my all! Dance, I must![3]

This is the heart of the incarnational artist—one who freely pours into and gives away the gift of beauty placed within him by the Holy Spirit. In incarnational ministry, the creative becomes the hands and feet of Jesus Christ. Every dance, a movement of Christ's feet walking this earth. Every brushstroke, a touch of Jesus' hand. Every word spoken or written, a prophetic Divine Word straight from the heart of the Father. Every creative inspiration, a gift placed within he or she who will cultivate it until that gift is to be released to others so desperately in need of his saving grace and unending love.

The Spirit-led Adventure

Sometimes the Holy Spirit stretches us. This is especially true as artists and creatives. Yet, we must heed the voice of the Spirit who guides us, for we never know what might happen when we do. Susan Echard is a prophetic artist, and she shared this remarkable story about an experience she had as she sought the heart of the Holy Spirit in what *she thought* was a disappointing art project. In speaking of the finished piece of artwork, she shares:

This isn't the most beautiful thing I have painted, but it might have been one of the most powerful.

At a weekly prophetic art meeting we did an exercise of painting with our hands. It was the first time I'd painted with my hands. I really didn't understand what I was painting. I just felt awkward and agitated as it came out. Everyone in the meeting painted beautiful paintings. Ummm, mine, not so much. I left the meeting feeling deflated and like I just didn't connect with the exercise.

The next morning I asked the Lord why I was still feeling this way and why my painting seemed off. He began to remind me what I did just a few hours before that meeting.

I work with "at risk" kids and horses. It's a therapy type program where we bring kids and horses together for healing. I was working with a 17-year-old boy who had spent most of his life in multiple group homes—dad incarcerated, mom addicted to drugs living on the streets, and his own issues with drugs. His life is a mess, to say the least. It was a tough day for this boy, and he wasn't going to stay for the session but he did.

The Lord proceeded to tell me that what this boy was feeling on the inside came out in my painting: his life was a turbulent swirling wave of emotions, and he felt tossed to and fro. I was shocked with what the Lord revealed to me. I was looking at it from an internal "me" standpoint, but it wasn't about me at all. It was about a boy who needed someone to intercede for him. I immediately prayed peace over his storms!

There is more the Lord took me through to intercede for this boy but I wanted to share this much with other prophetic artists. That there is always more to *why* we are painting and not so much about *what* we are painting. No matter what it looks like, try not to lean on your own understanding but trust the *why* and how it comes out of you. We can't begin to understand what is happening in the spirit when we create with the gift the Lord has given us.

I pray this encourages you to "get 'er done" when the Lord tells you to paint, draw, or create. There is a reason why…

You're bringing heaven to earth.

Beloved, *you* bring heaven to earth! Let that sink in! As Susan's testimony illustrates, we are often called to intercede for others through our artwork. There are many times when we feel baffled or frustrated by something that surfaces in our creative process, but those are the very times to seek the Lord's heart. As we adventure forward as God's creatives, we should expect these moments more and more. We may not always get answers, but if we trust the process, and more importantly, trust the Holy Spirit, we join the army of artists bringing heaven to earth.

Likewise, in our everyday encounters we must also understand that the smallest action can have a huge impact on another. Throughout the gospels we find Jesus "on his way" when he stops to heal or minister to someone along his journey (see Lk 17:11). In the same manner we need to be prepared to stop on our way to "someplace else." As my friend Michelle Thielen always says: "Interruptions often turn into divine appointments. We need to create enough space and margin in our days to be interrupted."

Knees to the Earth

Our role as artists, creatives, and worshipers should drive us to our knees. Whether we are seeking healing for our own hearts or for the hearts of others, we need to lead lives with our knees to the earth in a posture of heartfelt prayer. We cannot live apart from his presence, we cannot be healed apart from his presence, and we cannot heal others apart from his presence. For some of us, we literally will have knees to the earth. For others, it may be brush to canvas, feet to stage, finger to shutter, pen to paper, voice to music or character, or hands to clay as we seek Jesus through our creative process.

We are nearing the end of our healing adventure together. This prayer from Ephesians 3:14-21 (NLT) is my prayer over you as you continue to dig more deeply into God's Word and find abundant, resurrection life therein:

When I think of all this, I fall to my knees and pray to the Father,
the Creator of everything in heaven and on earth.
I pray that from his glorious, unlimited resources
he will empower you with inner strength through his Spirit.
Then Christ will make his home in your hearts as you trust in him.
Your roots will grow down into God's love and keep you strong.
And may you have the power to understand, as all God's people should,
how wide, how long, how high, and how deep his love is.
May you experience the love of Christ, though it is too great to understand fully.
Then you will be made complete
with all the fullness of life and power that comes from God.
Now all glory to God, who is able, through his mighty power at work within us,
to accomplish infinitely more than we might ask or think.
Glory to him in the church and in Christ Jesus
through all generations forever and ever! Amen.

Listen to: "Gracefully Broken" by Matt Redman (ft. Tasha Cobbs Leonard)

Digging Deeper Into...

John 9: God's Glory in Us	Page 209
I Samuel 1 & 2: A Life of Sacrifice	Page 213
Genesis 37—50: Recovery, Redemption & Restoration	Page 216
Psalm 30: Celebrating the Victory of the Cross	Page 220
Exodus 3/Mark 13: Staying Alert, Awake & Amazed	Page 223

Benediction of Hope — Page 226—227
In the Cave by Jody Thomae

Next Steps: Resources for Your Healing Journey & Endnotes — Page 228

Coloring Page "Flame of Love" by Pauline Mae Blankenship — Page 229

Digging Deeper: God's Glory in Us

Read: John 9

Many times throughout our healing journeys we ask…

Why did God allow this to happen to me?

This is a valid question and one worth wrestling with. This passage will provide *some* answers, but please realize that many answers won't come until we are face-to-face with the One Who is Beyond Our Understanding, until we fall in adoration before the throne, and all the pain of this earth is instantly healed by the Lamb Who Was Slain.

Let's start by placing this passage in context. It follows Christ's teaching during the Feast of Tabernacles where the lighting of lamps was a symbolic part of the ritual ceremonies.[4] Previously in 8:12 Jesus proclaimed:

I am the light of the world.
Whoever follows me will never walk in darkness, but will have the light of life.

In the darkness, we cannot see. As the Light of the world, Jesus comes to give sight—even in the darkest places of our journey. Here in chapter 9 the disciples happen upon a blind man and ask Jesus, "Who sinned?" Jesus answers them, repeating, "I am the light of the world" (9:5).

Face-to-face with the blind man, Jesus spits on the ground and makes mud to put on his eyes. Just as Jesus was *sent* as Messiah to the world, the man is *sent* to wash in the Pool of Siloam, which also means *sent*. An interchange with the blind man and the religious leaders ensues, and they toss him out of the synagogue. Notice how the "sent ones" are called to lead others out of darkness. Also notice how they are often thrown out of the presence of their religious context—and into the presence of Christ. Jesus uses this encounter to speak of spiritual blindness, of which these leaders are guilty. Soon, the blind man makes his profession of faith and falls in worship before the Son of Man, his Healer and Savior. By the Light of the World, the blind now see! Amazing grace!

Now let's return to the question at hand. Verse 9:3 is commonly referred to among Bible scholars as the "purpose clause." While the disciples were more concerned with who sinned, in our day and age, it is *this* statement that disturbs us most:

…but this happened so that the works of God might be displayed in him.

And, if we're honest with ourselves, it gives rise to this candid response:

So the trauma and wounding I have endured in life was inflicted on me by God
so that he can display glory through my experience?
Am I to believe this was *on purpose*?

Some may balk at my transparency here, but I want to be honest about how this passage, at first read, may sound to those who have been deeply hurt. This is a stumbling block for many.

Bible scholars offer helpful insight. For example, Gary Burge offers a different translation that links the phrase to the following verse like this: "Neither this man nor his parents sinned," said Jesus. "But so that the work of God might be displayed in his life, we must do the work of him who sent me while it is still day."[5] This certainly changes the meaning of this clause. And yet it still does not answer the question of suffering. Other scholars offer a long list of reasons for our suffering:

- Original sin (humankind's rebellion in the garden allowed evil to be released and now we collectively live under its consequences);
- God is calling us to repentance (sin in our own life leads to natural negative physical, emotional, and spiritual consequences);
- God is testing or growing our faith (our faith is strengthened as we rely on him in the storms of life);
- For the sake of our spiritual health (sometimes a doctor must wound to heal);
- The enemy is wreaking havoc on our lives (remember how he seeks to kill, steal, and destroy);
- Temporary suffering is endured for a greater redemptive purpose (Jesus, as well as Jeremiah, John the Baptist, Paul, Stephen, and many others suffered and were promised care after death, and their stories stand as a witness to God's redemptive plan);
- For God's glory (as this passage and Job both reveal);
- Hardships conform us to the image of Jesus (we follow him in suffering, as we die to our old nature);
- Some suffering is punishment for sin or punishment of the sins of our parents or previous generations (generational sins);
- As we endure we prove our faithfulness and obedience to God (we see this over and over in scripture and in the stories of the martyrs).[6]

This list might be helpful and perhaps begins to make *some* meaning of our suffering. I can look back at my life's suffering and site examples that align with many of these. I'm sure you can too. As research into trauma-related illness can attest, understanding *why* you suffered and accepting its greater purpose allows one to find deeper healing.[7] If you struggle to understand, prayerful consideration of the list above may be helpful.

Of course, while understanding is helpful, ultimately it is in moments of discovery in the presence of Our Great Physician that will truly mend our hearts back together again. The truth is we often feel rejected by God when bad things happen. Scholar Craig Farmer encourages us: "The chief end of all our misfortunes is this: to be aroused to call on God that our faith might be strengthened and that God might be glorified in our deliverance."[8] Scholar Rodney Whitacre continues:

> Our rebellion has brought disorder to every aspect of our existence, and the way back to the beauty and peace and order of his kingdom leads through suffering, but we should ask God to use it to further his purposes in us and through us. Some lessons only become ours in reality through suffering and the relationship with God that results from these tests.[9]

We learn through holy encounters with a Living God wooing us back into his presence, to correct not only our misalignments, but our misgivings and misjudgments, as well. In those places we are strengthened, and our faith in him grows. The way back to beauty is undeniably a road that leads through the valleys of the shadow of death—death of our old sinful nature; death of our stubborn ways; death of our sinful grasping to fulfill our longings. As much as God would like us to learn these lessons the easy way, we are so bent and broken by the enemy's attack on our lives, it is difficult. If we are to be adventuring forth as God's wounded healers, we must face our own crosses. The beauty of the cross is not the cross itself: it is that Christ would willingly sacrifice himself for the glory of God and the salvation of mankind. We must enter the dark and quiet tomb where God's wonder-working power resurrects us to new life.

I have learned on this journey that things in the natural often reflect what is going on in the spiritual. As I write this chapter, death surrounds my family, friends, and community—in many destructive ways and a variety of forms. That is the reality of the world in which we live—death threatens to set up its encampment around us. Yet Jesus the Breaker has already broken through! Even as it appears that we are encircled by death, by suffering, by great tragedy, there is a different reality taking place—one that must be viewed with heavenly eyesight. In the natural there is death, but in the heavenly realm those with broken bodies have been given new glorified ones. Those who have suffered rejection, pain, and violation are held in the healing embrace of a Loving Father. Those who have lingered here on earth in pain and disease run with great strength into Heaven's throne room! We cannot view life with earthly eyesight—we must see with heavenly vision.

Like the blind man, we must submit to the healing process of the Savior—mud and spit and being blindly sent to a place we cannot see. Others help us as we follow his instruction. In our obedience, and in the process of being washed clean, we find our sight. With renewed vision we declare:

One thing I know: I once was blind but now I see!

In the midst of swirling questions—our own and others—we speak the truth of our encounter with Jesus. And then, when we meet him face-to-face, we proclaim: "I believe!" and we fall at his feet in worship.

The healing journey, the abundant life of adventure, is one that requires us to come before him again and again. Over and over we bring our shattered broken pieces, and one by one he mends them together again—*kintsugi* of the soul. While scholarly lists are helpful and give us wisdom and understanding, in the end we must come before Jesus and allow him to heal us. With each wound brought to memory, we rely on the Holy Spirit to take us into a place where we pour out our lament before God and grieve our many losses. At the end of ourselves, Christ comes and shows us a different reality—one that does not change the past but allows us to move anew into the future. We forgive. We speak blessing. We give praise! We tell our testimony so others can find healing, wholeness, and freedom for themselves.

Saint Irenaeus once taught that, "The glory of God is man fully alive, and the life of man is the vision of God." With heavenly eyesight we see God's vision for our lives. As we find healing and wholeness, we begin to adventure forward. Fully alive and awake with him, we reveal his glory.

(continued next page)

Using the quotes from Farmer, Whitacre, and Irenaeus as your prompts as you begin to explore through creativity, won't you join me in this prayer?

Invite the Holy Spirit into this moment.
Ask the Lord Your Shepherd (Yahweh Rohi) to guide you as you pray.
Ask the Lord Who Sanctifies (Yahweh M'Kaddesh) to purify your imagination and help you picture, sense, or create a place of protection and provision around you and to join you in that place.
Ask the God of Vengeance (Jehovah Gmolah) to set right all that the wrong that has been done to you.
Ask the Lord the Breaker (Jehovah Happores) to break through before you as you pass through the gate to a life of restoration, healing, and hope.
Ask the Lord Your Healer (Yahweh Rophe) to lead you into deeper and greater healing.

Lord I come before you in the midst of my suffering. I am blind. I have walked this earth without vision. I cannot see. I cannot make sense of my suffering, but I trust that you can. Oh Sent One, send me to the pools of your grace, love, and mercy. And as I wash away the mud and spit of this world, may I see as you see. Lord, I desperately need heavenly eyesight. I don't understand why these things have happened to me. I need your vision to truly understand its meaning and purpose. I rely solely on you to help me see. I come before you again and again and submit to your healing process. I walk the road to beauty and peace and order in your kingdom through the valley of my suffering. As my faith in you grows, I know I will come out on the other side—fully awake, fully alive!

Only by Your Power and the Power of Your Mighty Name, Jesus, Amen.

Watch on YouTube: "Lauren Daigle: Trusting God in the Midst of Grief" posted MyCBN and
Listen to: "Trust in You" by Lauren Daigle
"Mended" by Matthew West

Digging Deeper: A Life of Sacrifice

Read: I Samuel 1–2:11 & 2:18-21

The story of Hannah is an incredible story of God's redemption in brokenness. When read in light of what we've learned, it becomes a poignant example of all we've studied. Hannah means "favor," though it would seem that she's far from favored. In Ancient Israel, having children gave women a place and position in their family, tribe, and community. If you were barren, you were often alienated. While Hannah had a husband who loved her dearly, which certainly helped, it didn't keep her from the harming insults of the "rival" wife. According to Bible scholar David Tsumura, "It is noteworthy that the Lord's closing of Hannah's womb was the reason why Peninnah …provoke[d] her severely, while on the other hand, despite it, Elkanah loved her."[10] Her troubles caused one to harm her and another to love her even more. However, it didn't matter that Elkanah loved her, for his other wife tortured her with harmful words. This was her wounding.

So what does she do with her wounds? She takes them to the Lord:

> *In bitterness of soul Hannah wept much and prayed to the Lord. (1:10)*

This is a bitterness that resides deep in her bones. We find her pouring out her lament before the Lord in such a deep and fervent way she is accused of being drunk. Tsumura notes:

> The sense is that Hannah was fully absorbed in the presence of the Lord, forgetting herself and, for a long time, not knowing who was watching. …The expression 'pouring out my soul' denotes not simply an inward state of one's heart or mind, but an involvement of the whole being.[11]

This isn't a pretty lament—her whole body is involved as she weeps before God. Her "pouring out" assumes the metaphor of a vessel, a drink offering, being emptied to the last drop at the Lord's altar. She has refrained from drinking wine, and yet she pours out her soul like wine, emptying its contents fully with reckless abandon.

As she laments, she encounters God through Eli the priest, who bestows blessing and promise over her life. In time, God fulfills his promise, and a precious child is born. As Hannah goes to present Samuel to the Lord as promised, she pours out another offering to the Lord in the words of her beautiful prayer found in I Samuel 2. So much of what we've encountered in scripture throughout this book is echoed in her words! God has brought justice and healing to Hannah!

Yet it is not without sacrifice. Her wounding is healed, but it still costs her. God doesn't demand it, but still she fulfills her vow—even though giving up her son might've been the most difficult thing she's ever had to do. In her obedience, her son grows up to be the powerful prophet of Israel. A proud mother she must have been!

Life in Christ requires sacrifice. We must mourn our losses—even those losses that occur as a result of the sacrifices God is calling us to make. It isn't easy. But God didn't promise easy. He does, however, promise to be with you, to never forsake you, to shelter you, and to protect you with his love. The Christian life is about sacrifice—we sacrifice our old self, our sin nature, our will, our plans, our entire lives for the sake of knowing him (Phlp 3:8-10).

A thousand years after Hannah gave her son as a sacrifice to Israel, another woman gave up her child as a sacrifice to all. *This child* altered the course of history! A sword pierced that child's side, just as a sword pierced his mother's heart. Imagine the scene at the foot of the cross. You've seen it depicted in artwork and film. The mother Mary can barely stand as she watches her child hang naked upon a cross he surely didn't deserve. In the midst of her greatest wounding, the piercing of her soul, her son looks to her and gives her another son, John, who stood at her side (Jn 19:25-27). *In the midst of his anguish, Jesus noticed her!* Do you understand? Jesus is dying an excruciating death, and yet he stops to acknowledge his mother's pain. In his *own* pain, he sees *her* pain. What a remarkable moment!

Do you not realize it is the same for you? In his moment of greatest degradation, humiliation, and unbearable pain, Jesus looks to you in your greatest moment of wounding—the moment that pierces your soul and leaves you with more questions than answers, a moment that utterly makes no sense at all—and *he sees you!* He acknowledges your agonizing grief and gives you something new in the place of all you've lost. Jesus, our Restorer!

Now, John wasn't Jesus. He wasn't her son, birthed of her own body. And yet, the knowledge that Jesus saw her and still attended her needs is overwhelming. He saw the piercing of her soul and made provision and protection for her, even amidst his own suffering. God cannot make our worst moments disappear: they happened and cannot "unhappen." But, if we will allow him, he will bring a new thing that offers provision and protection—if we will allow it. Isaiah 43:18-21 promises us this:

> *Forget the former things; do not dwell on the past.*
> *Behold, I am doing a new thing!*
> *Now it springs up; do you not perceive it?*
> *I am making a way in the wilderness and streams in the wasteland.*
> *...I provide water in the wilderness and streams in the wasteland,*
> *to give drink to my people, my chosen, the people I formed for myself*
> *that they may proclaim my praise.*

This new thing is not like the old—it is *new*! It will *look* different, *be* different. But if you perceive it, you will see a way in the wilderness places of your life, a stream in the wastelands of your woundings, and a drink of living water that will cause you to proclaim his praise.

Steven Curtis Chapman is an award-winning Christian recording artist. Many are familiar with the heart-breaking story of the accident that took his young daughter's life in 2008. He shares that one of the things that carried him as he grieved was "proclaiming truth," especially through these words from the song *Blessed Be the Name of the Lord* by Matt Redman:

> You give and take away.
> My heart will choose to say, blessed be the name of the Lord.[12]

Chapman shares: "I just kept saying it. I kept singing it and whispering it. I'd go where nobody could hear me, and I screamed it until I didn't have a voice left, and every time I did, it was like I would feel something pull me back a little bit from that abyss…"[13] What a powerful lament: to speak, sing, whisper, scream until you have nothing left; to continue in a doxology of "blessed be" even when your heart is ripped from your chest. And in the midst of that beautifully broken lament, God pulls you back from the abyss.

Where are the wilderness and wasteland places in your life? Will you now look to the Lord as he hangs on his own cross of suffering and surrender those places to him? If you allow him into your surrendering, offer him your sacrifice, pour out your offering upon his feet, he will meet you there. In your brokenness, there is still beauty, beloved. He wants to rebuild, repair, restore, reclaim, renew, resurrect, reconcile, and redeem. Are you willing to surrender the shattered pieces of your broken heart so he can re-create you into his work of art, the *kintsugi* of his own masterful creation?

Using the questions and scripture passage above as your prompts as you begin to explore through creativity, won't you join me in this prayer?

Invite the Holy Spirit into this moment.
Ask the Lord Your Shepherd (Yahweh Rohi) to guide you as you pray.
Ask the Lord Who Sees (El Roi) to look upon his child as you cry out to him.
Ask the Lord Who Sanctifies (Yahweh M'Kaddesh) to purify your imagination and help you picture, sense, or create a place of protection and provision around you.
Ask the Great I Am (Ehyeh) to remind you that he is indeed right there with you.
Ask the Lord the Breaker (Jehovah Happores) to break through before you as you pass through the gate to a life of restoration, healing, and hope.
Ask the Lord Your Healer (Yahweh Rophe) to lead you into deeper and greater healing.

Master Artisan and Creator, this sacrifice is so hard, so against everything in my nature. And yet you call me to it. I can barely stand under the breaking of my will, the burden of carrying a cross you never meant for me to carry. Help me release this to you as I continue my healing journey with you. Over and over, you ask me to sacrifice my life to you, to pick up your cross and carry it, but I struggle, Lord. It is so incredibly painful. The outcome of sin in this world has caused this life to be broken, but only in you can I trade ashes for beauty. I give you the shattered places of my deepest being. I pour out my lament before you. I look to you hanging on the cross and hear your words of provision and protection over me as I lose myself in you. All that I am is yours. I have nothing left, but you. You are doing a new thing. Help me perceive it. Help me see your way in the wilderness and your streams of living water in the wastelands of my life. I am your chosen, created and formed for you so that I might give you praise.
In the Name of Jesus Who Hung on the Cross in My Place, Amen.

Watch: "Barlow Girl—Porcelain Heart" posted by Birdiej89 on YouTube
(notice how her tears wash away the shattered places of her soul)
Then listen to: "You Are for Me" by Kari Jobe
"King of Love" by Steven Curtis Chapman

Digging Deeper: Recovery, Redemption & Restoration

Read: Genesis 37 & 39—50

I realize this is a great deal to read, but there is *so much* to discover in this story of trauma and redemption. Let's dig in!

Jacob/Israel's family is wrought with dysfunction from the beginning. Joseph is a tattle-tale, and his brothers hate him. I'm not sure if the tattling is a result of his brothers' harsh treatment or their hate is a result of his tattling, but either way this dysfunction leads to what amounts to human trafficking. Joseph is stripped of his robe and thrown into a cistern. Naked and afraid, he lies in this pit until sold into slavery by his own flesh and blood. Consider his trauma—it is intense and very real.

But God has his hand on Joseph's life at every turn. Sold to Potiphar as a slave, he is soon elevated to the highest position in the household. But God has other plans for Joseph, and he finds himself in a cistern of another sorts—prison—where of course, he is elevated again. The cupbearer slights him, only to remember him later, and now brought before the Pharaoh, God helps Joseph interpret his dreams. Elevated again! I told you God had plans for Joseph, and despite setback after setback, wounding after wounding, Joseph is placed and positioned time and time again by God's mighty hand.

I suspect Joseph masked the pain of his trauma with over-achieving workaholism, and initially it served him well—it would even seem God was using it to position him in the very place where his wounds could later be healed. Eventually he comes face-to-face with the brothers who had stripped and trafficked him. In his own dysfunction, he fails to reveal himself and leads them through a series of tests and tricks. It sometimes seems as if he is waffling between reconciliation and revenge. Three times the brothers are sent to Joseph, three times one or all of them are imprisoned, and finally in a "third-times-a-charm" sort of way, Joseph unveils his identity, and they begin the journey of reclamation.

In her essay "Joseph's Journey: From Trauma to Resolution," Bible scholar Meira Polliack examines this story in light of trauma, PTSD, and memory. She points to many indicators within the story of the trauma, its results, and eventual resolution in Joseph's life. Polliack proposes that the memory had become lodged in Joseph's brain and as a result, he could not integrate the event into his life narrative. Unable to reconcile this event, his pain reveals itself through his actions as "symptoms" typical of those that suffer from PTSD.[14] These symptoms include: frequent bouts of weeping; removing himself from triggering situations with his brothers; his "uncontrolled oscillation of his feelings and reactions,"[15] and his need to "reenact" or "relive" moments of trauma by imprisoning his brothers over and over.[16] Even his recollection of the dreams in 42:9 shows how he has suppressed memories that were potentially wounding. Yet while his brothers "forget" (or fail to recognize) him, he "remembers,"[17] and it all comes flooding back.

Polliack writes: "Recovery from trauma has been compared to a marathon run, a prolonged and painful process that consists of several cardinal stages, including the creation of a safe environment, remembrance, mourning, reconnection, and telling."[18] Isn't this exactly what we've been doing through our creative process? We must remember and mourn. To reconnect to the lost places within, as well as the people around us in order to tell our story. As we begin to find answers to some of the whys of our trauma, we discover meaning and purpose in our pain.

When we discover our calling as wounded healers in this world, we find greater depths of wholeness and healing in our lives. Joseph is a wounded healer. As one "wounded" he faces the horrific trauma of his life of being trafficked, wrongly accused, and imprisoned. And yet as "healer" traveling this journey of healing, he finds greater purpose in all that has occurred. In Joseph's words we see this purpose:

> *And now, do not be distressed and do not be angry with yourselves for selling me here, because it was to save lives that God sent me ahead of you. …God sent me ahead of you to preserve for you a remnant on earth and to save your lives by a great deliverance. So then, it was not you who sent me here, but God. Gen 45:5, 7-8*

When Joseph realized there was a greater purpose behind his suffering, he was on his way towards greater healing. If he hadn't walked a journey of suffering, he wouldn't have been in a place to rescue his entire family from famine. As they embrace and weep (45:14-15) there is a reconnection, especially with his closest brother Benjamin. In your life, you may not be able to reconnect with those who've harmed you, but watch for God to bring others into your life to provide the connection you need.

Joseph is then reunited with his father Jacob and is able to protect his family through seven years of famine. At his death Jacob is able to bless Joseph with these powerful words that continue to give meaning and purpose:

> *Joseph is a fruitful vine, a fruitful vine near a spring, whose branches climb over a wall.*
> *With bitterness archers attacked him; they shot at him with hostility.*
> *But his bow remained steady, his strong arms stayed limber,*
> *because of the hand of the Mighty One of Jacob,*
> *because of the Shepherd, the Rock of Israel,*
> *because of your father's God, who helps you,*
> *because of the Almighty, who blesses you with blessings of the skies above,*
> *blessings of the deep springs below, blessings of the breast and womb.*
> *Your father's blessings are greater than the blessings*
> *of the ancient mountains, than the bounty of the age-old hills.*
> *Let all these rest on the head of Joseph,*
> *on the brow of the prince among his brothers. (49:22-26)*

His brothers shot arrows of hostility at him, but by the grace of God he remained steady and was blessed time and again.

Finally at the end, his brothers ask for forgiveness and bow low before him fulfilling his dream from many years ago. Read 50:16-21 again, taking note of 20-21:

> *But Joseph said to them, "Don't be afraid. Am I in the place of God? You intended to harm me, but God intended it for good to accomplish what is now being done, the saving of many lives. So then, don't be afraid. I will provide for you and your children." And he reassured them and spoke kindly to them.*

His father's words of blessing fulfilled as he stands, a prince among his brothers.

It's so easy to ask, "Why me, God?" when looking at our history of wounds and trauma. And yet, sometimes I wonder if God would answer us back,

> "Why not you, child? My son certainly suffered. Why would you expect any less? The enemy is set on your destruction, but have I not filled you with my Spirit? Have I not brought you healing and restoration in many areas of your life? What the enemy has intended for evil and for suffering, I have turned to good, to fulfill my plans and purposes in this world. Just as Christ's suffering brings many sons and daughters to restoration and deeper relationship with me, so too will yours."

Beloved, there is a greater purpose to your pain. Stop right now and take a moment to breathe in his presence, his purpose, his peace. The Great Physician is here with the Balm of Gilead (Jer 8:22) for the wounded places within. There *is* meaning and purpose.

We often quote Jeremiah 29:11 for reassurance in our lives, but there is so much more to that verse. Continuing through verse 14 we read:

> *"For I know the plans I have for you," declares the Lord,*
> *"plans to prosper you and not to harm you, plans to give you hope and a future.*
> *Then you will call on me and come and pray to me,*
> *and I will listen to you.*
> *You will seek me and find me when you seek me with all your heart.*
> *I will be found by you," declares the Lord,*
> *"and will bring you back from captivity. I will gather you from all the nations and places*
> *where I have banished you," declares the Lord,*
> *"and will bring you back to the place from which I carried you into exile."*

Call on him. Pray to him. Seek after him with all your heart. The Lord longs to bring you back from your places of exile. He longs to break through the gate before you:

> *Your leader will break out and lead you out of exile,*
> *out through the gates of the enemy cities, back to your own land.*
> *Your king will lead you; the Lord himself will guide you. Mic 2:13 (NLT)*

It's an adventure, to be sure!

(continued next page)

Using the scripture passages as your prompts as you begin to explore through creativity, won't you join me in this prayer?

Invite the Holy Spirit into this moment.
Ask the Lord Your Shepherd (Yahweh Rohi) to guide you as you pray.
Ask the Lord Who Sanctifies (Yahweh M'Kaddesh) to purify your imagination and help you picture, sense, or create a place of protection and provision around you.
Ask the Lord the Breaker (Jehovah Happores) to break through before you as you pass through the gate to a life of restoration, healing, and hope.

Great Physician, our Lord the Breaker, come and heal my wounds. I cry out to you. I pray to you. I seek you with all my heart. Oh Balm of Gilead, heal my wounded soul. Help me find greater purpose and meaning in all that has happened in my life. Though the enemy has intended to harm me, you intended to accomplish the saving of many lives as I walk this journey with you. Help me be the wounded healer you have called me to be. Strengthened and renewed in your healing presence, I press on toward the goal to win the prize for which God has called me heavenward in Christ Jesus (Phlp 3:14). May I find my prize in you and you alone.

In the Name of Jesus Christ the Breaker, Amen.

Listen to: "Though You Slay Me" (featuring John Piper) by Shane & Shane
"Thy Will" by Hillary Scott
"Rise" by Danny Gokey

Digging Deeper: Celebrating the Victory of the Cross

Read: Psalm 30

Psalm 30 is one of my favorite psalms. A song of celebration and a personal testimony of thanksgiving and praise, the psalmist has a story of healing to tell, and he wants to shout it aloud. Scholar Artur Weiser notes that the writer is most likely an artist: "Not only the way in which the poet is capable of giving striking and graphic expression to his varied emotions and of making others partners of his own experience, but also the fine construction of this poem, suggest that he is an artist to whom it is given to speak impressively of the things which move his heart."[19] Father God has removed his garments of mourning and despair and clothed him instead with joy—as Weiser points out, an outward expression of grief traded in for an inward emotion that expresses itself outwardly.[20]

As artists on the healing journey, we too must share our testimony of God's faithfulness and Christ's victory on the cross to others so desperately in need of his healing grace and mercy. As artists, worshipers, and creators of beauty we have a voice that is different from others around us, for our voice reverberates in people's spirits. Like the artist above, we must sing his praises and not be silent. Remember Polliack's statement from our previous study? "Recovery from trauma has been compared to a marathon run, a prolonged and painful process that consists of several cardinal stages, including the creation of a safe environment, remembrance, mourning, reconnection, and telling."[21] Psalm 30 is an example of the final stage: telling.

I pray Christ's healing power is meeting you and releasing you from broken places in your past. It is not always an easy process. Considering the wounds and offenses we've piled up, it's not a fast process either. Yet God's timing is perfect, and he's with us for the long haul. We grieve, weep, and mourn through the watches of the dark night of our soul, and joy comes in the morning!

Nouwen beautifully captures the essence of Psalm 30 in his book *Turn My Mourning Into Dancing*. He points to a life of grace, prayer, and love that meets us in the everyday moments of life: "As we dance and walk forward, grace provides the ground on which our steps fall. Prayer puts us in touch with the God of the Dance. We look beyond our experience of sadness or loss by learning to receive an all-embracing love, a love that meets us in everyday moments."[22] Then Nouwen makes this powerful statement filled with truth and mystery:

> *Who can say where the mourning ends and the dance begins?*[23]

Can we trust God's character enough to believe that our mourning will certainly turn to dancing? That perhaps there is dancing even in our mourning? Zephaniah 3:17 says God rejoices over us with singing. The word translated "rejoices" in the Hebrew means to spin around under the influence of intense emotion, indicating that God dances over us with much celebration and emotion. Perhaps the God of the Dance has been wooing us into a healing dance of his all-embracing love all along? Surely the line between mourning and dancing is thin and blurred!

Celebrating the victory of the cross is the final step in our healing journey. When Jesus enters into our most tragic moments he brings the kind of healing that only he can bring. As he frees us from the captivity of unforgiveness and revenge, we can begin to celebrate the victory of the cross as we pour out our praise and thanksgiving to the Great Physician. Then we take up the courage of a wounded healer and begin to share our testimonies of God's faithfulness as his wounded healer. I believe this is key in celebrating the victory of the cross! For what is a celebration if it's not shared?

In the end, like the psalmist above, we must let go of our enemies, tell our testimony to others, and sing our praises to our Healer, Redeemer, and Restorer. Our entire healing process is firmly and deeply rooted in the work of Jesus Christ on the cross and in his resurrection. In his death, all the sins of the world and all the wrong against us were nailed to the cross on Calvary. From the cross Christ cried:

"It is finished!"

and then he released and entrusted his spirit into the loving hands of his Father (Jn 19:30; Lk 23:46).

His friends lovingly placed his lifeless body in a borrowed tomb. Now, we don't know exactly what happened there in that place of death and sorrow, but on that greatest of the great gettin' up mornings, the stone was rolled away, and he walked out of that tomb! In his resurrection, he demonstrated his power over sin, death, and hell.

The cross could not kill him!

The tomb could not hold him!

He is alive!

In that moment, the cross and the tomb were changed from a symbol of mourning to a symbol of joy, celebration, and dancing. Jesus extends his nail-scarred hands towards us to touch and see. We match our own scars to his and all our wounds together cry,

Hallelujah! He is alive! I am alive!

As you create today, picture Jesus reaching his nail-scarred hands to meet yours as he calls you into his divine dance. Picture Jesus changing your mourning into dancing. Dance with freedom and abandon!

(continued next page)

Using the visualization and scripture passages as your prompts as you begin to explore through creativity, won't you join me in this prayer?

Invite the Holy Spirit into this moment.
Ask the Lord Your Shepherd (Yahweh Rohi) to guide you as you pray.
Ask the Lord Who Sanctifies (Yahweh M'Kaddesh) to purify your imagination and help you picture, sense or create a place of protection and provision around you and join you in that place.
Ask the Lord Your Healer (Yahweh Rophe) to lead you into deeper and greater healing as you celebrate the victory of the cross.

God of the Dance, today I choose to take your nail-scarred hands and join you in the dance. I choose to dance through the power of the strong name of Jesus of Nazareth. I celebrate with you Father God and praise you for your work in my life. Thank you for walking with me on this healing journey. Please continue to guide my steps on a path that leads to health, wholeness, and restoration and to bring health to my mind, body, and spirit. Where there is disease and illness, I cut it off and declare healing in every cell of my being through the spilt blood of Jesus Christ, my Lord and Precious Savior.

Lord Jesus, thank you for the cross and the tomb. I praise you for the victory that is mine through your death and resurrection. I praise you—for my wounds are yours and your victory is mine. I praise you for freedom, and I will not be silent anymore! I will sing, dance, paint, sculpt, play, act out, weave, and create my story of your great love, and I will tell everyone of how you've saved me and healed me. I give all my wounds to you, Lord, for your glory and not my own. All my wounds cry, "Hallelujah! He is alive! I am alive!"

In the Name of He who Lives, Jesus Christ the Messiah and King, Amen.

Listen to: "Dance Before You (Psalm 30)" by Jody Thomae
"Alive and Well" by Cindy Morgan
"Praise the King" by Cindy Morgan

Digging Deeper: Staying Alert, Awake & Amazed

Read: Exodus 3:1-10 & Mark 13:31-37

In Exodus 3 we find Moses on the far side of the desert tending the flock of his father-in-law. Long past are his palace days of being treated with princely honor after being plucked from a floating basket in the Nile River by the Pharaoh's daughter. Moses, which means "the one drawn from the river" (2:10): the one who was rescued from deep waters; the one who will turn the Nile water red; the one who will one day soon lead his people—his true people—to cross the sea on dry ground. It is interesting to note that in 2:19 Moses is referred to as an Egyptian, not a Hebrew—his identity is still tangled up in all he is running from. Yet here in his encounter at the burning bush, he comes face-to-face with the God of his Hebrew people—the Great I AM!

Scripture tells us that he saw flames of fire within a bush, but the bush wasn't consumed. The Message seems to capture the wonderment of the moment:

> *Moses said, "What's going on here? I can't believe this!*
> *Amazing! Why doesn't the bush burn up?"*

There in that place of amazement, God calls his name: "Moses! Moses!" It's as if God is saying, "Moses, the one who is drawn from water, let me show you a fire that burns but doesn't consume. Let me show you your true identity." From water to fire. Bible scholar William Johnstone explains the symbolism of the burning bush for Moses: "It is a message of reassurance to him, a sign of personal empowerment, under seemingly endless uncompromising circumstances, to endure the searing intensity of the awesome vocation to which God calls him, despite natural frailty."[24] This burning bush is not merely a sign for this moment, but a sign for his life's calling.

Moses removes his sandals in reverent obedience. As God reveals both his and Moses' true identities, Moses hides his face in fright. Johnstone reveals: "This experience, the recovery of the fundamental theological tradition of his own people that God now makes personally known to him, overwhelms him. He hides his face, too afraid to look at God."[25] It's as if in this moment of God calling him to his true identity, Moses isn't quite ready to come to terms with it. Yet, as he comes face-to-face with the true God of his fathers, his amazement turns to surrender, obedience, and worship. But the Great I AM, still has more to say:

> *I have indeed seen the misery of my people…*
> *I have heard them crying…*
> *I am concerned about their suffering…*

He says the same thing to you, beloved!

So often the Lord speaks—in both simple and astounding ways—and we fail to turn aside from our daily anxieties and distractions to be amazed. In our opening chapter, we were encouraged by Ephesians 5:14:

> *Awake, O sleeper, and arise from the dead, and Christ will shine on you.*

Our hearts have been awakened—now we must remain awake!

In Mark 13, Jesus tells us to remain awake and alert through the Parable of the Watchmen. Once he uses the Greek word *blepo*, which means to take care, watch, pay attention, be on the lookout. Three times he uses the word *gregorevo*, which means to stay awake, refrain from sleep. Jesus isn't referring to physical sleep here—he is referring to the state of your spirit. We must take care that our spirits stay awake and alert. This is an attitude of watchful preparedness. We must be like watchmen on the wall and stay alert to what Jesus Christ is doing all around us. The same message in Luke 21:34 says:

Be careful, or your hearts will be weighed down
with carousing, drunkenness and the anxieties of life,
and that day will close on you suddenly like a trap. NIV

But be on your guard.
Don't let the sharp edge of your expectation get dulled
by parties and drinking and shopping.
Otherwise, that Day is going to take you by complete surprise,
spring on you suddenly like a trap. MSG

We must not allow our hearts to get weighed down or the sharp edge of our expectation to be dulled by the distractions of this world. Our hearts, minds, and spirits must stay awake in order to hear and see the Holy Spirit's movement in this world. This is true in both big and small ways. Keeping our eye on the big picture, we must stay alert to what God is doing across the globe, around our country, and in our communities and churches.

As artists, creatives, and worshipers, we have eyes that see and ears that hear mysteries and wonders to which others have become blind or deaf. It is our role to be "revealers" of beauty in a dark and murky world. As we have traveled this journey of healing together and will continue to travel throughout our lives, we realize that healing, wholeness, and freedom is a "present and not-yet" reality. We live our lives as travelers that *have been* healed, *are being* healed, and *will be* healed. Moreover, as wounded healers we invite others along on the journey.

How can you as an artist or creative reveal his beauty so that others can be awakened to Jesus' great love for them? How can you bring about a spirit of worship where heaven meets earth in the thin places of our sacred gatherings? How can you use your creativity to remain awake and amazed in his presence? How can you invite others into that sweet healing presence you have found? These are questions you need to ask yourself. *How will your redemption be lived out in fulfillment in your life?*

Hard work in healing leaves you with a sense of wholeness and fulfillment, but soon life and the enemy will bear down on you to steal your newfound freedom. Reread what Johnstone said above about the burning bush as a symbol for Moses. Just like Moses, we need the "burning bush" symbols of our desert places to serve as a reminder of God's empowerment in our lives and ministry. The burning bush was the symbol of empowerment that carried Moses through the setbacks he would encounter as he lived his life in service to God, the Great I AM he met on the far side of the dessert that day. Consider the life of Moses. Pharaoh hated him, his own people grumbled, complained, and turned away at the slightest temptation or provocation. Even his own brother and sister turned against him at times. Moreover, he didn't even get to enter the Promised Land! If anyone was in need of a symbol of empowerment, it was Moses!

Throughout this book you have entered into the creative process again and again. Now at the end of this book, you might have one single creation or a whole series of creations that have emerged as beautiful symbols of your healing journey. Allow this creative work to be your "burning bush" symbol. Let it empower you as you live a life of service to the Great I AM. Stay alert, awake, and amazed!

Colleen Briggs is a wonderful, thought-provoking artist. Accompanying a stunning painting entitled "Arise," she writes these words of deep truth:

> Suffering has a way of whittling the world down into compact space with infinite feeling. But what if there, in the negative space, the space around what is, there is something more? What if it is actually Love, standing there on the compact grave of buried memories of what was stolen and lost?
>
> And, then, what if Love has the power to cry, "Arise!" and it pulls you up out of the dirt, into the sun, into looming space so broad and free it takes your breath away?
>
> And, then, what if Love is able to confiscate and crown you with all that space? What if all that emptiness becomes a living, breathing mantle of empathy, possibility, exponential love to give away to others?
>
> Then, Love will accomplish its mighty agenda.
>
> Resurrection.
>
> Don't give up. The time will come when you will clearly hear, "Arise."[26]

Are you listening, Beloved? He's calling you to adventure… in His presence!

Using the words of artist Colleen Briggs, as well as the questions and scripture passages as your prompts as you begin to explore through creativity, won't you join me in this prayer?

Invite the Holy Spirit into this moment.

Ask the Lord Your Shepherd (Yahweh Rohi) to guide you as you pray.

Ask the Lord Who Sanctifies (Yahweh M'Kaddesh) to purify your imagination and help you picture, sense or create a place of protection and provision around you and join you in that place.

Ask the Lord Your Healer (Yahweh Rophe) to lead you into deeper and greater healing as you celebrate the victory of the cross.

Oh Great Love, I see you standing there on the compact grave of buried memories of what was stolen and lost, and I hear you cry, "Arise!" I feel you pulling me up out of the dirt, into the sun, into looming space so broad and free, it takes my breath away. Oh Love of my heart, confiscate the space of my long buried memories and crown me with a space filled with the glory of your Sonshine. Help my emptiness become a living, breathing mantle of empathy, possibility, and exponential love to give away to others. I allow you, Great Love, to accomplish your mighty agenda: Resurrection! I will not give up. I will not be shaken. I will stay awake, alert, and amazed in your wonder of your beautiful presence.

In the Name of the Lion and the Lamb, Jesus Christ, Amen.

Listen to: "Wonder" by Bethel
"The Lion and The Lamb" by Big Daddy Weave

Beloved of God,

Do you remember our opening story of the inquisitive cub and his sleepy mama bear? She told him a legend: the Legend of the Snowdrops. In that story there was a battle between the Winter Witch and Lady Spring, and the snowdrops emerged from the frozen ground through a single drop of blood that fell from the precious finger of Lady Spring.

Surely you realize the legend echoes another story? A story of legendary proportions to be sure! Yet, it is no legend. From the serpent's menacing hiss heard in the garden many thousands of years ago, there arose a battle between good and evil. That battle raged on until Christ was pierced and his blood fell to the ground, declaring Jesus victorious over the enemy. Just as the elegant, white flowers emerged from a single drop of Lady Spring's blood, there in that place of Christ's suffering, a new beauty sprang forth.

In many ways, that battle still rages on—in the depths of our souls, in the broken places where the enemy seeks to take ground that's not his. Like Snowdrops that break through the cold and wintry ground, Jesus Our Breaker shatters the cold and wintry places within our spirits, rising before us, the King at our head. May he lead us into a life of creative adventure as we read our final benediction.

Thank you for joining me on this healing journey. It has been an honor to walk alongside you. May Jesus Our Breaker lead us ever onward!

Godspeed from your fellow wounded healer,

A Benediction of Hope

In the Cave
by Jody Thomae

"Mama?" Cub whispers into the den's deep darkness.

"Mama? Are you awake?" he whispers more loudly.

"I am now, little one," mumbles Mama Bear, sleep heavy in her voice. "What are you doing awake?"

"I can't sleep," answers Cub, yearning touches the fringes of his words. "Tell me about Spring again," he says as he snuggles deeply into her coarse fur, letting it wrap around him like blades of grass he can just barely remember.

"Spring starts when the Snowdrops come up and push back the snow," she begins.

"How do snow drops push back snow?" he asks puzzled, remembering the early snow that came in flakes, not drops. "That doesn't make any sense, Mama." He is certain her empty stomach is causing her confusion.

Mama Bear smiles as she pictures her every word, "Snowdrops are flowers, silly bear—the very first flowers to bloom each year. They bloom so early that they must push themselves up through piles of snow that stubbornly refuse to melt. Their beautiful, white blossoms hang delicately from emerald stems and silently shout of the coming Spring."

Cub turned his head to gaze up at her—eyes filled with curiosity and wonder.

She continued, "Legend tells us that Snowdrops were birthed from a battle between the Winter Witch and Lady Spring. One year, when Lady Spring arrived to take her rightful place, the Winter Witch refused to give up her reign over the frozen earth. In the midst of the brutal battle, the Witch pierced Lady Spring's finger and a tiny drop of blood fell to the earth. The blood drop melted the bitter snow and a Snowdrop sprang up in its place, declaring Lady Spring victorious over the Winter Witch."

"I think I'm gonna like Snowdrops, Mama" said Cub, wistfully wanting winter's end. His body begins to settle into the stillness.

"After the Snowdrops come the Crocus—lavender and purple and white. And then the red tulips and yellow daffodils. Then, finally then, the trees begin to bud: new leaves forming on every branch."

"The trees grow new leaves?" questions the curious Cub.

"Yes, the Creator Spirit makes all things new," her voice echoes with knowing wisdom.

"What color are the leaves, Mama? Are they red and orange and yellow?" his voice begins to drift off as he fights back sleep.

"No, baby. They are green—the color of new life."

Next Steps: Resources for Your Healing Journey

An Army Arising: Why Artists are on the Frontline of the Next Move of God by Christ John Otto

An Artist's Arsenal: 40 Days to Equip and Empower Warrior Artists by Christ John Otto

Bezalel: Redeeming a Renegade Creation by Christ John Otto

Endnotes

1. Originally shared on Facebook, Matthew graciously agreed to allow me to share his thoughts with you here. The Las Vegas Contemporary Dance Theater can be found at www.lvdance.org.
2. Donna Godwin can be found on at: www.facebook.com/DonnaGodwinART
3. Originally posted April 18, 2016 on Facebook, Randall has kindly given permission to share again here. Many who know Randall have been encouraging him to collect his thoughts for a book. Won't you join me in praying that into existence, and keep your eyes out for God to answer that prayer? See www.danceaddeum.com.
4. Burge, *John*, 271.
5. Ibid., 272-273.
6. Whitacre, *John*, 236, and Farmer, *John 1-12*, 339.
7. See for example, "Acceptance and Commitment Therapy for Veterans With PTSD" by Claudia J. Dewane, DEd, LCSW published in Social Work Today, May/June 2012 Issue, Vol. 12 No. 3 P. 14. Accessed September 28, 2016 at: www.socialworktoday.com/archive/051412p14.shtml
8. Farmer, 339.
9. Whitacre, 237.
10. Tsumura, *Samuel*, 114.
11. Ibid., 121.
12. Matt Redman, "Blessed Be Your Name," ThankYou Music, 2002.
13. Steven Curtis Chapman, quoted at: www.stevencurtischapman.com/about. Accessed October 17, 2016.
14. Polliack, "Joseph's Journey," 153.
15. Ibid., 157.
16. Ibid., 159.
17. Ibid., 154-155.
18. Ibid., 161.
19. Weiser, *The Psalms*, 267.
20. Ibid., 272.
21. Polliack, 161.
22. Nouwen, *Turn my Mourning*, 14.
23. Ibid., 15.
24. Johnstone, *Exodus 1—9*, 73.
25. Ibid., 75.
26. See www.colleenbriggs.com/2016/10/11/arise. Accessed October 12, 2016. I encourage you to explore Colleen's artwork, as well as how she is using her artist's heart to affect change in the world.

BIBLIOGRAPHY

Beal, Lissa M. Wray. *Apollos Old Testament Commentary, Vol. 9: 1 & 2 Kings*. Downers Grove, IL: InterVarsity Press, 2014.

Bednarowski, Mary Farrell. *The Religious Imagination of American Women*. Bloomington, IN: Indiana University Press, 1999.

Blige, Mary J. *No More Drama*. MCA Records, 2001.

Bock, Darrell L. *Luke*. Downers Grove, IL: IVP Academic, 1994.

Bovon, Francois. *Luke 1: A Commentary on the Gospel of Luke 1:1-9:50*. Minneapolis, MN: Fortress Press, 2002.

Broyles, Craig C. "The Psalms of Lament." In *Dictionary of the Old Testament, Wisdom, Poetry & Writings*, eds. Tremper Longman III and Peter Enns. Downers Grove, IL: InterVarsity Press, 2008, 384-399.

Briggs. Colleen. Excerpt from "Arise." October 11, 2016 post on www.colleenbriggs.com, 2016.

Brooks, David. "The Shame Culture." *The New York Times*, mobile addition, March 15, 2016. Accessed September 15, 2016 at: www.nytimes.com/2016/03/15/opinion/the-shame-culture.html

Brower, Kent. *Mark: a Commentary in the Wesleyan Tradition*. Kansas City: Beacon Hill Press, 2012.

Brueggemann, Walter. *Praying the Psalms: Engaging Scripture and the Life of the Spirit*, second edition. Eugene, OR : Cascade Books, 2007.

Buller, Bob. "Prophets, Prophecy." In *Dictionary of the Old Testament Pentateuch*, eds. T. Desmond Alexander and David W. Baker. Downers Grove, IL: InterVarsity Press, 2003, 664.

Burge, Gary M. *The NIV Application Commentary: John*. Grand Rapids, MI: Zondervan, 2000.

Butler, Trent C. *Luke: Holman New Testament Commentary*. Nashville: Holman Publishers, 2000.

Chapman, Steven Curtis. Quoted on his webpage: www.stevencurtischapman.com/about. Accessed October 17, 2016.

Chen, Pat. *The Depths of God: Walking Ancient Paths Into His Presence*. Shippensburg, PA: Destiny Image Publishers, 2003.

Cogan, Mordechai. *I Kings: a New Translation with Introduction and Commentary* (Anchor Yale Bible Commentary). New Haven, CT: Yale University, 2001.

Edwards, James R. *The Gospel According to Luke*. Grand Rapids, MI: William B. Eerdmans, 2015.

Escontrías, Heather. "Holy Saturday." By the author, 2016.

Farmer, Craig S. *John 1-12 (Reformation Commentary on Scripture: New Testament IV)*. Downers Grove, IL: InterVarsity Press, 2014.

Fitzmyer, S.J., Joseph A. *Romans: the Anchor Bible Commentary, Volume 33*. New York, Doubleday Dell Publishing Group, 1993.

Garland, David E. *Luke: Zondervan Exegetical Commentary on the New Testament*. Grand Rapids, MI: Zondervan, 2011.

_____. *The NIV Application Commentary: Mark*. Grand Rapids, MI: Zondervan, 1996.

Gaventa, Beverly Roberts. *Abingdon New Testament Commentaries: Acts of the Apostles*. Nashville, TN: Abingdon Press, 2003.

Gero, Mandy L. "A Reflection…Solemn Praise." Abiding Perspectives, 2015. www.abidingperspectives.com.

Goldingay, John. *Psalms (Volume 3: Psalms 90-150)*. Grand Rapids, MI: Baker Academic, 2008.

Graffagnino, Tom. "High Places that Deceive." In *Wilderness to Water*. Ashland, OH: Bookmasters, 2014. www.withoutexcusecreations.net.

Greathouse, William M. *Romans (a commentary in the Wesleyan Tradition)*. Kansas City: Beacon Hill Press, 2008.

Green, Joel B. *The Gospel of Luke*. Grand Rapids, MI: William B. Eerdmans, 1997.

Greenberg, Mark and Bessel A. van der Kolk. "Retrieval and Integration of Traumatic Memories with the 'Painting Cure'." In *Psychological Trauma*, ed. Bessel A. van der Kolk. Washington DC: American Psychiatric Press Inc., 1987.

Greig, Pete. *God on Mute: Engaging the Silence of Unanswered Prayer*. Ventura, CA: Regal Books, 2007.

Hafemann, Scott J. *2 Corinthians: The NIV Application Commentary*. Grand Rapids, MI: Zondervan, 2000.

Hebrew-Greek Key Word Study Bible: New International Version, ed. Spiros Zodhiates. Chattanooga, TN: AMG Publishers, 1996.

Henderiksen, William. *NT Commentary: Luke*. Grand Rapids, MI: Baker Book House, 1978.

Jacobson, Rolf A., Nancy Declaisse'-Walford, Beth Laneel Tanner. *The Book of Psalms*. Grand Rapids, MI: William B. Eerdmans, 2014.

Johnstone, William. *Exodus 1—9: Smyth & Helwys Bible Commentary*. Macon, GA: Smyth & Helwys Publishing, 2014.

Joseph, Sara. *Gently Awakened: the Influence of Faith on Your Artistic Journey*. Sisters, OR: Deep River Books, 2013. www.christian-artist-resource.com.

Kidd, Sue Monk. *When the Heart Waits*. San Francisco, CA: Harper & Row, 1990.

Lawrence, Brother. In *Practicing His Presence* from the Library of Spiritual Classics. Jacksonville, FL: The SeedSowers, 1973.

The Legend of Bagger Vance, directed by Robert Redford, 2000. Based on a book by the same title by Steven Pressfield. New York: Avon Books, 1996.

L'Engle, Madeleine. *Walking on Water: Reflections on Faith and Art*. Colorado Springs, CO: WaterBrook Press, 1980.

Levine, Baruch A. *Numbers 21—36: a new translation with introduction and commentary (The Anchor Yale Bible Commentary)*. New Haven, CT: Yale University Press, 2009.

McKenzie, Steven L. *1—2 Chronicles: Abingdon Old Testament Commentaries*. Nashville, TN: Abingdon Press, 2004.

Mulholland, M. Robert. *Shaped by the Word*. Nashville, TN: Upper Room Books, 2001, revised edition.

Norris, Kathleen. *Dakota: A Spiritual Geography*. New York: Ticknor & Fields, 1993.

Nouwen, Henri J.M. *The Dance of Life*. Notre Dame, IN: Ave Maria Press, 2005.

_____. *The Wounded Healer*. London: Darton, Longman and Todd Ltd., 1994.

_____. *Turn My Mourning Into Dancing*. Nashville, TN: W Publishing Group, 2001.

Ortega, Fernando. *Father of My Heart*. Urgent Records, 2009.

Parry, Robin. *Lamentations*. Grand Rapids, MI: William B. Eerdmans, 2010.

Patty, Sandi. *Via Dolorosa*. Word Records, 1990.

Payne, Leanne. *The Healing Presence: Curing the Soul Through Union With Christ*. Grand Rapids, MI: Hamewith Books, 1989, 1995.

Petterson, Anthony R. *Haggai, Zechariah & Malachi: Apollos Old Testament Commentary*. Downers Grove, IL: InterVarsity Press, 2015.

Polliack, Meira. "Joseph's Journey: From Trauma to Resolution." In *Genesis*, eds. Athalya Brenner, Archie Chi Chung Lee, and Gale A. Yee. Minneapolis, MN: Fortress Press, 2010, 147-174.

Redman, Matt. *Blessed Be Your Name*. ThankYou Music, 2002.

Richardson, Jan. "Blessing for a Whole Heart." In *The Cure for Sorrow: a Book of Blessings for Times of Grief*. Orlando, FL: Wanton Gospeller Press, 2016.

Rothschild, Babette. *The Body Remembers*. New York: W.W. Norton & Company, 2000.

Sailhamer, John H. *NIV Compact Bible Commentary*. Grand Rapids, MI: Zondervan, 1994.

Seal, Dean J. "Forgiveness 360: Three Stories of 'Letting Go'." In *ARTS: The Arts in Religious & Theological Studies, Vol 25:3*, ed. Kimberly Vrudny, 31-38. New Brighton, MN: Society for the Arts in Religious and Theological Studies, 2014.

Seamands, David A. *Healing for Damaged Emotions*. Chicago: David C. Cook, 2015.

Seifrid, Mark A. *The Second Letter to the Corinthians*. Grand Rapids, MI: William B. Eerdmans, 2014.

Shapiro, Deb. *Your Body Speaks Your Mind*. Boulder, CO: Sounds True, 2006.

Shoop, Marcia W. Mount. *Let the Bones Dance: Embodiment and the Body of Christ*. Louisville, KY: Westminster John Knox Press, 2010.

Spencer, Richard A. "Presence." In *Eerdmans Dictionary of the Bible*, ed. David Noel Freedman. Grand Rapids, MI: Wm. B. Eerdmans, 2000, 1081.

Tannehill, Robert G. *Abingdon NT Commentaries: Luke*. Nashville, TN: Abingdon Press, 1996.

Tanner, Beth Laneel. "Psalm 57" and "Psalm 91." In *The Book of Psalms*, by Nancy DeClaisse'-Walford, Rolf A. Jacobson, Beth Laneel Tanner, ed. Robert L. Hubbard, Jr. Grand Rapids, MI: William B. Eerdmans, 2014.

Terrien, Samuel. *The Psalms: Strophic Structure and Theological Commentary, Vol, 1 (Psalms 1-72)*. Grand Rapids, MI: William B. Eerdmans, 2003.

Thomae, Jody. *God's Creative Gift—Unleashing the Artist in You*. Eugene, OR: Wipf & Stock, 2013.

Thompson, Curt. *Anatomy of the Soul: Surprising Connections between Neuroscience and Spiritual Practices that can Transform Your Life and Relationships*. Carol Stream, IL: Tyndale House, 2010.

Tsumura, David Toshio, *The First Book of Samuel*. Grand Rapids, MI: William B. Eerdmans, 2007.

van der Kolk, Bessel A. "The Body Keeps the Score: Approaches to the Psychobiology of Post Traumatic Stress Disorder." In *Traumatic Stress: The Effects of Overwhelming Experience on the Mind, Body and Society*, eds. Bessel A. van der Kolk, Alexander C. McFarlane, and Lars Weisaeth. New York: The Guilford Press, 1996.

_____. *The Body Keeps the Score: Brain, Mind and Body in the Healing of Trauma*. Westminster, London: Penguin Books, 2015.

Waggoner, Brenda. *Fairy Tale Faith*. Wheaton, IL: Tyndale House, 2003.

Wardle, Terry. "Dysfunctional Behaviors & the Cross." In *The Ministry of Inner Healing Prayer* teaching materials. Ashland, OH: Institute of Formational Counseling, 2002.

_____. *Healing Care, Healing Prayer*. Orange, CA: New Leaf Books, 2001.

_____. *People of the Presence*, workshop at Sunbury United Methodist Church in Sunbury, Ohio, April 6-9, 2016.

_____. *Strong Winds & Crashing Waves*. Abilene, TX: Leafwood Publishers, 2007.

_____. *Wounded: How to Find Wholeness and Inner Healing in Christ*. Abilene, TX: Leafwood Publishers, 2006.

Wells, Sarah M. "The Antique Rocking Chair." In *Pruning Burning Bushes*. Eugene, OR: Wipf & Stock, 2012.

Westerholm, Stephen. "Clean and Unclean." In *Dictionary of Jesus and the Gospels*, eds. Joel B. Green and Scot McKnight. Downers Grove, IL: InterVarsity Press, 1992.

Whitacre, Rodney A. *John: the IVP New Testament Commentary Series*. Downers Grove, IL: IVP Academic, 1999.

Young, Wm. Paul. *Crossroads*. New York: FaithWords, 2012.

About the Author

Jody Thomae has been involved in worship arts ministry since 1997, serving as a worship arts ministry pastor, worship leader, creative arts director, and worship dance team director. She has coordinated artistic involvement in church services and regional worship events through dance, drama, poetry and fine arts, and performs, teaches, and leads workshops in the area of creativity, spirituality, embodied prayer, and healing movement. She leads worship at local seminars, retreats, and women's events and is a guest lecturer on creativity, embodiment, and spirituality for Healing Care Ministries and HCM International.

Her passion is for the revelation of God to be made more real through: 1) the prophetic use of the arts in church, and 2) creativity in formational and healing ministry. It is her desire to portray the message of Christ's desperate and unfailing love for His people to help sustain the hearts of the broken and weary. She is particularly interested in the reclamation of the body in the healing of trauma and works in the area of embodiment with survivors of abuse, addiction, and trauma.

Also part of the *Bible Studies to Nurture the Creative Spirit Within* series, her first book, *God's Creative Gift—Unleashing the Artist in You* is another interactive, in-depth devotional Bible study similar to *The Creator's Healing Power*. Print and digital copies are available through Amazon or Wipf & Stock. Signed copies of Jody's books are available for purchase through her Square store at: squareup.com/market/jody-thomae. They are also available in bulk amounts for your creative arts ministry team or group study through Square.

Jody also has a devotional CD called *Song of the Beloved*, which is a collection of simple acoustic music recordings with readings from scripture and *The Imitation of Christ* by Thomas à Kempis. It is designed to lead you through a time of confession into quiet meditation and rest in the arms of your Savior and King, Jesus Christ. It is available through her Square store, as well as iTunes, Spotify and other music outlets.

For additional creative resources and inspiration, visit Jody at:
www.jodythomae.com
www.facebook.com/JodyThomae

Jody can be reached via email at:
jodythomae@zoominternet.net

Made in the USA
Coppell, TX
24 April 2020